AFTER THE TRADITION

AFTER

ESSAYS ON

THE TRADITION

MODERN JEWISH WRITING

by Robert Alter

E. P. DUTTON & CO., INC. NEW YORK 1969

These essays were published in slightly different form in a variety of periodicals, to whose editors grateful acknowledgment is made:

Book Week: Review of *The Gates of the Forest* by Elie Wiesel. (May 29, 1966). Reprinted by permission of *Book World.*

Commentary: "The Genius of S. Y. Agnon" (August, 1961); "Israeli Writers and Their Problems" (July, 1962); "Sentimentalizing the Jews" (September, 1965); "Poetry in Israel" (December, 1965); "Confronting the Holocaust: Three Israeli Novels" (March, 1966); "The Apocalyptic Temper" (June, 1966); "Malamud as Jewish Writer" (September, 1966); "Sabbatai Zevi and the Jewish Imagination" (June, 1967); "Jewish Dreams and Nightmares" (January, 1968); "Hebrew Between Two Worlds" (April, 1968).

Dædalus: "The Israeli Novel: Language and Realism." Copyright © 1966 The American Academy of Arts and Sciences. Reprinted by permission.

Hadassah Magazine: "The Novels of Elie Wiesel" (April, 1966).

Judaism: "*The Days of Ziklag:* The Assessment of an Ideology" (Winter, 1961).

Midstream Magazine: "The Kidnapping of Bialik and Tchernichovsky" (June, 1964); "The Stature of Saul Bellow" (December, 1964).

Saturday Review: "Nobel Prize-Winners: 1966—S. Y. Agnon" (December 6, 1966).

Grateful acknowledgment is made for permission to quote from the following material:

The Chocolate Deal, by Haim Gouri, translated by Seymour Simckes, published by Holt, Rinehart & Winston, 1968.

Dangling Man, by Saul Bellow, published by Vanguard Press, Inc. Copyright, 1944, by the Vanguard Press, Inc.

The Fixer, by Bernard Malamud, published by Farrar, Straus & Giroux, Inc. Copyright © 1966 by Bernard Malamud.

Herzog, by Saul Bellow, published by The Viking Press, Inc. Copyright © 1961, 1963, 1964 by Saul Bellow.

Not of This Time, Not of This Place, by Yehuda Amichai, translated from the Hebrew by Shlomo Katz, published by Harper & Row, Publishers, Inc., 1968.

"An Old Manuscript." Reprinted by permission of Schocken Books, Inc., from *The Penal Colony,* by Franz Kafka. Copyright © 1948 by Schocken Books, Inc.

Selected Poems of H. N. Bialik, edited by I. Efros, Bloch Publishing Co., New York.

"A Sense of Smell," "Till Now," and "A Whole Loaf," by S. Y. Agnon. Reprinted by permission of Schocken Books.

To Miriam and Dan

CONTENTS

PREFACE

The excitement caused by the rise to prominence in American literature during the 50's and 60's of writers of Jewish origin is easy enough to understand though in some ways difficult to justify critically. This sudden new ascendancy of Jewish writers was implicitly interpreted as a turning point both in the development of American culture and in the general cultural relationship of Jews to Western societies. When imaginative writers are expected in this way to offer through their work evidence or even validation for large historical trends, they are likely either to disappoint their audiences bitterly or to become the objects of tendentious misrepresentation, their artistic importance exaggerated, their cultural antecedents falsified or misleadingly stressed. Both these responses—occasional disappointment and frequent overestimation—have been elicited by those writers whose work simultaneously affirms (in many cases merely flaunts) their identity as Jews and as Americans.

One inference frequently drawn from the new movement seems sound enough: that the WASP cultural hegemony in America is over. On the whole, this would appear to be a good thing, since variety is by and large a healthy condition in art, and since writers no longer have to feel constrained to betray some part of themselves by masquerading as members of the "dominant" cultural group in the forms of literary expression they adopt. It seems rather doubtful, however, that the period of WASP hegemony will now be followed by a golden age of productive cultural pluralism. The vogue of Jewish writing, quickly exhausting its artistic possibilities, offers many indications that it may be falling into a declining phase of unwitting self-parody, and what will follow it on the American literary scene is by no means clear.

The literary phenomenon I have been describing is still often referred to as the "Jewish renaissance," a term which confesses the need of many American Jews to see in the new literature proof of the cultural viability and vitality of their own anomalous position as self-conscious Jews and comfortably acculturated Americans. It is precisely because they were looking in the new novels and short stories for an authentication of their own existence that many members of the great, nonintellectual, Jewish book-buying public were shocked and hurt to find writers representing their institutions as shams, their communities suffused with pettiness, spite, lust, hypocrisy, and pretense—just as human communities always have been. Intellectuals, on the other hand, both Jewish and Gentile, were inclined to see American Jewish writing as a powerful expression of that tenuous culture of marginality in which Jews are supposed, somehow, to combine the "moral insights" of age-old Jewish tradition with the new sensitivities produced by the position of vulnerable exposure in which Jews since the Enlightenment have typically found themselves.

Modern Jewish writers, then, both in this country and elsewhere, have been imagined for various reasons as heirs of a great tradition, when actually the very nature of their literary enterprise bespeaks the fact that the tradition has become alien, irrelevant, or at least profoundly ambiguous to them. The influence of traditional Jewish experience on American writers like Bellow and Malamud is for the most part peculiarly tangential, however conspicuous it may sometimes be in their work. To other Jewish writers, such experience is a matter of indifference, or, in certain cases, alas, something largely unknown that is consciously faked; and even Hebrew and Yiddish writers like S. Y. Agnon and I. B. Singer, who are steeped in the world of tradition, often express in their imaginative work an acute ambivalence toward that vanished world of piety.

I would suggest that Jewish life since the entrance of the Jews into modern culture may be usefully viewed as a precarious, though stubborn, experiment in the possibilities of historical continuity, when most of the grounds for continuity have been cut away. The serious literature produced by Jews in this period draws its distinctive creative energies from the modern Jewish predicament and at the same time revealingly documents that predicament in all its pained self-contradictions and confusions. In the essays that follow, therefore, I have tried to offer careful literary evaluations of the writers and works discussed, and in so doing I have also tried to see how this literature reflects or helps us to imagine more candidly the troubling root-problems of modern Jewish existence.

If an experiment in continuity or survival has been going on, it is now chiefly centered in two geographical locations in which the conditions of the experiment differ substantially— Israel, where the majority culture is Jewish and the common language derived from the language of Jewish tradition, and America, where the Jews are a vocal minority within what is supposedly a pluralistic culture, and where the medium of literary expression is not an indigenous Jewish language. Despite this tidy antithesis, the two forms of the experiment are plagued by many of the same ambiguities and at times reveal unsuspected affinities. Some observers, like the distinguished French sociologist, Georges Friedmann, have argued that Israel and America merely provide two different backgrounds for the same underlying process of assimilation: there Jews are ceasing to be Jews by becoming Israelis, as here they cease to be Jews by becoming Americans. Such formulations have a seductive neatness, against which I implicitly argue in several of the essays, as I would also argue against the opposite position of some Zionists that assimilation is, by definition, impossible in Israel, inevitable (when the Jews are not persecuted) elsewhere.

In any case, I am persuaded that Jews in America and Israel, because of their different yet complementary cultural predicaments, have much to learn from each other, and I think that juxtaposing Hebrew literary activity with the literature created by Jews in other languages can have the effect of throwing both into a sharper and more meaningful perspective. Most of the writers in both groups have been impelled by some need to define themselves in relation to—or sometimes willfully against—a common historical tradition, and the ways in which they differ and resemble each other are, it seems to me, often suggestive. The same basic concerns, then, literary and existential, moved me to deal with Jewish writing in both Hebrew and in other languages, though the essays on Hebrew literature are necessarily somewhat more descriptive, since I of course assumed that American readers would be largely unfamiliar with both the Hebrew writers and the nature of the Israeli literary situation.

Since this is a collection of essays initially written for periodical publication, there naturally are writers pertinent to the subject not included simply because the occasion to deal with them did not present itself. I should like to make clear, however, that the question of literary Jewishness is by no means equally relevant to all writers of Jewish descent, many of whom would merely be distorted by being forced into this particular context. It would never have occurred to me, for example, to write an essay on Norman Mailer while involved with the concerns of this book because Mailer's Jewish origins have only the most marginal bearing on his work as a writer. The figures I discuss, therefore, represent a sampling of those writers for whom a serious question can be raised of a relation to some kind of Jewish tradition, whether literary, religious, or national.

Literature in general seems to have the effect of intensifying the contradictory attitudes with which we all live, and this would appear to be true of modern Jewish writing in an especially transparent way. On the one hand, this literature has itself embodied on occasion much of the fakery and self-deception which the whole modern notion of "Jewishness" encourages, and, on the other hand, it has demonstrated most impressively how the literary imagination can serve as an instrument of unflinchingly honest self-confrontation. It was ultimately in the hope of showing something of this significant tension of contradiction that I wrote these essays.

The majority of the pieces offered here first appeared in *Commentary*, and I would like to thank its editors both for the congenial forum they have made available to me and for the permission to reprint the essays. I would also like to thank the editors of *Book Week, Daedalus, Hadassah Magazine, Judaism, Midstream,* and *Saturday Review,* for permission to reprint material that originally appeared in their pages. Most of the essays are presented with only very minor changes from their original versions, though in a few cases, where I felt that certain qualifications or amplifications were called for, I have not hesitated to prefer accuracy of statement now to the historical record of what I may have thought, or inadvertently implied, four or five years ago. The translations from the Hebrew in the essays are my own, with the exception of the excerpts from Sholom J. Kahn's anthology, *A Whole Loaf,* which are quoted in "The Israeli Novel—The Two Generations."

R.A.

Berkeley
March, 1968

I Varieties of Jewish Experience

JEWISH DREAMS AND NIGHTMARES

What have I in common with Jews? I have hardly anything
in common with myself and should stand very quietly in a
corner, content that I can breathe.—Franz Kafka, *Diaries*

There is something presumptuously proprietary about the
whole idea of sorting out writers according to national, ethnic,
or religious origins, like so many potatoes whose essential characteristics can be determined by whether they come from Idaho
or Maine. Obviously enough, the primary focus for useful criticism of any original writer must be on the stubbornly individual
imagination that has sought to articulate a personal sense of self
and world through the literary medium, and this attention to
individual peculiarities rather than shared characteristics is especially necessary in understanding serious writers since the middle of the last century, so many of whom have been alienated in
one way or another from their native social groups. Indeed, as
Kafka's chilling confession of self-estrangement reminds us,
some of the most troubled, and therefore representative, modern writers have been alienated from themselves as well,
haunted by the fear that every affirmation or act of communication was a falsification, a betrayal.

Nevertheless, the onerous question of the writer's background persists. One justifiably speaks of Melville, Hawthorne,
even Poe, as essentially American writers, for their achievement
cannot be intelligently grasped without an awareness of its
intimate relationship to the common social and cultural experience of nineteenth-century America. Even more strikingly, the
Jewishness of writers like Mendele, Peretz, and Sholom Aleichem obviously has the greatest relevance to any serious assessment of their literary enterprise because their fictional worlds

are shaped out of the stuff of East-European Jewish life, its language, its folklore, its religious traditions, its social realia. With Jewish writers, however, the attempt to attribute literary qualities to ethnic origins is in many instances acutely problematic. The Jews, in any case a perplexing group to define, become almost perversely elusive as the process of modernization spreads after the French Revolution. It is by no means clear what sense is to be made of the Jewishness of a writer who neither uses a uniquely Jewish language, nor describes a distinctively Jewish milieu, nor draws upon literary traditions that are recognizably Jewish. If one were to compile an anthology of all the unabashed nonsense written by literary critics over the past fifty years, a good many pages would have to be devoted to what has been advanced about the Jewish values, vision, and world view of a wide variety of apostates, supposed descendants of Jews, offspring of mixed marriages, or merely assimilated Jews, from St. Theresa and Heine down to Proust and even J. D. Salinger.

One cannot, however, simply discount the possibility that some essentially Jewish qualities may adhere to the writing of the most thoroughly acculturated Jews. Most readers have sensed in at least some of these "post-traditional" or "transitional" Jewish writers certain modes of imagination or general orientations toward art and experience that seem characteristically Jewish, even where the writer scrupulously avoids all references to his ethnic origins. The difficulty, of course, is to translate such vague intuitions into clear descriptive statements about what actually goes on in the literary works.

I was led to ponder again this intriguing but treacherous question of Jewish literary identity by an essay of Leslie Fiedler's, "Master of Dreams," published in the summer, 1967, issue of *Partisan Review*. What Fiedler sketches out in his essay might be described as a single grand mythic plot which, in sundry variations, modifications, and reversals, is presumed to underlie all Jewish literature, and, apparently, all Jewish cultural activity as well. Fiedler's point of departure is the Joseph story in Genesis, which he interestingly characterizes as a "dream of the dreamer, a myth of myth itself." Joseph, whose troubles begin because of his own seemingly grandiose dream, makes his way to power by interpreting the dreams of others and so translates his original dream into dazzling fact, his fathers and brothers—and virtually the whole world besides—bowing down to him as viceroy of the mightiest king on earth. In the light of this communal dream of the Joseph story, Fiedler sees the Jew's characteristic cultural role as a vendor of dreams and an interpreter of dreams to the world, that is, as poet and therapist (in Fiedler's anecdotal English, "My Son the Artist" and "My Son the Doctor"). The Jewish sons who become poets, according to this account, continue to pursue the original myth of myth: their fictions are about the attempt—what some of them now recognize as a doomed attempt—to make the splendid dream literal fact, and their fictional surrogates are even frequently called upon to resist the temptations of a Potiphar's wife in order to remain faithful to the dream they bear within them. Fiedler concedes that there are wide differences in the literary forms adopted by Jewish writers, but he suggests that they all belong to a single tradition both because they all participate in a Joseph-like myth of myth, and because they share a distinctive purpose, which, in keeping with the double role of the biblical master of dreams, is "therapeutic and prophetic."

Before I speak to the issues raised by this interpretation—and the hasty account of it here hardly does justice to its athletic ingenuity—I would like to point out a general characteristic of Fiedler's critical enterprise which this essay makes particularly clear. Fiedler's criticism has a paradoxical doubleness of effect. On the one hand, because his favorite critical activity is the relentless pursuit of archetypes, an ill-considered literary fashion of the fifties that went out with the Eisenhower Administration, there is often an odd hint of datedness in what he writes, despite the swinging, up-to-the-minute prose he affects. One senses in Fiedler, on the other hand, a peculiar venturesomeness and energy of imagination that set him off from the academic myth-mongers of the fifties, indeed, that endow his work with a perennial fascination. The main impulse of

Fiedler's criticism is neither analytic nor evaluative but poetic:* the fidelity it most steadily preserves is not at all to the works or figures discussed but to its own inner coherence as a poetic invention.

The treatment of the biblical subject in "Master of Dreams" suggests a useful analogue for Fiedler's criticism— Midrash, the early rabbinic method of homiletic exegesis. One possible way of describing Midrash is as the art of imaginatively connecting things intrinsically unconnected, and the same could be said of much that Fiedler has written. Since for the creators of the Midrash the entire Bible, together with the Oral Law, exists in one eternal, divinely revealed present, everything is potentially an intricate commentary on everything else. One needs only the recurrence of, say, a verb-root in a verse in Genesis, in Isaiah, and in Psalms, to see the later statements as explications, developments, fuller revelations of the earlier one. When, for example, the Midrash Bereshit Rabba tells us that Abraham's "splitting" of wood for the sacrifice of Isaac was answered on a grand scale by God's "splitting" of the Red Sea for his descendants, our real knowledge of the relevant verses in Genesis and Exodus has not been augmented, but what we may enjoy is following the trajectory of the interpretative imagination from point to point, not unlike the delight we take in the linking of ostensible disparates that is effected through poetic metaphor. This procedure is not so far removed from that of modern archetypal criticism, which in just such an instance might easily speak not of verbal continuities but of "the recurrence of the cleavage motif," with or without Freudian innuendos.

Fiedler is more subtle and inventive than most mythopoeic critics in his articulation of archetypes, but he clearly shares

* In a recent essay, "My First Gothic Novel" (*Novel*, fall, 1967), Fiedler has, while modestly claiming for himself a place with the great critics of the ages, asserted, "I am, almost above all else, an evaluating critic." What this means, though, is that he expresses emphatic opinions about the writers he discusses, not that he offers, in the manner of serious evaluative criticism, reasoned and persuasive criteria for assessing literature.

with the medieval Midrash an indifference to historical perspective which allows him to speak of the varied literary productions
of far-flung times and places as one eternal system, and he is
thoroughly midrashic in his readiness to establish through the
merest hint of an association a "real" connection between
things. Thus, there is actually not the faintest suggestion in the
biblical story that Joseph is either a poet or a therapist. He
interprets dreams for purposes at once practical and divine, but
surely not to cure anyone, while the common association between dreamer and poet which Fiedler invokes is not even
vaguely intimated in the biblical account. Though Fiedler would
have us think of Joseph as a prototype of both Freud and
Kafka, it makes better sense on the grounds of the text itself to
imagine Joseph rather as a sort of ancient Near Eastern RAND
Corporation figure—the Jewish intellectual as government
planner, manipulating that great Pharaonic power structure
from the top, managing, through his two Seven-Year Plans, to
centralize control of land and economic resources to a degree
unprecedented in Egyptian history. If Fiedler's own bold anach-
ronisms invite anachronistic response, this, too, is in the
ahistorical spirit of midrashic interpretation: the rabbis did not
hesitate to represent Joseph as an earlocked talmudist applying
himself to the subtleties of the Law in the study-house of
Shem, and by the same logic he can be given a Viennese beard,
a passion for literary self-expression, or a knowledge of com-
puter mathematics.

There is, then, a special fascination in Fiedler's criticism,
but as in the case of the ancient Midrashim, we may sometimes
want to qualify that fascination with an adjective like "quaint."
The real question raised by his whole scheme of an archetypal
Jewish myth of myth is not whether it is firmly anchored in the
biblical story but whether it is really helpful in locating and
identifying a distinctive Jewish movement in Western culture,
and in this essential regard I cannot see that it has any utility at
all. On the contrary, it seems to me to encourage a common
error much in need of correction. For there has been a tacit
conspiracy afoot in recent years to foist on the American public

as peculiarly Jewish various admired characteristics which in fact belong to the common humanity of us all. The Jewish folk is imagined as possessing a kind of monopoly on vividness, compassion, humor, pathos, and the like; Jewish critics and novelists are thought to be unique in their preoccupation with questions of morality; and now we are asked to believe that the Jews have all along exercised a privileged control over the cultural market on dreams.

When Fiedler characterizes the Joseph story as "the dreamer's own dream of how, dreaming, he makes it in the waking world," and then goes on to represent modern Jewish writing as a varying account of the difficulties of "making it" through dreams in actuality, he is describing not a distinctively Jewish imaginative mode but the central tradition of the novel, from *Don Quixote* to *Lolita.* Cervantes had hit on a new set of literary terms to encompass a new, radically disorienting world (the one we still inhabit) by inventing a dreamer who madly and persistently tried to live out his shining dream in a gray existence stolidly resistant to dreams and intolerant of their perpetrators. The model of the heroically unhinged Don, progenitor of a genre, is followed by Stendhal's Julien Sorel, Flaubert's Emma Bovary, Dostoevski's Prince Mishkin and his Raskolnikov, Melville's Ahab, George Eliot's Dorothea Brooke, Gide's Lafcadio, Joyce's Stephen Daedalus as well as his Leopold Bloom—in fact, by the protagonists of most of the substantial novels written over the past two centuries. One might of course seize on the conjecture of some literary historians that Cervantes himself was a Marrano or the descendant of converts from Judaism, but this would be to succumb to a kind of philosemitic version of the *Protocols of the Elders of Zion* as an explanation of Western culture. According to such a theory, which seems to be tacitly assumed by many critics, the main currents at least of modern culture all derive from subterranean Jewish sources: a tenuous connection through three Christian generations with Jewish forebears is supposedly enough to infect the writer with a uniquely Jewish imagination, and this in turn he passes on to the Gentile world around him. (Fiedler applies much the same logic to fictional characters in describing the hero of *An American Dream* as an "essentially" Jewish figure by arbitrarily identifying him as a compound of two projected characters in Mailer's unwritten long novel, one Gentile and the other one-quarter Jewish, which then enables him blithely to assert that "Stephen Rojack . . . is half-Jewish, since in the world of myth a quarter Jew plus a full Gentile equals a half-Jew.") All this is undoubtedly somewhat less incredible than the obverse theory that the Jews have secretly seized control of Western civilization in order to destroy it from within, but it resembles the *Protocols* myth in reshaping observable realities to fit the contours of collective fantasy.

It is not the Jewish dreamer in Exile but the writer at large who "thinking only of making his own dreams come true, ends by deciphering the alien dreams of that world as well," and the "prophetic" and "therapeutic" ends which Fiedler assigns to Jewish writers are in fact the general aims of most serious European and American writers at least since the middle of the nineteenth century. The Joseph scheme works all too well in too many cases, whether we apply it to the writer's life or to his literary creations. Who, for example, could be closer to the archetype of Joseph than Charles Dickens, a master of dreams who determined from early youth to realize a great dream of worldly success and achieved it by creating and selling dreams to the millions—"the artist as tycoon," in F. W. Dupee's telling phrase—even to acquiring the very Gads Hill mansion he had envisaged from afar as a boy? The prophetic and therapeutic impulse in Dickens' novels hardly needs comment at this point in time, and it is equally clear that in the works of his maturity, by bodying forth in fiction his own dreams, he was interpreting the collective dreams of a culture to which part of him remained permanently alien, from his descent into the pit of the blacking warehouse as a child to his glorious assumption into the palaces of the great.

Or, using this same mythic touchstone to identify characteristically Jewish literary inventions, one might justifiably conclude that the most remarkable American Jewish novel is neither *Call It Sleep* nor *Herzog* but Ralph Ellison's *Invisible Man*. Ellison prefaces his book with a dedication to Morteza Sprague, "a dedicated dreamer in a land most strange," which is a neat description of the archetypal Joseph himself and also accurately characterizes Ellison's protagonist. The novel begins and ends with a dream and many of the intervening episodes are strikingly dreamlike, for the protagonist is at once attempting to escape a nightmare and realize a dream of worldly success, on the world's own meretricious terms. His slow recognition of who he really is—"I am your brother Joseph," one almost hears him saying in the poignant scene where he realizes his deep kinship with an evicted Harlem couple—involves a rejection of the false dream, a perception of the extent to which the nightmare is reality. In this version, it is at the end of his long journey from home that he is cast into a dark pit, Joseph-like, by those who should be his brothers, and he promises us that he will emerge from these depths with a new unillusioned strength. There are even Potiphar's wives to mislead this young man with a vision on his progress through a land most strange. In contrast to the three sexual partners of Steve Rojack—that highly supposititious "mythical" Jew—who are improbably seen by Fiedler as Potiphar's wives, the two white seductresses in *Invisible Man* are really imagined as alien women who, by using the hero for their own gratification, would thrust him into a false role, would unwittingly involve him in a symbolic betrayal of himself and his people. It is difficult, finally, to think of a novel written by a Jew that is as intent as this one to enunciate a prophecy and effect a kind of therapy. The young Negro, by working out the visions that haunt him, ends up deciphering the darker dreams of American society as well. It is entirely appropriate that the novel should conclude with a long dream-like sequence charged with intimations of apocalypse, the nightmare now galloping across the waking world, and that this episode in turn should be followed by a formal, allegorical dream of apocalypse, prophesying doom to America if it does not act quickly to redeem its own humanity.

The tracing of archetypes is a pleasant enough pastime, but

its value as a means of making useful literary identifications is dubious. Ellison himself has stated the matter succinctly in objecting to another archetypal interpretation of his novel: "archetypes are timeless, novels are time-haunted." If we are to discover any clue to the connection between a writer's origins in a particular group and the nature of his work, we must begin in time, which is to say, we must take history seriously into account. The case of Kafka, whom Fiedler cites as the great modern paradigm of Joseph as artist, the Jewish son as dreamer, takes us to the heart of this whole issue. No other Jew who has contributed significantly to European literature appears so intensely, perhaps disturbingly, Jewish in the quality of his imagination as Kafka. Though he never introduces explicitly Jewish materials into his work, though he never really writes "about" Jews (even symbolically, I would argue), most readers of *The Trial, The Castle, Amerika,* and the shorter parables and fables, have sensed that this peculiar mode of fiction would never have occurred to a Christian imagination. One is struck by the emphatic difference of Kafka's work from the various kinds of fiction that have been predominant in the European novel, but it is not so easy to determine whether or how that difference is Jewish.

To think of Kafka as a Joseph-figure will not really help us, for reasons which I hope I have already made clear. The invocation of that archetype does not, for example, enable us to distinguish between Kafka and Dickens, a writer whom he admired and imitated, and who shared with him a "Jewish" preoccupation with failed relationships between fathers and sons. Critics have made a variety of other suggestions about the Jewishness of Kafka's fiction, some of them comical, some interesting, some perhaps even credible. To begin with, there has been a general rush to align Kafka with various Jewish cultural traditions, without regard to the degree of familiarity he may actually have had with them. The fact that Kafka is both a Jewish writer and an arcane one has invited a certain degree of loose talk about the "kabbalistic" elements in his work, though he had no direct knowledge of the Kabbalah, and the Germanized home in which he grew up was hardly the sort where he could have picked up very much of it through oral tradition. More plausibly, comparisons have been drawn between the Hasidic folktale and the parable form Kafka favored in which the order of action is so often inscrutably miraculous. The biographical evidence, however, suggests affinity rather than influence. Kafka was fascinated by whatever he learned of Hasidic lore, but the better part of his acquaintance with it took place toward the end of his life, through his friendship with Georg Langer and then from his reading of Buber's early compilations, especially *Der grosse Maggid*, which did not appear until 1922. Again, a good many critics who have never studied a page of the Talmud have not hesitated to describe the peculiar questioning movement of Kafka's prose as "talmudic," but there is virtually no real similarity, and in any case Kafka's knowledge of the Talmud, until his last years, was confined to quotations passed on to him by those of his friends who had once studied in the East-European *yeshivot*. One is free to suppose, of course, that Westernized Jews as a rule simply continue to talk and think in talmudic fashion, but such a supposition can be made only out of ignorance of both the Talmud itself and the way modern Jews actually talk and think.

Heinz Politzer, in his book, *Franz Kafka: Parable and Paradox*, links Kafka's fiction somewhat more probably with a still older mode of Jewish literature. Politzer compares Kafka's spare, taut tales, which repeatedly generate a sense of fatal significance in the events narrated, to the narrative method of the Hebrew Bible. Picking up the notion developed by Erich Auerbach of the biblical story as a tale "fraught with background," Politzer argues that in Kafka's enigmatic fictions one can observe this same general effect of starkly drawn surfaces which suggest a heavy pressure of dark meanings behind them that are never spelled out by the narrator. In Kafka, he goes on to say, as in the ancient Hebrew stories, the characters are at once impersonal and more than personal, uncannily representative in their very distance and peculiarity, inviting multiple interpretation by leading us to think of them as our surrogates in a cosmic drama. Kafka certainly read the Hebrew Bible in translation intently, occasionally even alluded to aspects of his own experience in biblical terms, and at the end of his life he was learning to read it in its original language. It is at least plausible that his familiarity with the Bible helped him work out his own characteristic narrative art; in any case, he must have discovered in it a compelling imaginative kinship. Such notions of kinship, however, can be adopted for the needs of precise literary analysis only with great caution, for they are but a step away from assuming a Hebrew Imagination over against a Greek Imagination as timeless categories, which, of course, would bring us back through another door into the wide-and-woolly realm of myths of culture.

Critics less interested in Kafka's treatment of literary form than in his moral, philosophical, and theological concerns have associated him not with Jewish literary traditions but with the distinctive values and assumptions of historical Judaism. Thus, the absence of any radical disjuncture in Kafka between spirit and flesh, this world and the next, even between the prosaic and the miraculous, has been attributed to his Jewish background, which, it must be admitted, is a suggestive idea if not altogether a demonstrable one. The fact, on the other hand, that moral or spiritual obligations in Kafka so often take the form of commandments from an unreachable authority and frequently necessitate torturous interpretation, can obviously be connected with Kafka's personal awareness of rabbinic Judaism, and represents a particularly Jewish formulation of a general spiritual predicament. Still clearer is the condition of exile—for Jews, a theological category as well as a historical experience—which underlies all of Kafka's major fiction. It is this, above all else, that commentators have quite properly stressed in identifying the distinctively Jewish note in Kafka: if modern literature in general is a literature that adopts the viewpoint of the outsider, Kafka, as the alienated member of an exiled people, is the paradigmatic modernist precisely because he is a paradigmatic Jew.

The general validity of this familiar idea is, I suppose, unassailable, but its usefulness is limited because of the very fact that in its usual formulation it remains so general. "Exile" tends to be applied to Kafka and to other Jewish writers as an evocative but unexamined abstraction with a supposedly fixed meaning, when in fact exile meant different things to different Jews at various times and places, and for most of them, at least until fairly recently, it was quite distinct from alienation, a concept with which many literary critics automatically identify it. It makes sense, therefore, to try to state in concrete terms how this particular writer seems to have encountered the experience of exile and then how that encounter enters into the substance of his imaginative work.

Living in Prague, Kafka of course belonged to a very special kind of double exile—a Jew in the Austro-Hungarian Empire and a German writer in a Czech city. His position, moreover, as an employee in a state-sponsored insurance agency extended his initial sense of himself as a suspect intruder: at his office he was, as he pointedly phrased it, the single "display-Jew" in a "dark nest of bureaucrats," and so every workday forced upon him at least the negative awareness of Jewishness as a condition of being unwanted, mistrusted, transparently dependent on the favor of others. At the same time, Kafka was acutely conscious of Jewish history and Jewish peoplehood, even without any deep knowledge of the former or very much external involvement in the latter, until the Zionism of his last years. He was inclined to view the Jews of his own generation as in fact transitional, standing uncertainly at the irrevocable end of a long process of Jewish history, but this sense of belonging to a twilight period seems to have had the effect of sharpening his interest in the history and culture of his people. The Yiddish theater in Prague, for example, held a fascination for Kafka out of all proportion to the artistic merit of the plays it presented because he saw in it the living manifestation of an uninhibited, self-sufficient folk culture, unlike anything he had known personally. The very idea of Yiddish literature continued to attract him—he carefully read and took notes in his diary on Pines's *Histoire de la littérature Judéo-Allemande*—because with its obvious stress on "an uninterrupted tradition of national struggle that determines every work," he envisaged it as an alluring antithesis to that anguished exploration of a private world which writing inevitably was for him.

The case of Kafka, the acculturated Jew, shows how a man may feel his way into a body of collective history through his very consciousness of being outside it: Kafka brooded over the experience of the people from whom he derived, and I would argue that certain key images and states of awareness that were the product of European Jewish history exerted continual pressure on his imagination as he wrote. In this connection, there is one passage in his recorded conversations with the Czech writer Gustav Janouch that is especially revealing. Janouch had asked him if he still remembered the old Jewish quarter of Prague, largely destroyed before Kafka could have known it; this, according to Janouch, is the reply he received:

> In us it still lives—the dark corners, the secret alleys, shuttered windows, squalid courtyards, rowdy pubs, and sinister inns. We walk through the broad streets of the newly built town. But our steps and our glances are uncertain. Inside we tremble just as before in the ancient streets of our misery. Our heart knows nothing of the slum clearance which has been achieved. The unhealthy old Jewish town within us is far more real than the new hygienic town around us. With our eyes open we walk through a dream: ourselves only a ghost of a vanished age.

This remarkable statement is a kind of spiritual autobiography, a summary of what the awareness of being a Jew meant in Kafka's inner life; at the same time, it might be observed that what he has in effect described here is the imaginative landscape of all three of his novels—the hidden alleys and sinister attics of *The Trial,* the medieval squalor and confusion of the courtyards, the dubious inns and devious byways in *The Castle,* and even the new-world landscape of *Amerika,* which begins with skyscrapers but breaks off in a dark and filthy garret where the protagonist is held prisoner. The world of Kafka's novels incorporates the maddening impersonality and inscrutability of modern bureaucracy in an image of an insecure medieval community derived from a ghetto Kafka remembered obsessively without ever having known

Let me emphasize that the recognition of such a connection may tell us something about the genesis of Kafka's enigmatic fictions but it is by no means a key to their meaning. What Kafka's imaginative intimacy with the Jewish past did was to give a special shape to the imagery and a particular sharpness to the edge of feeling in his work, but the work is surely not intended as a representation of Jewish experience. It is, for example, a serious misplacement of emphasis to describe *The Castle*, as a few critics have done, as a Zionist myth of an outcast in search of a land, though the novel would not have been conceived in the terms it was and would not carry the conviction it does without Kafka's concrete imagination of uncertain steps and glances along the ancient streets of Jewish misery. Or again, to insist that the eternally exiled hero of "The Hunter Gracchus" is an avatar of the Wandering Jew would be to force a hauntingly elusive tale into the predictable contours of allegory. It seems wiser to say that Kafka's general and untranslatable fable of a wanderer through awesome eternity is imagined with such disturbing intensity because of the presence in the writer of Jewish memories, personal and collective, out of which he could create this particular "ghost of a vanished age" walking open-eyed through a dream of damnation. It is not as an archetypal Jew that Gracchus speaks at the end of the story, but the words and images his inventor chooses for him resonate with the experience of rejection and exclusion of many generations: "Nobody will read what I say here, no one will come to help me; even if all the people were commanded to help me, every door and window would remain shut, everybody would take to bed and draw the bedclothes over his head, the whole earth would become an inn for a night." It is one of those unsettling moments in Kafka when, in the retrospectively ironic light of history, we see the recollection of the past as a grimly accurate prophecy of the future, too.

Another major theme of Kafka's, which he often connects with the situation of the outsider or pariah, is the irruption of the inhuman into the human, or more generally, the radical ambiguity of what seems to be human. While this movement of his imagination was obviously energized by the tensions and fears of his own private neuroses, it seems to me that his notion of a convergence of inhuman and human frequently draws on his hallucinated memory of the Jewish past. Even in a bizarre story like "A Report to an Academy," which is so far removed from any overt reference to Jews, I would contend that Kafka's fictional invention is formed on a kind of "analogical matrix" of his experience as a transitional Jew. The scientific report, one recalls, is that of a gifted ape who has managed "with an effort which up till now has never been repeated . . . to reach the cultural level of an average European." In the torturous confinement of a cage so small that he could neither stand nor sit in it, the idea had dawned on the ape of getting out by imitating his captors, and he began, most appropriately, by learning to spit, and then to drink schnapps by the bottle, an act which at first violently repelled him. In retrospect, the ape stresses again and again that he finds no intrinsic advantage in being human: "there was no attraction for me in imitating human beings; I imitated them because I needed a way out, and for no other reason . . . ah, one learns when one has to; one learns when one needs a way out." Conversely, the ape makes no special plea for apehood; there may be nothing especially admirable in being an ape rather than a human, but, if one begins as an ape, it is at least an authentic condition, what one would naturally prefer to remain, other things being equal. When at the end of the report the ape adjures his audience, "Do not tell me that it was not worth the trouble," there is a quaver of doubt in his voice: cages are admittedly maddening to live in, but has he not lost a great deal by betraying his native self for a way out, selling his birthright, so to speak, for a mess of lentils?

Now, one of the distinctive qualities of a Kafka parable is that it has no paraphrasable "moral," and I would not want to transform "A Report to an Academy" into an allegory of assimilation. I suspect, however, that this fable which calls into question the whole status of humanity was initially shaped around Kafka's awareness of himself as part of the modern movement of Jews who had emerged from the confinement of ghetto life to join European culture, and that the ape's disquieting ambiguity about his own achievement flows from Kafka's insight into how much of themselves Jews had left behind in their former existence without even the compensation of genuine acceptance in the "human" world outside the cage. The very contrast between human and Jew was one that modernizing Jews themselves implicitly accepted in their desperation for a way out. The poet Y. L. Gordon's famous line, "Be a man outside and a Jew at home," summed up this whole self-negating mentality as it was articulated in the Hebrew Enlightenment, and Kafka himself must have been particularly struck by Gordon's formulation, for he copied it into his diary when he ran across it in Pines's history.

Typically, however, confusions between human and inhuman in Kafka terrify more than they perplex, and the imaginative core of that terror is often Jewish for this writer who lived so intensely with the fear and trembling of a vanished ghetto. The nightmarish little tale entitled "An Old Manuscript" is paradigmatic in this respect. Again, the terms of reference of the story are as universal as those of some ancient myth. A nameless town in a nameless empire has been taken over by fierce, implacable nomads who speak no recognizably human tongue. The Emperor remains a powerless spectator, shut up in his palace, a little like the symbolic King of banished sons in many of the midrashic parables, while the townspeople, in the person of the cobbler who is the narrator, confess their incapacity to cope with the terrible strangers:

> From my stock, too, they have taken many good articles. But I cannot complain when I see how the butcher, for instance, suffers across the street. As soon as he brings in any meat the nomads snatch it all from him and gobble it up. Even their horses devour flesh; often enough a horseman and his horse are lying side by side, both of them gnawing at the same joint, one at either end. The butcher is nervous and does not dare to stop his deliveries of meat. We understand

that, however, and subscribe money to keep him going. If the nomads got no meat, who knows what they might think of doing; who knows anyhow what they may think of, even though they get meat every day.

One does not have to invoke mythic archetypes to feel the bone and blood of Jewish memories in these ghastly images. Behind the nameless nomadic horsemen are dark hordes of Cossacks, Haidameks, pogromists of every breed—the alien and menacing *goy* in his most violent embodiments, speaking no intelligible language, obeying no human laws, even eagerly violating, as we learn in the next paragraph, the Noahide injunction against consuming the flesh of an animal while it is still alive. To the Jew trembling before the torch and ax and sword of the attacker, it seemed that the enemy quite literally could not belong to the same species, and so here the ironic displacement of inhuman and human of "A Report to an Academy" is reversed, the Jew, in the analogical matrix of this story, associated with vulnerable humanity, and the Gentile with inhuman otherness.

What should also be noted is that the story pronounces judgment on the passivity of the townspeople as well as on the stark bestiality of the nomads. Edmund Wilson has accused Kafka of "meaching compliance" with the brutal and unreasonable forces he means to expose in his fiction, but I think this misses the point, for the object of Kafka's "satire" (the term is applied by Wilson) is not only the inhuman powers but also man's pathetic inadequacy of response to them. To put this in terms of the ethnic background of Kafka's imaginings, he never sentimentalized Jewish history; though he was intrigued by the lore of his forebears and their unusual sense of community, he remained ruthlessly honest about the way Jews were. In the passage quoted, one can see a distinctly familiar response of Jews to violence and impending disaster—the attempt to buy off calamity, to temporize with it. (How sadly characteristic that the tradesmen of the community should answer the terrible challenge only by pooling resources to subsidize the principal victim of the invaders!) The story makes clear that this response represents a failure of courage and of imagination as well: in the face of imminent and hideous destruction, where bold, perhaps violent, action is required, the townspeople can muster no more than a piously impotent wringing of hands, a collection of donations, and the grotesquely timid understatement that "This is a misunderstanding of some kind; and it will be the ruin of us."

Kafka, in sum, addressed himself to the broadest questions of human nature and spiritual existence, working with images, actions, and situations that were by design universal in character; but his self-awareness as a Jew and his consciousness of Jewish history impelled his imagination in a particular direction and imparted a peculiar intensity to much of what he wrote, where the abstractness or generality of the parable is strangely wedded to the most concrete sense of actual experience felt and recollected. He could envision the ultimate ambiguities of human life in general with a hyperlucidity because he had experienced them in poignant particularity as a Jew. Out of the stuff of a Jewish experience which he himself thought of as marginal, he was able to create fiction at once universal and hauntingly Jewish.

All this is far from exhausting the question of how Kafka's antecedents enter into his writing, but it should at least suggest that there is no simple formulaic key for identifying the Jewish character of all Jewish writers. As I have tried to illustrate in the case of Kafka, one must always attend to the particular ways in which Jewish experience impinges on the individual, and this impingement is bound to differ in small things and large from one writer to the next. The varied materials of art itself, with their confusingly various connections with reality, are more recalcitrant, less pleasingly symmetrical, than the neat designs of archetypal criticism, but, in the final analysis, they are a good deal more interesting.

1968

SENTIMENTALIZING THE JEWS

The peculiar cultural phenomenon which some choose to call an American Jewish literary renaissance is by now showing signs of having overstayed its critical welcome: one begins to suspect that too much has been made of what may not have been such a significant or valid development in the first place. There is no question that a great many writers now active in America are of Jewish descent. This hardly justifies, however, those critics, readers, publishers, members of the organized Jewish community, and a few of the writers themselves, who all insist on the Jewish character of this literary activity in order to give weight to both its contemporary and traditional implications.

It ought to be self-evident, first of all, that a literary renaissance can take place only where there is a general cultural milieu alive enough to nourish an original, distinctive literature. A case in point is the extraordinary flowering of Hebrew poetry in Spain from the eleventh to the fourteenth centuries—a movement which has been seized on by some overly optimistic Jewish observers as an analogy for contemporary Jewish writing in this country. But a genius like Shmuel Hanagid, the poet-vizier of eleventh-century Granada, transcended his Arabic models in his contemplative personal lyrics and in his great battle poems not because of some mysterious Jewish "sensibility," but because his imagination could draw freely and variously on a living literary tradition that ran from Genesis to the Responsa. A necessary precondition for the literary renaissance created by Hanagid and his successors was a deeply rooted autonomous Jewish culture which could supply these sources of significant innovation from within the larger context of Arabic secular culture.

By contrast, the so-called renaissance of American Jewish literature has come into being out of what is, from the Jewish point of view, almost a complete cultural vacuum. Given the general state of Jewish culture in America, it is quite understandable that nearly all the American Jews who have become writers are just like other Americans, if not even more so. The typical involvement in Jewish culture consists of an acquaintance with *gefilte* fish and crass *bar mitzvahs*, a degree of familiarity with overstuffed Jewish matriarchs, and a mastery of several pungent Yiddish synonyms for the male organ. With such a cultural heritage at his command, the American Jewish writer is vaguely expected to produce imaginative work rich in Jewish moral insights, alive with Jewish fantasy, humor, and pathos, in a prose whose varied textures will reproduce the exciting differentness of "marginal" experience.

One of the stories in *Roar Lion Roar*, a first volume of fiction by Irvin Faust, includes a delightful incident that can be taken as a paradigm for the predicament of many American Jewish writers, especially the younger ones who have begun to publish recently. Myron Leberfeld, the teen-age protagonist of "Miss Dorothy Thompson's American Eaglet," has ventured forth from his native Brooklyn, impelled by wartime patriotism, to work on a Vermont farm. There he is confronted—for in such a setting, nothing less than a confrontation could be expected—by the inevitable farmer's daughter, who is, of course, a piece of quintessential America: backwoodsy, big-busted, good-natured, and irrevocably naïve. Rita Ann, a hospitable girl in any case, is thrilled by the idea of having so exotic a creature as a Jew in her own home. But she inadvertently confounds the newcomer when she turns to him with the request, "Myron, talk Jew to me." Myron, with a knowledge of "Jew" scarcely larger than Rita Ann's, rummages through his memory and finally seizes on a phrase recalled from a favorite German record of his aunt's: "Ish leeba Dick," he pronounces mysteriously.

> The effect was exhilarating. "Oh," Rita Ann moaned softly, "say that again."

"Ish . . . leeba . . . Dick."

"Oooh. What's it mean?"

This I remembered, at least to a point. "I love you . . . Dick."

Faust, whose stories are refreshingly free of portentousness, does not mean this encounter to symbolize anything, but the analogy to his generation of American Jewish writers is in some cases painfully close. These younger writers, appearing as they do after the successes of Bellow, Malamud, and Roth in the fifties and especially now after the spectacular popularity of *Herzog* and the remarkable revival of *Call It Sleep,* often end up playing the role of a pseudoexotic Myron opposite the American reading public's gaping Rita Ann. The one quality which seems most to distinguish Jewish writing in this country is its growing self-consciousness about its own Jewishness. Everyone is by now aware of the fact that literary Jewishness has become a distinct commercial asset, and at least Bellow and Isaac Bashevis Singer have shown that it can be an artistic resource as well. Some of the younger writers thus feel called upon to "talk Jew" in their fiction, but, unlike Myron in the story, they do not seem to realize either their own ignorance or the falseness of their position.

One clear symptom of this general condition are the palpably ersatz touches of Jewish local color that have been appearing with increasing frequency in recent novels and stories —garbled Yiddish, misconstrued folklore, plainly impossible accounts of synagogue services and religious observances. Faust again offers a convenient model in his "Jake Bluffstein and Adolph Hitler." The story is transparently a *conte à thèse* about Jewish self-hatred and the Jew's fascination with moral qualities dramatically antithetical to his own. This schematic presentation of a complex psychological phenomenon is embarrassingly inept because Jake Bluffstein, as even his name suggests, has been imagined with no more individuality or ethnic authenticity than the stereotyped Jew of a tired anecdote. Jake Bluffstein's thought and speech are flavored, if that is really the right word, with an oddly limited set of Yiddishisms—the usual obscenities, and a few words like *shikkah* (which Faust seems to think is Yiddish for "drunk") and *tzoris* (which is construed as a singular noun). The place of worship Bluffstein frequents is an androgynous sort of affair that is sometimes described as an old-fashioned *shul* and alternately spoken of as a "temple" with an Americanized rabbi. The entire story was obviously a mistake on Faust's part—he does considerably better with other materials—but it is a mistake which illustrates the compromised position into which many American Jewish writers have worked themselves.

In more general terms, what has happened over the last decade is that a new sentimental literary myth of the Jew has gained what appears to be general acceptance in American fiction and criticism. A sentimental literary myth usually represents the failure of a culture to come to terms with some vital aspect of its own life; most often, the culture responds to its own inadequacy by projecting its secret fears, its unadmitted desires or illusory fantasies of itself onto a patently unreal image of a figure from another culture. (One has only to recall the image of the South- or East-European slinking through Victorian fiction, dark, sultry, sexually potent and attractive, an embodiment of bold and perhaps unsettling possibilities of freedom.) Such myths are sentimental because they are not live responses to any observable realities but rather sets of contrivances—stock situations, characters, and images—intended to produce certain desired emotions or predetermined states of imagination.

To understand how a sentimental myth about the Jew has been fostered in recent American literature, we have to remind ourselves that the so-called American Jewish writers are—with rare exceptions—culturally American in all important respects and only peripherally or vestigially Jewish. It seems to me that this elementary fact needs a great deal of emphasis. We are accustomed to admiring the marginal man's supposed advantage in perspectives on the disparate worlds he straddles: so many great modern writers have been outsiders, the argument runs, and this has been preeminently true of the Jews. But the fact is that the role of the Jew—and especially the intellectual

Jew—as an outsider in American life has generally dwindled into an affectation or a stance of pious self-delusion.

Ironically, what most American Jewish writers are outsiders to is that very body of Jewish experience with which other Americans expect them to be completely at home. The result of this reversed situation is a reversal of the critical perspective which is an outsider's proverbial birthright. That is, the American writer of Jewish descent finds himself utilizing Jewish experience of which he is largely ignorant, and so the Jewish skeletons of his characters are fleshed with American fantasies about Jews. The result is a kind of double sentimental myth: the Jew emerges from this fiction as an imaginary creature embodying both what Americans would like to think about Jews and what American Jewish intellectuals would like to think about themselves. From the larger American point of view, the general assent to the myth of the Jew reflects a decay of belief in the traditional American literary heroes—the eternal innocent, the tough guy, the man in quest of some romantic absolute—and a turning to the supposed aliens in our midst for an alternative image of the true American.

Leslie Fiedler has for years been an ideologue of the new sentimental myth; *Back to China,* his most recent novel, because it illustrates the myth with the engaging clarity of a well-drawn comic strip, marks out most of the important guidelines that both generations of American Jewish writers seem to be using for their literary ideal of the Jew. Baro Finklestone, the hero of Fiedler's novel, is, predictably, an archetypal outsider—a Jew in Montana, an intellectual among the hicks, a square despite himself among hipsters, and so forth. Like all Jews who are allowed to be the protagonists of novels, Finklestone is an inveterate *shlemiel,* but in his very ineffectuality and muddleheadedness, he is also—Fiedler must insist—morally sensitive in a way that others are not. He is not just a well-meaning, perennially protesting liberal; he really cares about other human beings, he carries the world's guilt on his shoulders, and he is driven to a sort of self-immolation in an attempt to expiate that guilt. This last touch, incidentally, introduces the by-now-familiar motif of the Jew as Christ, which itself is a good indication of the degree to which the fantasy-image of the Jew in American fiction is American and Christian in its deepest imaginings.

Finklestone, as a moral preceptor without real disciples, also illustrates one version of the fashionable archetype with diagrammatic neatness in being a father in quixotic search of a son. (Here Leopold Bloom lurks in the background.) Since we no longer like to take our moral preceptors straight, Fiedler supplies his with elaborate camouflage. Finklestone is a compassionate and honest man—in the bed of his best friend's wife; a seeker for the truth—through the agency of mescaline. Like the heroes of many American Jewish novels, he alternates between the role of the zany and that of an updated version of the Hebrew sage, "caught between the impulse to play the clown and a resolve to act the professor." But one begins to suspect that the former role is intended mainly to make the latter more palatable. I, at any rate, become skeptical when Fiedler writes of his archetypal exiled hero that there is a "trace of something oriental about him which had made him feel always a visible stranger in the ultimate West." This sounds perilously close to Daniel Deronda, that well-meant but silly Gentile fantasy of the Jew as Mysterious Stranger, a dark, exotic figure from the East who has been through the crucible of suffering and emerged a creature of saintly gentleness, with unguessed inner stores of moral wisdom.

The general formula, in fact, for the Jew as literary hero in this new version of an old sentimental myth is Daniel Deronda with cap and bells, Daniel Deronda in the cool world or on the dissident fringes of academia, perhaps flouting conventional morality, certainly talking and acting bizarrely, but Daniel Deronda nevertheless. Whatever the particular twists, he is a man with a luminous past and a great if desperate dream for the future, his heritage of suffering and survival providing him with a unique adeptness in the ultimate science of knowing how to be.

Earl Rovit's *The Player King*, a first novel published in 1965, could serve as a textbook introduction to this whole literary image of the Jew. Rovit is a novelist with dazzling verbal gifts (in sharp contrast to all the other new writers) and with an artistic self-consciousness that is occasionally an asset but more often a serious impediment to his writing. His novel is framed by opening and concluding dialogues between the author and a Yiddish-accented alter ego. Moreover, there is an inner frame, the journal of a novelist who is presumably writing the principal story; and inserted between chapters of what one hesitantly calls the novel itself are parodies of imagined reviews of the book and a *Paris Review* interview with the author of *The Player King*. In all this literary talk, which is sometimes very bright and often quite funny, Rovit suggestively characterizes the myth in which his characters are caught up and out of which he—"vaudevillian of the interior consciousness . . . crucified clown of the esthetic high wire"—has contrived a distinctive narrative mode.

According to Rovit, or rather one of his several personae, the two great myths of Christian literature, Christ and Faust, the Victim and the Victimizer, are dead, and their place is now taken by the myth of the Jew, at once a grotesque figure of fun and an uncanny shaman-hero:

> The Wandering Jew has taken off his cloak (the mysterious greasy black of the ghetto, the usurer's pit, the worn entrails of the peddler's pack) and he is naked revealed for the first time. There is a white scar on his side which has sealed into a pious caricature of the comic mask. . . . The feet are strangely pale and long-boned, and he rolls from heel to ball in dark reminiscence of the Mourner's Chant.

There is unresolved irony here: it is hard to know just what is meant seriously and what satirically. This very irresolution is Rovit's way of hanging onto both the grotesque mask and the sentimental image behind the mask. But the mythicized Jew, sheltering in that "mysterious greasy black of the ghetto," is clearly present both in this passage and elsewhere in the novel, for all the ingenious disguises Rovit provides him.

"Mysterious" is notoriously a dangerous word to use in a novel, even half-ironically. It is usually a sign that the novelist is in some way asking us to assume complexities of feeling which his art has not in fact been able to evoke. In this connection, there is a very funny moment in *The Player King* which inadvertently points to the core of hollowness in the fashionable mythic version of the Jew. The protagonist discovers that the zipper of his fly won't close, and, shielding himself with a copy of *Ebony*, he makes his way to the nearest tailor, who he finds has just locked up for the day. When the little old Jew refuses to open the door, the stricken hero explains that "It's worse than trouble, it's tzoris I got." This is the magic tribal password: the door swings open and the tailor, grinning, answers, "Trouble is trouble, but tzoris—dat's someding else."

But is it really? The two words, of course, were created in different historical circumstances, each was gradually molded into its own particular contours of meaning by different kinds of experience. But the pressure of collective experience that has shaped the Yiddish word is scarcely present in Rovit's book: it is the word itself which is waved like a magic wand, just as in this and other novels the name or idea of the Jew is invoked and the naked invocation is expected to conjure up all sorts of images, from epiphany to pogrom, of a unique history and a unique moral heritage.

One of the most bizarre expressions of the sentimentality of this myth is the motif of conversion or quasi-conversion that has been improbably cultivated in American Jewish fiction. The model, of course, is the circumcision of Frank Alpine at the end of Malamud's *The Assistant*. There is something instructively peculiar about that act. Circumcision, after all, is a theologically serious matter; it means sealing a covenant in the flesh between a people and its God. But the idea of being a Jew in Malamud's novel—as is generally the case in American Jewish fiction—is shorthand for a set of moral abstractions: Jewishness is equated with an ethic of hard work, integrity, acceptance of responsibility, forbearance in distress, and so forth. Since there is no necessary connection between any of these qualities and being a flesh-and-blood Jew, the symbol inflicted on Frank Alpine's flesh seems gratuitous, or, rather, obtrudes as a merely symbolic contrivance.

More often, the conversion motif appears under the guise of discipleship. One clear example is the relation between Angelo DeMarco (another wayward Italian lad) and Sammy the orderly in Edward Wallant's posthumously published novel, *The Children at the Gate*. Angelo, who doesn't believe in the genuineness of feelings and would like to think of human beings as machines, is taken by Sammy on the rounds of suffering at his hospital to be taught the lesson of redemptive love. Sammy, in keeping with the general formula, has the mannerisms of the bizarre comedian: his mouth is full of obscenities, his past is queer and sordid, and he is generally suspect at the hospital. But of course he has a real Jewish Heart, and for all his bizarreness he is a true Jew, which, as one often discovers in American Jewish fiction, means that he turns out to be a true Christ—at the end of the book Sammy, impaled on a stake outside a hospital filled with false plaster Christs, imparts through his death the redeeming agony of love and life to Angelo. *The Children at the Gate* manages to be a moving book, but it would have been more completely honest, I think, if its ethical guide had more authentic credentials for his role than a command of Yiddish slang and a ghetto childhood.

Perhaps the most ingenious variant of the conversion motif is the metamorphosis of Nick Lapucci into Lipshitz in Jerome Charyn's recently published second novel, *On the Darkening Green*. (The Italians may begin to wonder why they should be made the object of all this fictional missionary zeal. Perhaps it is simply a matter of sociological convenience, since Italian and Jewish neighborhoods have often bordered on or overlapped each other.) Nick Lapucci has from the outset some suspiciously Semitic features: he is bookish, unathletic, an outsider in a neighborhood of tough (Jewish) kids, and, of course, he is something of a *shlemiel*. So he is ripe for symbolic conversion when he takes a job as counselor-jailer at a Jewish school for delinquent and retarded boys in upstate New York.

The requisite Jewish elements of grotesqueness are generously multiplied and unusually contorted in this novel. The upstate institution is run like a concentration camp by its director, Uncle Nate, a self-deluded sadist and Jewish chauvinist, a sort of comic-gothic version of Faust's Jake Bluffstein, the Jewish Nazi. Probably the most important person for Nick on the school's staff is Rosencrantz, who works for Uncle Nate as part-time chaplain, part-time chauffeur, and full-time thorn-in-the-side. A defrocked rabbi, he is one of the stock types of the new sentimental myth of the Jew, possessing in fine balance through his heretical-clerical status all the necessary qualities of grotesqueness and moral insight. He is way outside institutional Judaism, yet significantly linked with it. He is utterly unillusioned, yet he ultimately evinces faith in the possibility of becoming human. Though a lost soul himself, he somehow manages to be a guide to others. Virtually crazy, he is nevertheless reliable in teaching his Torah of stubborn survival and of the seductive danger of hate and violence to all men, the persecuted as well as their persecutors.

Nick's eventual success in becoming part of the weird society of wayward and deranged Jewish boys means, predictably, his entrance into the sphere of significant moral experience. The rebellion in which he participates with them is the moral climax of the novel because it demonstrates that real solidarity is possible and that people can muster enough concern for their own human dignity to protest being deprived of it. Charyn handles his bizarre moral microcosm imaginatively, but his inclination to treat the novel as parable unfortunately encourages the tendencies inherent in the sentimental myth to schematize and simplify moral issues. And his enlisting a Jewish group to serve as moral paradigm reinforces the fashionable conception of the Jew as primarily a symbolic entity: to become truly human one must become True Israel, like the elect in the Book of John.

Hugh Nissenson's A Pile of Stones, another recent first volume of fiction, is worth mentioning because it provides such a striking contrast to all the books we have been considering. Nissenson is, as far as I can recall, the only genuinely religious writer in the whole American Jewish group. His fiction represents an attempt to follow the twisting, sometimes treacherous ways between God and man; his stories reach out for Jewish experience in Eastern Europe, in Israel, and in America, in an effort to discover what Jews do with their faith in a God who so often seems conspicuous by His absence. Where other Jewish writers haul in forefathers by their pious beards to provide scenic effect or symbolic suggestiveness, the introduction of such figures in Nissenson's work is an act of serious self-examination: can the God of the kaftaned grandfather still be the God of the buttoned-down grandson, especially with the terrible shadow of the Holocaust intervening between then and now?

This exploratory relationship to Jewishness reflects an order of imaginative integrity lacking in the writers who end up merely using Jewishness, but it is not without its own artistic difficulties. Religious fiction—witness Graham Greene—is often problematic: it is probably easier on the whole to talk precisely and persuasively about encounters with transcendence in poetry than in narrative prose. Nissenson's fiction, moreover, seems to suffer from some of the intrinsic limitations of the modern intellectual's religion-in-the-head, culled from the pages of Buber, Heschel, Herberg, Tillich, Niebuhr, and the rest. There is an odd element of abstractness in his stories; they read like neatly arranged laboratory situations for testing out a series of problems of faith and theodicy. But whatever the drawbacks of this kind of writing, one senses that it is about something real, and that there is a necessary connection between the Jewishness of its subjects and what it has to say.

Nissenson, however, is obviously a rather special case. A *Pile of Stones* offers welcome relief but hardly an indication of a change in the current trend of American Jewish fiction. It allows one to hope for more writers who will try in varying ways to observe the Jew as a real human being, but what seems immediately in prospect is a continuing parade of Jews as holy sufferers, adepts of alienation, saintly buffoons, flamboyant apostles of love—in all the twisted, grinning masks of a literary convention that keeps literature from making imaginative contact with reality.

1965

THE APOCALYPTIC TEMPER

> We must get it out of our head that this is a doomed time,
> that we are waiting for the end, and the rest of it. . . .
> Things are grim enough without these shivery games. . . .
> We love apocalypses too much.—Saul Bellow, *Herzog*

As a rule, defining literary works in terms of timeless archetypes and looming cultural traditions turns out to be a pretty arid business. All it takes, after all, is a little learning, a little ingenuity, and the solemn determination to make a "discovery." Since our universities are increasingly filled with people who possess all these attributes, the hunt-and-peck system of archetyping has become, in the literal as well as the proverbial sense, mainly an academic exercise. But there are plainly times when the act of aligning a contemporary work with some broad configuration of the literary past can produce a clearer perspective in which to see the imaginative outlines of the work under consideration, the past explicating the present as the present adds its gloss on the past. For, despite the notion now so much in vogue of a dramatic break between our age and preceding ones, we bear with us, in ways we don't always realize, the spiritual freight of the past, sometimes staggering under that burden down blind alleys we might otherwise have avoided.

This kind of relevance of cultural past to cultural present was brought home to me with particular force by R. W. B. Lewis's recent essay on an apocalyptic mode of American fiction, "Days of Wrath and Laughter."* Although Lewis's purpose is to offer a careful description of a literary phenomenon, not really to evaluate it, his account of the apocalyptic strain in American writing had the effect for me of throwing into focus a vague sense I have had of an underlying inadequacy in much of

---

* The concluding essay in Lewis's volume, *Trials of the Word* (New Haven: Yale University Press, 1965).

our fiction and thinking over the last few years. Now, "apocalypse" is one of those words that has seemed so strikingly appropriate for the major literature—and, of course, the history—
of the past fifty years that it is more often sonorously invoked
than simply used. Lewis reminds us that it is also the name of a
book in the New Testament and argues that if the apocalyptic
vision of our writers is partly inspired by the nightmare of
modern history, it is as well a very particular kind of dark dream
passed down from the ancient world by religious and literary
tradition. What he tries to do in "Days of Wrath and Laughter," for the most part quite persuasively, is to make "apocalyptic" work as a useful term of literary classification by showing
how the specific content associated with that word by Christian
tradition has been utilized, reworked, transformed, to constitute a distinctive sub-genre of American fiction.

American culture, Lewis points out, has had a powerful
apocalyptic tendency from the days of its Puritan founders. In
the earliest stage, the apocalypse was more typically imagined as
millennial than cataclysmic; though this is hardly the way the
word is now used, Christianity does give warrant for brighter
views of the promised end—the Book of Revelations, we recall,
includes a vision of the Millennium and the New Jerusalem to
follow as well as the Seven Trumpets of Woe and the Beast
from the Abyss. By the middle of the nineteenth century, the
millennial gleam had altogether faded in the minds of many
serious American writers, leaving only a brooding sense of the
terrible imminence of the End. It is at this point that Melville,
in *The Confidence-Man*, creates a distinctive American version
of the apocalyptic myth: the imagined end of all things is in
this elaborately ironic presentation ludicrous as well as disturbing; the novelist alludes to it as he brings all the people of his
world into a state in which their pathetic absurdities are utterly
exposed. *The Confidence-Man* thus initiates in American fiction a tradition of what Lewis calls "savagely comical apocalypse": a line runs from Melville's steamboat of damned fools
through Mark Twain's *The Mysterious Stranger* to Nathanael
West's *The Day of the Locust*, finally splaying out in a variety

of novels of the fifties and sixties—Ralph Ellison's *Invisible Man*, John Barth's *The Sot-Weed Factor*, Joseph Heller's *Catch-22*, Thomas Pynchon's V.

One might characterize the mode of fiction common to these novels—though this is not a term Lewis uses—as a picaresque version of the apocalypse. Our civilization is seen by these writers as such a "colossal humbug," in Mark Twain's words, that it deserves to go to pieces, but not in the dignity of a grand smash: as the protagonist of *The Mysterious Stranger* goes on to say, "Only laughter can blow it to rags and atoms at a blast." Most of these novels work out some central action which is an updated variation on the scene from Revelations of the last loosing of Satan. Appropriately enough for a world that is no more than a stupendous fraud, the Prince of Lies appears as a picaresque role-player, a free-wheeling artist of disguise and deception whose intelligence, agility, and freedom from self-delusion may frequently elicit downright sympathy for his role as catalyst in the dissolution of a rotten existence. Melville's Confidence-Man, with his constantly changing masks, reappears in a variety of bizarrely protean figures in recent novels: Ellison's Rinehart, the Harlem preacher and pitchman of many faces; Barth's ubiquitous guide, Burlingame, expert of worldly knowledge and carnal corruption; Pynchon's mysterious lady of shifting identities, V., who is associated by Lewis with "the dark lady of the apocalypse, the Whore of Babylon." (Though Pynchon could hardly have been familiar with it, an equally apposite apocalyptic motif for V.'s world of people usurped by things is found in the legend of Armilus, the "Antichrist" of medieval Jewish apocalpyse, who is the stonyhearted spawn of intercourse between Satan and the Roman statue of a beautiful woman.)

Virtually all the books that fit this pattern have, I would say, a special kind of coldly glittering appeal to the imagination. Their sharp-edged laughter gives the appearance of cutting to the core of our culture's moral abscesses and so communicates a sense of pain inflicted to work a cure. At the same time, the picaresque exuberance of the comedy offers a welcome release for our deepest feelings of anxiety about the mad state of things in which we live: the play of inventive energy of many of these novels imparts a kind of desperate exhilaration, an excited feeling that this is the way the world ends, not with a bang but a caper. (My generalizations, of course, will not fit all the books in Lewis's grouping equally well. *Invisible Man*, despite major points of intersection with the comic-apocalyptic group, is in some ways a different kind of novel, finally more serious, I think, than the others mentioned.) All the writers, in sum, who account for the modern world through a harshly comic eschatology—and that description readily applies not only to novelists but to many contemporary poets and critics as well—would seem to fulfill ideally the characteristically modern notion of the function of art, to tell the terrible truth boldly, with intellectual verve.

What I would like to suggest is that, quite to the contrary, much recent American literature has told considerably less than the truth precisely because of the apocalyptic postures it has assumed. The excitement of apocalypses is seductive and may easily give the impression of profundity and imaginative daring where neither is present. No one can be altogether impervious to the jeweled flashes and lurid flames that illuminate those doomed landscapes of the Book of Revelations, but there is no other document in either the Old or New Testament so inhuman, so spiritually irresponsible, and the same negative attributes adhere to the modes of imagination that ultimately derive from Revelations.

It is a historical commonplace that Christianity was born out of the apocalyptic side of Judaism, but I think it is important to add that apocalypse is itself a decadent form of Judaism. Lewis, in the course of his argument, refers several times to an essay by Buber, "Prophecy, Apocalyptic, and the Historical Hour,"* but he does not make plain the fact that Buber's essay is a powerful exposure of the spiritual and moral weaknesses

---

* Available in English in the paperback selection, *Pointing the Way*, edited and translated by Maurice Friedman, Harper Torchbooks.

inherent in the apocalyptic imagination. The fundamental difference between prophecy and apocalypse, as Buber describes it, is between courageous engagement in even the most threatening history, on the one hand, and a total withdrawal, on the other hand, from a history that has become unbearable. The prophets of the Hebrew Bible, Buber reminds us, were not oracles; they evoked the future as vividly as possible because they believed that human actions could determine what the future would be, and they wanted desperately to affect their auditors' actions.

> The task of the genuine prophet was not to predict but to confront man with the alternatives of decision. . . . The prophetic faith involves the faith in the *factual* character of human existence, as existence that factually meets transcendence. Prophecy has in its way declared that the unique being, man, is created to be a center of surprise in creation.

By contrast, apocalyptic writers, ancient and modern, are not really interested in the facts of history or human nature because they scarcely believe anymore in either—or, to put it another way, because what they assume to be the essential facts of human existence are wholly known, and can be summed up in a brief sentence like "We are all marked with the sign of the Beast, and the End is near." Apocalypse, which means "uncovering" in Greek, is a perfectly appropriate name for this kind of literature because there are no genuine, human surprises in it, only a breaking open of seals, tearing away of masks, lifting of veils—nothing but "revelations" of what is already known. As Buber aptly puts it, "Everything here is predetermined, all human decisions are only sham struggles. The future does not come to pass; the future is already present. . . . Therefore it can be 'disclosed.'" Such disclosures may be impressive, but what we can *learn* from them about the complicated facts of our lives is at best limited.

Let me illustrate the applicability of Buber's analysis of the classic apocalyptic vision to the secular literature of our own century. Nathanael West's *The Day of the Locust* (for the title, see Revelations 9:1–11) offers a memorable image of the

dehumanized Average Man of modern society in the grotesque
Iowan hotel clerk, Homer Simpson, a character at first merely
pathetic but in the end suddenly destructive. In E. M. Forster's
distinctly unapocalyptic *Howards End*, we have a roughly analogous representation of the new common man, hopelessly
warped by modern culture, in the self-educated insurance clerk,
Leonard Bast, "one of the thousands who have lost the life of
the body and failed to reach the life of the spirit." What
Homer Simpson makes us repeatedly aware of is his symbolic
freakishness, the ineradicable mark of the Beast upon him.
What Leonard Bast makes us aware of is the complex, knowing
intelligence with which he is conceived by the author and continually reexamined, re-presented. West isn't really interested in
the facts about Homer because they are so simple and so
known—Homer is merely the perfect product and paradigm of
American society's insidious sterility, a man totally alienated
from his own intelligence, his body, from the very experiences
he undergoes. For Forster, on the other hand, all the facts
about Leonard Bast are terribly important: we learn the particular ways in which society forms him and in which he misguid-
edly forms himself, and by observing this pitiful yet somehow
likable creature we discover the ambiguities and self-decep-
tions in our own aspirations for "culture," our own liberal-intel-
lectual attitudes toward the deprived classes. *The Day of the
Locust* is a brilliant book, but its achievement is of a lesser
order—finally, I think, because of the schematic imagination
which its apocalyptic assumptions impose.

There is no room for real people in apocalypses, for when a
writer chooses to see men as huddled masses waiting to be
thrown into sulfurous pits, he hardly needs to look at individual
faces; and so it is not surprising that recent comic-apocalyptic
novelists should fill their worlds with the rattling skeletons of
satiric hypotheses in place of fully fleshed characters. The impersonality, however, of apocalyptic writing is merely a symptom of its fundamental deficiency, and I think Buber is right in
placing central emphasis on a failure of nerve, a determination
to opt out of the challenges, complexities, and threats of his-

tory: "Wherever man shudders before the menace of his own work and longs to flee from the radically demanding historical hour, there he finds himself near to the apocalyptic vision of a process that cannot be arrested." If this weakness, which Buber claims to be the core of apocalypse, would seem in some way contradicted by the uncompromising strength of apocalyptic indictments, both in the old visions and in the new savage comedy, it is well to keep in mind an intuition of D. H. Lawrence's about the spiritual tenor of the Book of Revelations: "The Apocalypse . . . is repellent because it resounds with the dangerous snarl of the *frustrated, suppressed* collective self, the frustrated power-spirit in man, vengeful." Lawrence, as usual, states the case at once profoundly and with polemic provocation. The vehemence bespoken by his italic emphasis is directed not only against the chapel-going folk of his Christian boyhood, but also against an impulse in his own residually Christian religious imagination which he struggled to overcome, and it is perhaps the presence of apocalyptic rage within himself that explains the sureness of his insight.

The instance of Lawrence suggests why this whole question has particular relevance to our own time and place. American culture may be in many ways secular and humanist—or perhaps posthumanist, as that most apocalyptic of critics, Leslie Fiedler, has recently argued—but it is decisively post-Christian in some of its important aspects. Whether a writer's ancestry is Christian or Jewish makes little difference, as the presence of West and Heller among our neoapocalyptists should indicate: the imaginative modes which the American writer often, perhaps even typically, draws upon are deeply embedded in a Christian world view, a Christian ethics and politics.

Apocalypse was of course a Jewish invention, but I suspect that even in its first great period of flourishing it was championed for the most part by Jews like John the Baptist who went out into the desert to eat locusts. Yet even if it may have commanded wide enthusiasm in that age of profound spiritual unrest, the fact is that the historical consensus of Judaism largely rejected it in favor of competing "translations" of the vision of man and history articulated by the prophets. The point, to be sure, should not be overstated. The idea of a "normative" Judaism is an invention of the apologists, and in the many shifting streams that make up Jewish belief a powerful current through to the beginning of the modern era has been apocalyptic. The fact, however, that Judaism was often very far from the rationalistic, this-worldly faith modern Jews like to imagine, does not entirely vitiate the familiar attempt to distinguish it from Christianity on roughly these grounds. Unmitigated apocalypse could never be altogether central to the Jewish vision of history, and despite the strength and persistence of apocalyptic belief in certain circles, Jewish tradition offered alternatives that generally enjoyed greater popularity as well as higher institutional priority. It is these alternatives that seem especially worthy of attention in our own age, caught up as it is in the dread and anticipation of the end to come.

Christianity, on the other hand, has never been able to free itself wholly or comfortably from the basically apocalyptic nature of its beginnings. As far as one can safely infer historical fact from the record in the Gospels, Jesus appears to have conceived himself as a kind of prophet but more essentially as an "apocalyptic messiah," in the pointed phrase of the late Yehezkel Kaufmann. A new kind of claimant to the throne of David, he brings, like the prophets, an ethical message, but, at least as prominently, he brings dire predictions of an imminent end of time, when, just as in Revelations, the chosen will shine like the sun while the mass of offenders, as Jesus repeatedly warns, "will be thrown into the blazing furnace, the place of wailing and gnashing of teeth." This is quite different from both the prophetic threats of national disaster and the prophetic "days to come" (*aharit ha-yamim*, usually translated with a most misleading eschatological implication as "the end of days") because man has no control over what will happen. He can only prepare himself—individually, not as part of a society made up of mutually responsible members—for the impending moment. In the prophets, God works through man in history, with the promise of bringing history to a fulfillment; in Jesus' teaching,

God stands poised to lop off history, suddenly, in the night.

The contrast between what Judaism and Christianity typically did with the prophetic impulse is strikingly illustrated in the different meanings attached to the term "kingdom of heaven" by Jesus and the early rabbis. In Jesus' mouth, of course, the kingdom is eschatological, something that will come *upon* man. In rabbinic literature the phrase appears as part of the idiom *'ol malkhut shamayim,* literally, "the yoke of the kingdom [or kingship] of heaven." When a man accepts the obligations of the Law, both written and oral, he is said to take upon himself the yoke of the kingdom of heaven. Law is thus grasped as the means to implement those grand prophetic visions of God's reigning in splendor on earth. The quality of the most ordinary man's life, then, the small and large acts that constitute his daily relationship with other men and with what is beyond men, have the power to make manifest God's sovereignty in this world. Nothing expresses more clearly Judaism's concern with "the factual character of human existence, as existence that factually meets transcendence" than the Jewish preoccupation with law. Although the analysis and expounding of the Law often became an intellectual game in its own right, losing touch with the initial religious impulse of the activity, its primary motive is nevertheless an urgent need to discover what the particular and varied meanings of revelation are as it impinges upon the realm of everyday experience. Perhaps this is one reason why Jewish law, despite extended contacts with the Greco-Roman world in its formative period, never developed an extensive vocabulary of abstractions. The language of the Talmud is remarkably concrete—I am tempted to say, almost novelistic in its focus on familiar particulars. There is no "party of the first part" and "party of the second part" but "Simon" and "Reuben"; one does not speak of "incurring liability for indemnification" or even of "creating a public hazard," but of the man who piles up his barrels so as to block a thoroughfare, or who leaves his pottery to dry on the roof in a place where prevailing winds blow.

This centrality of law, with its intricate involvement in the here and now, generally placed visions of the hereafter in a secondary role; this is one of the meanings of the traditional primacy of *Halakhah* over *Aggadah*, law over lore. Christianity, by contrast, having discarded the very principle of *Halakhah*, was left in the uneasy position of making *Aggadah* absolutely essential to its world view and therefore dogmatically binding—as it was never to be in Judaism—upon its adherents. There is, moreover, a clear connection between Christianity's rejection of law and its expectations of an imminent apocalypse. When Paul, in one of his demonstrations of the dispensability of the old Law, says (Romans 13), "Love cannot wrong a neighbor; therefore the whole law is summed up in love," he immediately adds that the entire earthly life we have known will soon be over: "In all this remember how critical the moment is. It is time for you to wake out of sleep, for deliverance is nearer to us now than when first we believed. It is far on in the night; day is near." The famous rabbinic precedent for Paul's statement— Paul, of course, had been a student of Rabban Gamaliel and may even have had this earlier formulation in mind—is Hillel the Elder's answer to the Gentile who challenged him to sum up the whole Law while his questioner stood on one foot: "Whatever is repugnant to you, do not do to your fellow man." Hillel's restatement of the injunction in Leviticus to love one's neighbor is, I would say, more realistic than Paul's, but the more important difference between them is in the three words Hillel adds to his maxim—*v'idakh zil g'mar* ("go learn the rest"). Basic principles are certainly worth stating, but if history is more than a dark night about to be broken by an apocalyptic dawn, one must face up to the endlessly complicated, humanly inevitable business of details; one must learn.

To move from the realm of *Halakhah* to that of *Aggadah*, we might note that Judaism's characteristic development of the prophetic vision was messianism, not apocalypse, for the differ- ence between the two is instructive. This is not to say that messianism and apocalypse have no significant connection; as a matter of fact, a whole cycle of post-talmudic messianic legends is suffused with apocalyptic motifs that ultimately derive from the same late biblical and Hellenistic Hebrew sources as the Book of Revelations. Nevertheless, the two modes of vision are different in kind because of the attitudes they take toward history and man's role in it. "Messiah" was originally a political term, and however heavily it was later overlaid with eschatological splendors by Jewish tradition, it was never wholly cut off from its connections with a Davidic dynasty destined to be flesh-and-blood rulers over the land of Israel. According to one often-cited talmudic view, "The only difference between this world and the Messianic Era is our present subjugation to foreign powers" (*Berakhot*, 34b). A century after Jesus' appearance as an "apocalyptic messiah," Rabbi Akiba supported the messiah-ship of Bar Kokhba, whose claim to that title was asserted through political activism, open rebellion against Rome.

As political alternatives came to seem less feasible, human participation in the great movement of redemption shifted more typically to the moral and spiritual life of the individual. This notion is perhaps most strikingly expressed at a later juncture in history in the kabbalistic doctrine that man hastens the redemption by gathering up in his acts and meditations the divine sparks scattered through our broken world. It is also a point stressed in many rabbinic legends, like the well-known tale of Rabbi Joshua Ben-Levi, who is sent by Elijah to the gates of Rome to speak to the Messiah. Ben-Levi finds the Messiah sitting among the poor of the city, binding and unbinding his wounds; he exchanges polite greetings with the tarrying deliverer, and then, in answer to his question, "When are you coming?" he hears a single word—"today." Puzzled, Ben-Levi returns to Elijah with the complaint that the Messiah has lied to him. "What he really said to you," Elijah explains, quoting a verse from Psalms to complete the enigmatic answer, "is, 'Today—if ye give heed to His voice' " (*Sanhedrin*, 98a).

The recurrent image of the afflicted Messiah sitting among the poor suggests something of the human warmth with which the Jewish folk imagination typically infused the messianic idea. Eschatology had a personal focus, not only in the figure of the Messiah, but also in his forerunner, Elijah, who was transformed in popular legend from the biblical man of righteous wrath to a beloved emissary of divine compassion. One awaits the apocalypse with an electric tremor of fear tinged with delight in destruction—the comic apocalyptists, of course, simply reverse these proportions. One awaits the Messiah with the joyful eagerness appropriate to the anticipation of a dear, human guest. Stories are told of pious Jews who would buy a new suit of clothes and lay it aside, never to wear, in order to have their holiday best ready to put on when the redeemer came. S. Y. Agnon, in a memorable account of his childhood in Galicia of the 1890's, re-creates the way in which the figure of his absent father and the awaited redeemer fused in his mind, so that when he went to sleep in his father's big bed, he would try to keep one ear pricked, to be ready to leap up if the ram's horn of the Messiah should sound during the night. Though the idea of redemption does imply setting things right on a cosmic scale, it was generally imagined by Jewish folklore in vividly personal terms, and this frequently saved it from the irresponsibility of apocalypses, in which the imagination tends to go skittering off into the upper reaches of the cosmos, there to view humanity abstractly, as swarms of odious insects, beetles, or locusts.

Now, the impress of such classic Jewish traditions on the modern Jewish literary imagination is, admittedly, for the most part negligible, especially in the case of writers not working in Yiddish or Hebrew. Where there is ignorance one can hardly expect influence, and even for many Israeli writers who have been exposed to the Hebrew source materials and some American writers who have culled them in translation from paperback anthologies, the classic Jewish views rarely rise from the paper-and-ink plane of book learning to become a vital mode of imagining man and history and their interrelation. From time to time, though, one does run across a significant exception, and, as in other matters, the exceptions are more instructive than the rule, since they show how a past different from the accepted one of Western culture can be immensely relevant to the needs of the present. For one of the chief advantages of the anomalous presence of the Jews, deeply implicated yet sharply apart, in two millennia of Christian civilization, is that they could sustain a culture whose development was roughly parallel to the majority culture, yet dramatically different, thus tracing against the curve of Christian history a series of lived-out alternatives to it. I scarcely need to add that the cultural life of our own time, with its peculiar habit of digging itself into circular ruts of constantly narrowing radius, could often benefit from alternatives.

It seems to me, for instance, that there is an essential connection between the fact that *Herzog* is Saul Bellow's most Jewish novel, in language, allusion, narrative materials, and that it is his great dissent from the intellectual vogue of "wasteland ideologies" and apocalypses. (Quite to the point is the fact that *The Waste Land* itself, the paradigmatic modern poem, is pervasively Christian, not merely in the motifs it employs, but in the nature of its basic assumptions about the life of the spirit. To cite a central example—the symbolic use of death, the whole myth of death and rebirth, presupposes a radical disjuncture between a sinful nature in man and his capacity for redemption which is profoundly alien to Judaism.) *Herzog* is Bellow's most autobiographical novel and that is both a strength and a weakness. But what is more to our purpose is that it is his most personal novel as well, in the sense I have used the word to distinguish messianism from apocalypse. Herzog continually attempts to counterpose against the great, killing abstractions of modern intellectual life the concrete particulars—poignant, saddening, ludicrous, sordid—that constitute the individuality, the vividly recollected specialness, of one man's life. His expressed hope for human value in an infinite and indifferent universe reflects the commonsense commitment to the world of familiar experience that has informed both Jewish law and Jewish messianism:

> And the peculiar idea entered my (Jewish) mind that we'd see about this! My life would prove a different point altogether. Very tired of the modern form of historicism which sees in this civilization the defeat of the best hopes of Western

religion and thought. . . . The question of ordinary human experience is the principal question of these modern centuries . . . the strength of a man's virtue or spiritual capacity measured by his ordinary life.

What Bellow has absorbed from the Montreal ghetto-milieu of his boyhood is a certain feel for experience, an imaginative tone, style, and viewpoint, but it is clear that he has not been touched by the impelling central myths of Jewish tradition, which more often than not had already dwindled into superstition and pious reflex in the immigrant generation from which he sprang. By contrast, Elie Wiesel, the remarkable writer who casts his novels in French, and his journalism in Yiddish and Hebrew, was brought up in a little town in Transylvania where, in the years before the war, a child could still be steeped in the lore of a reverent Judaism, fired by the passionate aspirations of Jewish mysticism; and his work testifies to the impressive sustaining power of the messianic vision. No one has more right to the apocalyptic viewpoint than someone who has gone through what Wiesel has. Auschwitz, after all, was and is a kind of end of the world for all of us—anyone who has read Wiesel's account of it in *Night* is likely to have the doomsday glare of its unspeakable ovens flickering somewhere in the back of his head for a lifetime. One of the extraordinary aspects of Wiesel's vision is that, even after directly experiencing this terrible turn of history, he refuses to look at the world in an apocalyptic light. Instead, each of his novels asks with agonized urgency how the Messiah could have so utterly failed his people, while at the end of his most recent book, *The Gates of the Forest*, the protagonist comes through painful quest to an affirmation—marvelously resonant against the novel's accumulated experience—of a transformed messianism, one in which man will have to dare to assume the whole burden of redemption:

Whether or not the Messiah comes doesn't matter; we'll manage without him. It is because it is too late that we are commanded to hope. We shall be honest and humble and strong, and then he will come, he will come every day, thousands of times every day. He will have no face, because he will have a thousand faces. The Messiah isn't one man . . . he's all men. As long as there are men there will be a Messiah. One day you'll sing, and he will sing in you.

The obvious difference between this messianic reconstruction of life after the war and the kind of savagely comical apocalypse in vogue in American fiction is that Wiesel's vision is founded on an act of faith and that of the comic-apocalyptic writers, on a complete failure of faith. It is commonly assumed that to avow a lack of faith is a sign of honesty, and this is obviously often the case. But to absolutize a lack of faith in man and history and project it into literature is, for an artist, an easy way out, an escape from the difficult responsibilities of his calling. Through a habit of nervous laughter over the world's going to pieces, we titillate ourselves and at the same time imperceptibly inure ourselves to the prospect, so that it may become just a little more likely. Conversely, by carefully attending to the bewildering human particularities of our world, with the assumption that they must and can be coped with, we may make it somewhat more likely that we can grab hold of history before it goes skidding off to that awaited End. We may all sometimes wonder whether the communicated word really has the power to help us change ourselves and our history. That it possesses such power has, in any case, always been Judaism's first implicit principle of faith after the belief in God, and it seems now as much as ever to be a principle of faith that is literally indispensable.

1966

SABBATAI ZEVI AND THE JEWISH IMAGINATION

> The Patriarchs came to the world in order to restore the
> primal integrity of the senses, and accomplished this with
> four of them. Then Sabbatai Zevi came and restored the
> primal integrity of the fifth sense, the sense of touch, which
> —according to Maimonides and Aristotle—is mankind's dis-
> grace, but which, through Sabbatai Zevi, became praise-
> worthy and glorious.—Eighteenth-century Sabbatian homily

Modern experience has taught us to recognize that in the particular past which we choose to rediscover, we discover ourselves—that is, we find out who we are and, in the older sense
of the word "discover," we reveal, or expose, ourselves. This, at
any rate, has repeatedly been the case since the eighteenth century, when people first began to look at the past in the full
lucidity of historical perspective, out of a steady awareness of
essential differences in the feel of human experience in different
ages. Thus, the rediscovery of the Middle Ages by English
writers in the last decades of the eighteenth century represented
a final turning away from the age of reason, or rather solid
common sense, that had begun with Hobbes, Locke, and the
neoclassical writers after them: symptomatically, the term
"Gothic," which was synonymous with "barbaric" for Pope and
Swift, came to suggest rich and alluring realms of passionate
adventure by the end of the century. In a similar way, the
fascination that the primitive past has held for the modern age,
since the time of Frazer, obviously reflects the underlying concerns and confusions of our own cultural predicament: out of a
sense of sapped vitality, we turn to dark wellsprings of archaic
life; out of a radical disenchantment with the weary and destructive course of Western history, we fill our inner vacuity
with visions of ages when that history had scarcely begun, of
places it never touched.

Now, in the varieties of Jewish experience undertaken since the French Revolution, it is the biblical past which has often served the purpose of focusing the self-awareness of the present. For the Reform movement in nineteenth-century Germany, the Bible was, of course, the source of those eternal verities that had been hidden or disguised by the encrustations of rabbinic law. There is, however, little attempt to reconstruct the life of the past imaginatively in this Reform use of the Bible as the artificial prop for a shaky ideology. In the early stages of modern Hebrew literature, on the other hand, the return to the Bible did involve a real immersion in the biblical past. The language of the new poetry and fiction, after all, was often the language of the Bible itself, in syntax, idiom, imagery; and many writers of the Hebrew Enlightenment struggled heroically to imagine anew, out of the bleakness and impotence of their lives in Exile, the sun-blessed warmth and vigor of life on the land when their forefathers tilled and defended it. There is an inner connection, therefore, between the literary return to the biblical past of the Hebrew Enlightenment and the physical return to the land of the Bible first envisioned by the proponents of *Hibat Zion* (Love of Zion) in the 1860's and fully realized by the Zionist movement. It is perfectly understandable that the Bible should still be given inordinate emphasis in Israel's schools and official cultural programs; implicit in the concentration on this particular stretch of the past is a rejection or at least depreciation of the long stretch of diaspora history which followed it.

The Bible alone, however, has generally proved to be a less than faithful mirror for the troubled face of the present, and Jews over the last few decades have attempted with increasing frequency to discover themselves through the recollected world of East-European Jewry—most notably through the evocation of Hasidism, which, as an enthusiastic movement of inner liberation, has provided the most congenial material for humanistic reinterpretation or simply for sentimental distortion. What may at first seem surprising is that a messianic movement which, despite some affinities with Hasidism, is in important respects its diametric opposite, a movement which completely contradicts our cherished notions of European Jewish life as an innocent sphere of quaint or touching piety, should also have a powerful hold on the modern Jewish imagination.

In circles that have remained closely in touch with Jewish history—which, by and large, has meant among readers of Hebrew or Yiddish—the figure of Sabbatai Zevi, the seventeenth-century pseudo-messiah, has in recent times possessed a strange magnetism. It is suggestive that Avraham Mapu (1808–1867), who initiated the Hebrew novel with a book set in the time of Isaiah, soon afterward began work on a novel called *The Visionaries* (of which only a fragment has survived) dealing with the Sabbatians. The subject has been treated by Sholem Asch (in Yiddish), by Israel Zangwill (in English), by Haim Hazaz (in Hebrew), and, of late, most impressively, by Isaac Bashevis Singer, again in Yiddish. In Jewish scholarship, moreover, during the past thirty years, Sabbatianism has become one of the great subjects of reasearch. Most of this activity has been directly influenced by Gershom Scholem, who first announced the program for a general reassessment of Sabbatianism in an essay written in 1937, *Mitzvah ha-Baah ba-'Aveirah* (the untranslatable Hebrew title, which alludes to a Sabbatian reinterpretation of a talmudic concept, might be roughly paraphrased as "The Way of Holy Sinning"); Scholem's two-volume work in Hebrew on Sabbatai Zevi, published in 1957, stands as one of the major achievements of modern Jewish historiography.

The impression one gets from the usual handbooks of Jewish history or from the standard encyclopedias—all of them based on the hostile and misinformed scholarship of the nineteenth century—is that Sabbatianism was merely a bizarre and transient episode in Jewish history. A deluded Turkish Jew, his brain addled by mystic studies, pronounces the ineffable name of God to an assembled congregation in Smyrna. After he persists in committing this and other forbidden acts, the local rabbis banish him, and eventually he makes his way to Palestine, where he meets up with a very young man called Nathan of Gaza, who, unlike Sabbatai Zevi, has a genius for both theology and propaganda. Nathan manages to convince the older man that he, Sabbatai, is the Messiah, son of David, something he seems inclined to have believed at times anyway, and the two begin to look fervently for the imminent unfolding of the redemption, perhaps in the next year, 1666. Sabbatai returns to Smyrna to announce his mission while Nathan, his "prophet," busies himself sending out emissaries to the far reaches of the diaspora, bearing the good tidings. Almost everywhere, masses of Jews respond to the call of redemption. Sabbatai Zevi proceeds to Constantinople, where his followers expect him to take the crown from the head of the sultan. Instead, he is imprisoned for inciting insurrection; after being detained in what proves to be grand state in the fortress at Gallipoli—the divinely appointed bastion, his followers believe, from which he will soon emerge for the last great battle with the forces of evil—he is summoned to judgment and offered the choice between death by slow torture and conversion to Islam; unhesitatingly, he assumes the fez.

Sabbatai Zevi's apostasy strikes Jews everywhere with the profoundest consternation and despair; in its aftermath, only small sectarian groups of the "faithful" cling to the belief in his messiahship, explaining that he has entered into the realm of defilement in order to redeem or conquer evil at its very source. Some of the faithful imitate their master by themselves converting; others engage in orgiastic rites in order to emulate the audacious plunge of the redeemer into the sphere of impurity. A century later, when the social, political, and intellectual horizons of the Jewish people begin to enlarge significantly with the advent of the Enlightenment and the French Revolution, Sabbatianism seems like a bad dream, a last sickly residue of what were still the Jewish middle ages.

In contrast to this general image of Sabbatianism, which owes much to the rationalistic bias of nineteenth-century Jewish historiography, Scholem has tried to understand the subject sympathetically, as a manifestation of religious consciousness, not merely of psychopathology. Above all else, he has sought to demonstrate that Sabbatianism, far from being a strange passing episode, is in effect the beginning of modern Jewish history. He is able to establish through a careful and exhaustive examination of contemporary documents that the proportions of Sabbatianism, both in the lifetime of Sabbatai Zevi and afterward, were far greater than the official "Jewish" versions of the events have led us to believe. During those hectic months of messianic jubilation before the apostasy, opposition to Sabbatai Zevi in all but a few places was negligible or simply did not exist. Revered rabbis, adepts of the Law, pillars of the various communities, believed without question in Sabbatai's messiahship; the minority who had doubts kept prudently silent for the most part in the face of the fervid enthusiasm of the Jewish populace. Until the apostasy, then, there was no Sabbatian "sect"; one must rather say that Sabbatai Zevi, with only minor exceptions, was the acclaimed Messiah of the Jewish people, from Yemen to Galicia, from Tunis to Amsterdam. Scholem also shows that very considerable numbers of Jews still adhered to the belief in Sabbatai, and the imminent redemption he would bring, for nearly a century after his death. The most essential point, however, of Scholem's revisionist history is that for a brief moment almost the whole Jewish people was convinced it was living in the presence of the dawning redemption—the *athalta d'geulah* —and that many would never again be able to accept their unredeemed, restricted lives as ghetto Jews in the same unquestioning way. A passage in which Scholem discusses the new relation to rabbinic law into which the Sabbatian experience thrust Jews touches on a crux of his argument and also reveals a chief source for his own fascination with the whole Sabbatian phenomenon:

> The believers were able to develop a new criterion with which to measure ghetto reality. This ghetto Judaism had been and was still upheld by the "infidels" who denied the Redeemer's mission, men who possessed the mere body of the Torah and not its innerness. It would not be long before some of the believers would come, whether in extreme or moderate forms, to a criticism of rabbinic Judaism. And that criticism, it must be emphasized, would be from within, not primarily dependent upon the influence of external causes and historical circumstances, like the criticism evoked in the period of the

French Revolution and in the age of struggle for political rights for the Jews. . . . And if the traditional forms no longer fit the paradoxical values upon which the movement stood, they would have to seek new and other expressions for their utopian Jewish consciousness. For their consciousness was Jewish and remained Jewish; even at moments of open conflict with the ruling powers of the traditional Jewish society, the believers did not seek to deny their historical Jewish identity from the start.

The general effect of Scholem's pioneering research into Sabbatianism is to turn inside out many of our preconceptions of what is Jewish and what is not. If we think of Jews as tough-minded rationalists, wryly ironic realists, Scholem shows us a whole people emotionally caught up in the most fantastic faith, men and women alike wildly dancing, rolling on the ground, foaming at the mouth, uttering prophecies. If we think of Jews as people living within tightly drawn lines of legal restriction and self-imposed restraint, Scholem shows us Jews casting off all bonds, entering, so they thought, into a new world of unlimited freedom where, according to the Sabbatian maxim, "the abrogation of the Torah is its true fulfillment." If we think of Judaism as a broad antithesis to Christianity in some of its most essential assumptions, Scholem shows us Jews insisting on the primacy of faith over works, Jews coming to believe in a trinitarian God of which the Son, or Messiah, is part, Jews arguing—with the traditional method and idiom of rabbinic discourse as well as of the Kabbalah—that the Messiah has taken upon himself seeming disgrace and outward defeat in order to redeem a sinful world. If our stereotype of the premodern Jew tends to be a puritanical figure, stern, pale, enveloped in somber cloth, following a faith in which the dominant symbols and institutional arrangements are masculine, Scholem discovers for us a Messiah who awakens the hearts of Jews to the possibilities of serving God through the pleasures of the body, who sings this poignantly sensual Spanish song to the *Shekhina* at the holy ark, Torah in hand:

> When I went up to the mountaintop
> When I came down to the river's edge

I met Meliselda
Who is the Emperor's daughter
Coming up from the bath
From the bath where she had washed.
Her face flashed like a sword
Her brows were like the bow
Her lips were like corals
And her flesh whiter than milk.

This is not to suggest that Scholem, the disciplined scholar
and patient reasoner, so clearly an "Apollonian" figure, is
preaching through his scholarship the adaptation of a "Diony-
sian" form of Jewish life. But what he construes to be the
vitality manifested in Sabbatianism is what especially draws him
to it, and it is this which he himself emphasizes in the preface
to his *Shabbtai Tzvi:* "The degree of vitality in these phenomena surprises us no less than the degree of daring in them,
and the eyes of recent generations have learned to see the spark
of Jewish life and the constructive longings even in phenomena
which Jewish tradition fought against with all its soul." Now,
vitality is a concept which, when it is not completely self-evident, becomes oddly elusive, and I must say that I find this to
be the case with Scholem. One man's vitality is another man's
sickness, as opposing interpretations of Sabbatianism vividly
illustrate. Scholem seems to connect vitality almost axiomati-
cally with antinomianism, though it could easily be argued that
antinomianism in general, especially as it moves toward the
unbridled excesses to which its inner logic drives it, is rather an
expression of cultural, moral, and psychological disintegration,
sharing with vitality only the superficial similarity of violent
motion. More plausibly, Scholem appears to associate vitality
with the return to the full life of the senses that is at least
implicit in the urgent messianic expectations of the Sabbatian
movement. If the early talmudic masters had taught their
disciples to imagine this world as an "anteroom" to the "main
hall" of a true world elsewhere, the Sabbatians thought they
were seeing the anteroom transformed before their eyes into the
inner hall of the palace, and so there is, paradoxically, a power-

ful impulse toward realizing the fullness of life here and now in the very movement so intoxicated with the heady mysteries of the divine Beyond. Finally, Sabbatianism is an expression of national vitality for Scholem because it begins to look like a movement of autoemancipation miscarried only because the age in which it occurred made its political implementation unfeasible: Sabbatai Zevi, the manic-depressive kabbalist, is no Theodor Herzl, but it is undeniable that at his call thousands upon thousands of Jews in all parts of the diaspora actually began to pack up their possessions and prepared to march after him to Zion.

"Vitality" has been a great will-o'-the-wisp of Hebrew literature at least since the time of Berditchevsky, Schneur, Tchernichovsky—the first generation of Hebrew writers to be influenced by Nietzsche—and I think that it is against this background that Scholem's emphasis on the vitality of Sabbatianism has to be seen. The Sabbatian movement plays much the same role in Scholem's imaginative vision—and he is a historian who clearly possesses such a vision—as the cults of Baal, Astarte, and Tammuz play in the poetry of Tchernichovsky and the latter-day Canaanites after him. Both the pagan gods and the more recent messianic movement embody possibilities of a dramatic "transvaluation of values" for the Jewish people, and Scholem in fact uses the Hebrew equivalent of that Nietzschean formula, *shinui 'arakhim*, more than once in describing the Sabbatian program. The Canaanite gods, however, are a convenient literary fiction, a cultural alternative borrowed from the outside that at best merely impinged once upon ancient Israel. Scholem's model of vitality, on the other hand, is the product of a process immanent in Jewish historical experience. The Sabbatians see themselves as the legitimate heirs of the Jewish past; even as they set about radically transforming the practices and values of Jewish tradition, "their consciousness was Jewish and remained Jewish." Scholem argues, moreover, that there is some causal connection between them and the nineteenth-century modernizing movements that sought to change the basic conditions of Jewish existence.

Scholem's encompassing interpretation of Sabbatianism is

so subtly developed that it is hard to know how much of it is
really cogent, how much merely seductive. The subject, at any
rate, has a seductive allure for him, and I think his relationship
to it is finally Faustian, as Faust in Part Two of Goethe's poem
plunges into the depths of the past to capture a beauty and
power that will always elude him. This, if I read him right, is
what S. Y. Agnon is suggesting about enterprises like Scholem's
in his remarkable tale, *Edo and Enam.** According to literary
gossip in Jerusalem, Dr. Ginath, the enigmatic discoverer of
unknown ancient cultures in the story, is in fact an oblique
allusion to Agnon's old friend, Gershom Scholem. (The character's name might be a clue: there is a medieval kabbalistic
work entitled *Ginath Egoz*, which, like all other kabbalistic
works has been discussed in print by Scholem. The word refers
to the "garden" of mystic contemplation.) Twice in the story, a
character wonders, jokingly, whether Dr. Ginath might not be
sitting in his room writing a third part to Faust. Ginath's key to
the mysteries of the primal past is, in a strangely denatured way,
erotic: in the somnambulistic Gemulah he holds the Helen of a
civilization older than Troy whom he will never really possess,
as Faust never really possesses Helen. There is something both
poignant and ghoulish in her love for him, his use of her; and
the intrinsic logic of their relationship brings them to mutual
destruction. If, at the end of the tale, Ginath leaves after him
the luminous life and beauty of the past he has captured in his
work for every man to "make use of its light," that final phrase
echoes another a few pages earlier about the ambiguous light of
the moon, magically linked to the doomed Gemulah, of which
the narrator must warn: "Happy is the man who can make use
of its light and come to no harm."

Agnon, in his symbolic treatment of the characteristically
modern quest for sources of renewal in the past, is concerned
with the ultimate spiritual dangers of such pursuits, but Scholem's own scholarly enterprise also has more immediate implications, and as a useful gloss upon them I would like to offer
another imaginative work in Hebrew, Haim Hazaz' play, *In the*

* Available in English in *Two Tales* (New York: Schocken,
1966).

End of Days. The Hazaz play, written in 1950, is in no way a
direct comment on Scholem, but it provides an instructive
parallel, making explicit the ideological message of Sabbatianism that seems to be implicit for Scholem. The action is set in a
German town during the time of Sabbatai Zevi's ascendancy.
Yuzpa, the fiery messianist who is eventually excommunicated
for his rebellion against the traditional order, can be taken, with
little qualification, as Hazaz' spokesman in the play, and the
doctrine he preaches is the annihilation of the Exile, which for
him means a tearing apart of the institutional bonds that held
life in the diaspora together: "The strength of the Exile is in
Torah, commandments, and the fear of heaven. . . . Torah
has been absorbed by Exile, has become synonymous with it."
It begins to be clear why Sabbatian antinomianism should be
associated with vitality, for all the heavy restrictions, sodden
with the weight of Exile, must be cast off in order to enter the
new world of freedom and life: "We will bury ourselves, a
burial of the dead, in license, in promiscuity and raw instinct, in
order to arise from the void and chaos of this world like the
sleepers of the dust who are destined to be resurrected, pure
and clean and seven times more alive."

Hazaz, let me emphasize, is not really interested in moral
anarchy but rather uses such anarchy as a dramatic symbol for
what he conceives as the desperate need to smash the Exile, to
extirpate all bonds and allegiances with the world of Exile. The
main referent of messianism in his play is not individual and
anarchic but collective and political. When Yuzpa interprets
Sabbatianism as a call for Jews to seize the reins of their own
destiny, we hear in his words a distinctly Zionist modernization
of the seventeenth-century movement; Scholem, as a meticulous
scholar, is careful to represent his subject in its own premodern
religious terms, but he often leads us to infer the same analogy
with the modern secular movement of redemption that is
forced upon us by Hazaz' protagonist: "Heaven is in our
hands . . . understand that, my friend, understand that. The
Redemption depends on us; more than on God Almighty and
more than on the Son of David, it depends on us. Not the

Messiah alone, but us as well, the whole people of Israel and
every single Jew! Great is the Redemption we possess, for we
ourselves have conceived it. . . . We decreed and He—must
carry it out."

Although I do not think that Scholem's superb scholarship
can justly be called tendentious, there is surely some connection
between his ideological commitment to secular Zionism and his
professional commitment to the study of Sabbatianism. If we
are generally accustomed to place the rise of Zionism in the
context of nineteenth-century European nationalism, Scholem's
reassessment of Sabbatianism emphasizes a powerful desire for
immediate national redemption working through the entire
people, an exhaustion of patience with life in exile, which are
not dependent upon external influences or the imitation of
European models. Scholem finally sees Sabbatianism as a prepa-
ration of the ground for modern Jewish nationalism, and he
even tries to establish a lineal descent—somewhat sketchily, it
must be said—from known Sabbatian families to the first
Jewish proponents of Enlightenment, who in turn prepared the
way for the beginnings of Zionism. Scholem has been vehe-
mently attacked on this point by Baruch Kurzweil, the Israeli
literary and cultural critic, who claims that it represents a
spurious attempt to legitimize secular Zionism in Jewish terms,
to set it up as the logical and authentic product of a process
working within Jewish history before its exposure to the great
innovating forces of the modern world. Kurzweil vigorously
denies any causal connection between Sabbatianism and the
Hebrew Enlightenment, though he bases his argument less on
historical documentation than on common sense—perhaps a
dangerous criterion in history—and on his deep personal conviction that Sabbatianism is a pathological "borderline phenomenon" from which little can be learned about Judaism in its
strength or about the Jewish people as a whole.

I cannot pretend to the competence needed to resolve the
complex question of Sabbatianism's role in the concatenation of
modern Jewish history, but it does not seem to me that the
proof of historical causation is indispensable to Scholem's im-

plicit argument for the contemporary relevance of his subject.
The ultimate importance of Sabbatianism for our age, even in
Scholem's case, is as a paradigm and not as an ancestor. In a
period when many conscious Jews are trying to sort out the
confusions of their own Jewish identity by a renewed confrontation with the variety of the Jewish past, the Sabbatians embody
possibilities of Jewish existence, lived in the fullness of "utopian
Jewish consciousness," which are—despite Kurzweil—imaginatively stirring, in any case challenging, and in certain obvious
ways deeply disturbing as well. We adopt figures from the past
as our contemporaries out of our own needs, regardless of the
lines of historical connection with them, and Sabbatai Zevi, the
grandly and pathetically deluded Messiah, reaching out for a
lustrous world of redemption over the precarious brink of an
abyss of anarchy, is, for better or for worse, a distinct contemporary.

The paradox of Sabbatai Zevi's contemporaneity is allied, I
think, to that of Isaac Bashevis Singer, a writer whose world is
older than the crumbling folio pages of a study-house Talmud
and yet has seemed to many readers as urgently modern as the
last inarticulate cry from the Theater of the Absurd. Singer has
none of Scholem's interest in the ideological inferences that
may be drawn from Sabbatianism, but its antinomian frenzy
constitutes for him a dark revelation of human nature and of
the character of the spiritual reality we inhabit. It should give
us pause to note that one of the greatest Jewish scholars of our
age and also one of our great Jewish imaginative writers have
been powerfully drawn to this same ambiguous subject. (This,
incidentally, is one of several respects in which Singer and
Agnon offer an instructive contrast. Agnon, for all his imaginative intimacy with spectral ambiguities, remains rooted in what
used to be called "normative" Judaism. Although Buczacz,
Agnon's native town, is one of a dozen places singled out by
Scholem as centers of underground Sabbatian activity for generations after the death of the false messiah, there is no trace of
the presence of Sabbatianism in all Agnon's fiction about the
Buczacz of bygone days, with the exception of the father of the

groom in *The Bridal Canopy*, whose grandfather used to eat a single pea on the fast of Tisha B'Av, hedging his bets, so to speak, on the late redeemer.)

One gets the peculiar impression that Sabbatianism plays a larger role in Singer's fiction than is actually the case. It is the subject of just one novel, *Satan in Goray*, and appears in the background of one other, *The Slave*, while most of the short stories are set in a period well after the conclusion of the Sabbatian movement. This impression, however, is not altogether mistaken because the Sabbatian experience serves as an implicit model or general analogue for what we have come to recognize as the distinctive Singer world, whatever its temporal setting—a world in which humanity, having burst the constricting bands of civilized restraint, hurls itself into a Witches' Sabbath of lust and self-debasement.

It is worth noting that Singer in *Satan in Goray* chooses to refashion Sabbatianism in the image of its final deterioration in the eighteenth-century orgiastic sect of the sinister Polish Jew, Jacob Frank. A few of the details of the novel, in fact, seem direct borrowings from the career of Frank, like the old castle in which the members of the sect gather at night to wallow to-gether in sexual abominations as a means of hastening the redemption. This is not a serious distortion of historical fact on Singer's part because Sabbatai Zevi's own selective but spec-tacular violations of the Law—perhaps more appositely here, of taboo—clearly pointed the way to a nihilistic rebellion against all moral inhibition. What Scholem observes in contrasting the Sabbatian paradox of the Messiah's apostasy with the Christian paradox of the Messiah's crucifixion might be an appropriate motto for the moral world of much of Singer's fiction: "The paradox . . . of apostasy . . . leads straight into the bottom-less pit; its very idea makes almost anything conceivable." While many modern novelists have written under the shadow of Ivan Karamazov's warning that if God does not exist every-thing is permissible, the somber implication of Sabbatianism spelled out here is more strictly appropriate to Singer's world, which remains unquestionably sacramental, suffused with the presence of divinity, but a divinity that may be ultimately ambiguous, that repeatedly threatens to become a satanic inversion of itself. Singer, in other words, is lucidly aware that the moral abyss opened up by Sabbatianism is also a metaphysical abyss; as Scholem aptly sums up the movement in his chapter on it in *Major Trends in Jewish Mysticism*, "To the Sabbatians all reality became dialectically unreal and contradictory. . . . Their God no less than their Messiah bears the mark of such self-contradiction and disintegration." It is surely Singer's artistic realization of this threat of self-contradiction in the ultimate nature of reality that, more than anything else, explains his anomalous "modernity."

Modern literature has in certain memorable instances chosen to search out strange continents and alien races for the dramatic symbols of the Heart of Darkness in all men. Singer's Sabbatians, by contrast, confront the Jew with a kind of unsettling intimacy because they are, historically, part of the Jew—as thoroughly Jewish as any kaftaned, earlocked, pious figure in Peretz or Sholem Aleichem. They represent, to borrow a pointed idiom of the Kabbalah, the *Sitra Aḥra*, the Other Side of oneself. Singer's attitude, moreover, toward his sundry devotees of the demonic is not finally moralistic, and this is probably what most disturbs those of his Jewish readers who have vociferously objected to his "negativism." We might note in this connection that the attitudes of the pious "Tale of the Dybbuk," the epilogue to *Satan in Goray*, are not identical with those of the novel as a whole. If the moralizing narrator of the Tale denounces Reb Gedaliyah, the leader of the heretics, as a "son of Belial and entirely wicked," the figure of the arch-Sabbatian in the novel itself is somewhat more ambiguous. Reb Gedaliyah is, of course, a bestial man (his body is matted with hair, covered with rolls of fat) who eventually leads his followers into extreme acts of bestiality; but he is aso a ministering spirit to the sick, a teacher of speech to the stammering, laughter to the melancholy, simple joy to the young. There is an essential element of *playfulness* in Reb Gedaliyah that provides a paradoxical continuity between his exuberant geniality, his almost

Falstaffian love of mischief, and the moral obscenities he perpetrates. What he promises his followers, after all, is a world of pure spontaneous play, where there is no right or wrong, pure or impure, permitted or proscribed. Singer is horrified by the utopia of depravity Reb Gedaliyah envisages, and yet he is also at moments responsive to the Sabbatian's dream of an unchecked flow of self-fulfilling life. *Satan in Goray* is finally an unresolved novel because the forces of anarchic release it dramatizes cannot be contained by the moral imagination that shapes plots, do not admit of readily conceived human resolutions.

According to a kabbalistic tradition adopted by the followers of Sabbatai Zevi, there are two Torahs: the Torah of the Tree of Knowledge, Good and Evil, which has been revealed to us, and the Torah of the Tree of Life—manifestly, beyond good and evil—which the redeemer is to reveal. Because the common image of the Jew has been a figure clinging to the first Torah, the man bound by the Law, there is a special piquancy in Sabbatianism's antithetical image of the Jew committed to a Torah which is all life, unfettered by any law. The serious danger, however, in such alluring antitheses is that life becomes arbitrarily associated with the abandonment of restraints and hence death with the general notion of imposing limits. The experience of the more extreme Sabbatians, culminating in the Frankists, and again, the fate of vitalistic ideologies in modern political history, suggest that the quest for life, so conceived, may produce only its opposite, and that it is the human vocation to try to realize life to the fullest within necessary limits. Perhaps from this ultimate viewpoint there is a greater truth in Singer's fictional version of Sabbatianism than in Scholem's massive reconstruction of it, for Singer knows in the very quick of his imagination what Scholem understands finely but often seems unwilling to concede—that the would-be redeemer opened the gates to a world of chaos, not of redemption.

1967

HEBREW LITERATURE AND THE PARADOX OF SURVIVAL

> This "new literature" is the death-rattle of the 19th century, just as the Kabbalah and Hasidism were the death-rattle of the Dark Ages.—M. Z. Feierberg, *Whither?*

There is something peculiarly depressing about most modern Hebrew literature written in the diaspora. The reasons for this general effect of persistent dreariness are in certain cases obvious, in others obscure, but, taken together, they can tell us a good deal about the peculiarity of the Hebrew literary enterprise of the last two centuries, and they may also suggest something about the unsettling ambiguities of Jewish existence since the Emancipation.

I would imagine that there are few people who have gone through the accepted stages of a modern Hebrew education—in Israel, in the secondary schools, in America, in the various Hebrew teachers' institutes or colleges of Jewish studies—who do not feel a certain chill in the soul at the thought of the long hours spent over the pages of Mapu, Smolenskin, Y. L. Gordon, Feierberg, Berkowitz, Fichman, and all those other Russian- or Polish-born writers of labored prose and swollen verse. There was a time when I attributed the bleakness exuded by these Hebrew texts quite simply to their deficiency as works of art, but it seems to me now that this explanation is both incomplete and imprecise.

Modern Hebrew literature is so transparently vulnerable to negative criticism and invidious comparisons that hostile commentary is often merely truistic, in some ways almost an impertinence. The first Hebrew novel, for example, Avraham Mapu's overwrought biblical romance, *The Love of Zion*, appeared just two years before *Madame Bovary*: the artistic difference between the two being roughly that between Joyce Kilmer's "Trees" and *Paradise Lost,* comparative evaluations are, to say the least, superfluous. What on the contrary strikes me now about modern Hebrew literature in Europe is the breathtaking anomaly in the very fact of its existence, and how much of substance it managed to achieve despite its unlikely circumstances. It was never more than the activity of a brave handful, somehow surviving in little coteries gathered in the interstices between the old Jewish world and modern European society, men with a kind of crazed love for a three-thousand-year-old language that no one—themselves included—spoke, breathing the air of a hypothetical culture invented in their own imaginations. Yet this spectral Hebraizing milieu was able to sustain itself uncannily through individual writers and small groups of faithful followers centered around a series of literary journals, from Moses Mendelssohn's Berlin to the Warsaw of David Frischman and the Odessa of Ahad Ha-am. By the first decade of the twentieth century, the new literature had produced one poet of unquestionably major stature (Bialik), one impressively original novelist (Mendele), and a few other writers in whom at least glimmerings of genius could be discerned. By the same time, all this anomalous literary activity had helped bring about the first beginnings of a Hebrew-speaking milieu in Palestine, where Hebrew literature would eventually lead an existence, for better and for worse, *k'khol ha-goyim* ("like all the nations").

There was, then, a powerful impulse working through the Hebrew literary movement on European soil which can properly be called creative, and I shall try to describe later the distinctive nature of this Hebrew imagination of renewal that achieved so much even in the sphere of action. At one time it was common to speak of the new Hebrew creativity in ringing tones as a marvelous "rebirth" or "national renaissance." Though terms of this sort have some obvious applicability, they carry with them a good measure of ideological exaggeration or simplification, as the best of the modern Hebrew writers themselves often felt. The typical Hebrew literary text of the pre-Palestinian period is rather likely to impress the reader with a sense of terrible sterility, a quality that stands in strange contradiction to the creative *élan* which modern Hebrew literature is supposed to embody. This sense of sterility cannot be entirely explained by the badness of the individual works, for one often finds it, or at any rate something akin to it, in writers of real imaginative force and integrity (Feierberg, U. N. Gnessin, Y. H. Brenner, even a good deal of Mendele, Bialik, and Tchernichovsky).

Let me suggest, to begin with, that the relationship between language and reality in modern Hebrew literature gives it a general bias quite different from that of other literatures. This relationship itself amounts to an inner contradiction in modern Hebrew writing which became a source of elation or despair as it was perceived in varying lights by the writers. Modern European literatures, despite the notable exceptions of certain movements and individual writers, have characteristically tended to bring the word of written art closer to the word spoken or otherwise used in actual experience. Literary language since the early Renaissance moves toward a greater degree of specification than it had typically exercised in the past; traditional hierarchical distinctions between sublime and low styles are progressively blurred; the sound and look and feel of everyday life begin to play a new central role in serious literature. One indication of this general movement is the fact that in England, from Donne to Eliot, every important revolution in poetic diction was proclaimed as a return to "natural" speech, to the language of "real men and women."

The initial movement, on the other hand, of modern Hebrew literature was in all these regards headed in virtually the opposite direction. It is suggestive that the new Hebrew literature begins to flourish in the several decades after the French Revolution, during the very period when the novel was rapidly becoming the dominant genre in European literature. That is to say, while European writers were seeking expression more and more in a genre where language could be made to adhere with a new closeness to the rhythms and contours of familiar experience, the writers who adopted Hebrew as an instrument of secular literary expression were choosing a language that was not even a vernacular, that had scarcely any vocabulary to describe the bare physical facts of urban, industrializing societies. Most of the earlier modern Hebrew writers, moreover, preferred the lofty—and as they thought, "pure"— style of the Bible to the rabbinic Hebrew that had been in continuous written use in Jewish communities for centuries, so that the enormous distance between the language they wrote and the world they inhabited was still further magnified.

This striking contrast between Hebrew and European literature depends ultimately on opposing views of the efficacy— really, the ontological status—of literary language. One can detect among serious Western writers over the past two centuries a growing skepticism about the ability of language to embrace reality. If we can in any way engage reality through words, many writers seem to feel, some kind of violence, something unheard of, must be done to language; at any rate, the words to which we frequently turn will not be high-sounding, or fixed in formulaic order by literary tradition, but rather the words once spurned by literature because of their banality, their bizarreness, their scientific neutrality, their ugly or sordid associations, their rawness. The prominence of obscenity, for example, in the rhetoric of contemporary American fiction can be partly explained as a desperate last assault on reality with what seems to some writers the only kind of vocabulary that has not become misleading, dishonest, empty, or irrelevant. The very idea of obscenity, on the other hand, is unthinkable in Hebrew literature until its most recent Israeli phase, because this whole literary movement begins with a turning toward the sanctified verbal formulas of ancient literary tradition, in the belief that beauty of a conspicuously lofty sort is necessarily the vehicle of truth.

The Haskalah, or Hebrew Enlightenment (roughly, from 1784 to 1881), was animated by what might be regarded as a secular survival of the classic Jewish idea that Hebrew was the language in which the world was created. As the old faith in the divine source of the Bible rapidly slipped away, the new Hebrew writers clung with paradoxical fervor to a belief in the langauge of the Bible as a model of aesthetic perfection and an instrument through which all the fullness of the cosmos could be apprehended. One paradigm for this touching innocence and enthusiasm of belief is a poem by Solomon Levisohn (1789–1821) entitled *Ha-M'litzah* ("Hymn to Poesy"). Now, it is true that enraptured hymns to beauty are a commonplace in European poetry during the latter eighteenth and early nineteenth centuries, but there is an important difference here. The subject of Levisohn's poem, strictly speaking, is not the heavenly muse or the divine idea of beauty, but rather poetical language. *M'litzah*, which in current Hebrew usage has become a wholly derogatory term, means "lofty language," or even more specifically, "poetic phrase." In Levisohn's poem it is the poetic word itself that spans the universe, working wonders, planting joy and aspiration in the hearts of men, melting the warrior's fierce wrath into love (this at the time of the Napoleonic Wars!), even holding sway over the animal and vegetable kingdoms in some obscure hyperbolic fashion. The poetic word, in short, has become a cosmic force, not only a delegate but virtually the surrogate of God: "Like streams / Of mighty waters bursting from / The womb of everlasting mountains, so they [the words of poetry] sweep on / With their vast tumultuous roar, and who / Can withstand the surge of their might?"

This is of course turgid stuff, in the original as well as in translation, but the Hebrew does manage to achieve a certain grand ring—though always with a suspicion of hollowness—because the subject of the poem, *m'litzah*, is also its chief instrument of expression. In typical Haskalah fashion, Levisohn's language is a pastiche, or more generously, a mosaic, of biblical phrases, and as such it represents a rhetorical achievement of a very peculiar sort. Such poetry is above all a reveling in the high phrases of a grand tradition, and whatever charm it held for its composers and its contemporary readers must be explained through the enthusiastic inventiveness and energy with which the poet reconstituted the familiar, affectionately recollected language of the Bible. It is hard for anyone unacquainted with this tradition to imagine the kind of delight a Hebrew

reader could take in a piquant combination of a phrase from
Job with one from Psalms, or in the creation of a line that
would perfectly simulate the style of Isaiah without actual
quotation; even the use of a rare biblical variant of a familiar
word or the tricking out of a common root in an odd grammati-
cal form could be a source of aesthetic pleasure. The Hebrew
language itself was a magical thing for the early readers of
modern Hebrew literature, and the art of the poet hovered
somewhere between the ritualistic gestures of a high priest and
the technical deftness of a prestidigitator.

It is here that the inner contradiction to which I alluded
begins. The writers of the Haskalah, and even some of their
successors in more recent times, started from the assumption
that the Hebrew language, if used with a full sense of aesthetic
decorum, was uniquely suited to express the most fundamental
truths of creation and the eternal qualities of human nature. In
fact what Hebrew proved to be for the Haskalah writers and for
many of their successors was something like the all-absorbing
Glass Bead Game in Herman Hesse's *Magister Ludi*—an activity supposed a key to the nature of reality that is in practice a
refined but arid intellectual pastime, an elaborate deployment
of pleasing patterns within a closed system. The point is not
merely that Hebrew of this sort had no vocabulary to deal with
the prickly particularities of everyday experience. What is far
more serious is that these tissues of lofty phrases, woven by
Central- or East-European Jews in the torment and turbulence
of nineteenth-century existence, may have expressed the adolescent idealism and bookish fantasies of the men who used
them, but certainly little of their adult inner life. Or, alternately, one might say that such addiction to merely verbal
values prevented many people from having much adult inner
life. Literature of this sort, in other words, becomes a means of
avoiding self-confrontation or honest self-exposure, a way of
escaping the complexities of life through the intoxication of
language.

A poem like Levisohn's "Hymn to Poesy," then, is pathetic
and—despite its ecstatic mood—finally depressing, not simply

because of its lack of subtlety or originality but because of its complete airlessness, and though this poem is perhaps an excessively neat illustration of the general phenomenon, a whole century of Hebrew compositions, in both verse and prose, resemble it to one degree or another in the stifling bookishness of their atmosphere, in being only marginally expressions of real human experiences, for all their earnestness. It is worth adding that the disturbing insulation of literary language from actual experience has proved to be more than a curious passing episode: the ghost of *m'litzah* still haunts many Hebrew writers, especially the older ones, and even in Israeli novelists as gifted as Haim Hazaz and S. Yizhar, verbal virtuosity too easily becomes a substitute for literary imagination. In the public rhetoric, moreover, of many Israeli political leaders and cultural dignitaries, unblushing *m'litzah* flourishes as of old, so that one is often tempted to conclude that it is easier to say absolutely nothing grandiloquently in Hebrew than in any other language.

The contradiction in the modern literary use of Hebrew that I have been describing in terms of its supposed utility as an instrument of knowledge could also be put in terms of the relationship of the language to Jewish history. The usual assumption made about the revival of the old poetic Hebrew is that it was itself an act of national renewal, a return through language to the people's life-sources located deep in the period when the nation was rooted on its own land. "Buds of Rebirth," a poem by Aaron Kaminka (1866–1950) on the early Zionist settlements, offers a logical complement to the Haskalah conception of Hebrew; Kaminka sees the noble language of the Bible with engaging simplicity as a concrete agent in history, just as Levisohn before him imagined it as the most real cosmic force. "Who gave you being, lovely buds?" Kaminka asks, alluding to the new settlements. "Was it the verses of Isaiah buried here in the earth / That sprang from the dust and bloomed into thousands . . . / Or was it Ruth and the Song of Songs that left their fair phrases [*m'litzot*] / Hidden here, to become in the magic moonlight / Living souls?"

This Zionist notion of the power of the Hebrew language

has of course a degree of plausibility wholly lacking in the earlier Haskalah notion. It is true in a sense that the words of Isaiah, especially in their literary revival, helped stir the minds and hearts of men to create those new settlements. What enthusiasts like Kaminka failed to see is how drastically qualified such attributions of historical causation to language must be, and how terribly ambiguous the revival of an age-old tongue was for Jewish intellectuals in the throes of modernity, threatened with the loss of their own religious and cultural identity. It is the ambiguity, however, that sensitive Hebrew writers began to feel more keenly as the nineteenth century waned, and that was stressed by them with growing frequency in the early twentieth century. For the adoption of Hebrew as a modern literary language eventually had the effect of polarizing outlooks on the prospect of Jewish survival. On the one hand, obviously enough, participation in the Hebrew revival could involve a sense of sharing in a real miracle of cultural resurrection, and could inspire in some individuals—one still occasionally encounters them—a loyal enthusiasm for all things Hebrew that borders on fanaticism. For a few writers, on the other hand, the commitment to Hebrew became a naked exposure to an inexorable sharp edge of despair. Having chosen to express themselves in the classic language of Jewish culture, they were located at a unique vantage-point from which to see the progressive erosion of that culture from within. At the same time, they were made painfully aware both of the lack of resonance of their Hebrew words in the larger community of Jews, and of the tenuous connection of their necessarily esoteric words with the vast world of change and dislocation in which all of Europe was caught up. They clung to the language of Jewish tradition because an authentic continuation of their identity as Jews was a first existential necessity for all of them, but what could one think of the possibilities of continuation when the very language they tried to sustain rang hollow, seemed painfully irrelevant to the post-traditional world? Often, then, the language of old and new beginnings seemed to be the language of the bitter end.

This note of forlornness in modern Hebrew literature is struck as early as Y. L. Gordon (1830–1892), the most prominent Haskalah poet, in a plaintive piece with the self-explanatory title, "For Whom Do I Labor?" While the poet sees himself "writing poems in a forgotten language," the obscurantist older generation of Jews holds poetry in contempt, and the young people leave on the high road to assimilation; the poet, then, is led to wonder whether he may be "the last of the singers of Zion" and his audience the last Hebrew readers. History has of course laid to rest Gordon's doubts at least about the physical survival of a Hebrew audience, but his question would be asked again by Hebrew writers a generation later with a new awareness of the troubling problem of authenticity in survival.

Hebrew literature around the turn of the century, though referred to in the standard literary histories with unwitting irony as the "period of renascence," exhibits in many notable instances a distinct *fin de siècle* mood, and no one expresses that mood more poignantly than the novelist Yosef Haim Brenner. In his *Beside the Point,* a work whose title suggests the frustrated flailing-out that writing was for him, one character is moved to ask: "Look, the Holy Temple has been destroyed for all time, and what are we, its priests, doing among the ruins?" The question could serve as a somber motto for Brenner's generation of Hebrew writers, but it also has a persuasive applicability to a broad spectrum of post-traditional movements of Jewish revival, whether religious, cultural, political, or ethnic. Such movements, whatever their particular programs, have not generally been willing to admit this kind of radical, self-doubting criticism, for so much of modern Jewish life has been founded on tendentious evasions and self-congratulatory apologetics. In this regard, however, the unique strength as well as the weakness of modern Hebrew literature makes itself felt: in Hebrew, for reasons I have tried to indicate, it can be either treacherously easy or excruciatingly difficult to deceive oneself about the nature and future of Jewishness.

Paradoxically, when Hebrew literature comes of age morally and artistically around the turn of the century, it is even more depressing than it was before, though for different reasons. The literature of national rebirth at last finds its true subject, what the writers know in their bones, can hold tight in the close of their imagination, and that subject is, in a word, death. If Haskalah phrasemaking is airless because the only experience it provides is a hermetically sealed literary one, the fiction and poetry of Feierberg, Brenner, the early Y. D. Berkowitz, Bialik, and many of their contemporaries have the airlessness of the tomb because that is what the real world had become for these hyperconscious Jews. Such writers, discovering out of their own struggle to renew Hebrew that Jewish history had entered into an awful cul-de-sac, produced a literature in which the prevalent mood was exhaustion, the dominant imagery claustrophobic.

One symptom of this general condition is the fact that from the latter nineteenth century well on into the Palestinian period, there is so little persuasive youthfulness in Hebrew literature. One finds, to be sure, a kind of callow or presumptuous adolescence, which some writers, like the late Zalman Schneur, managed to sustain till their dying day, but more self-critical figures typically passed from this stage of adolescence into shriveled old age sometime after their eighteenth birthday. Bialik's recurrent theme of the "theft of youth," like so much else in his work, expressed the experience of a whole culture; and time after time one sees young Hebrew poets, even those imbued with the idea of a Nietzschean revival, bemoaning the grayness of their lives, the wasting of their strength, their forlorn state in an existence which denies them love and joy.

This sensibility of decrepitude could, at its worst, be merely the occasion for personal self-pity, or, more impressively, it could be simultaneously a reflection of and percipient penetration into a process of dissolution immanent in Jewish life—one which the sundry Jewish apologists and romanticizers of the *shtetl* have chosen to ignore or avoid. The prose of the Haskalah had been typically satirical, assuming that the ills of Jewish life were measurable divergences from a sane standard (that of modern Gentile Europe) and so could be corrected by a rational program of education and social reform. The criticism of Jewish life in later Hebrew writers is more profound because it does not impose extraneous standards, begins not from the bias of satire—though its effect is often grimly satiric—but out of the need to describe as faithfully as possible the way things are. Here, for example, is how Brenner, in a story called "The Jerusalemite," depicts a small-town Russian synagogue of sixty years ago:

> The windowpanes had become dark. The oven-bricks were rubbed smooth by the abrasion of generations, the bench-boards worn thin by countless sitters. The little bulging lecterns seemed to have grown heavier through long usage. The edges of the tables were splintered and pockmarked, gouged with tatooed inscriptions and jackknife carvings. The pages of the books were crowded with marginal comments and notes; they looked damp with sweat.
>
> The ceiling was lower now. The brass candelabra that were suspended from it, all their sockets befouled with tallow-drippings, had a coating of verdigris. The crooked walls were enveloped in gloom, covered with a layer of dust. Over everything there hovered an ancient spirit of sorrow, of everlasting melancholy; everything was immersed in the longings of the moribund, the yearning of the lost.

The description of physical objects overlaid in this fashion with the traces and smudges of human use—setting as a revelation of cultural style or lived experience—is of course a familiar device in nineteenth-century European fiction. But in writers like Balzac and Zola, such rendering of scene generally shows the imprint of human energy and will, however crude or misdirected, on the world of things. What is clear, on the other hand, in Brenner's description of the synagogue is that all energy has been sapped, all will has long since subsided into the futile longings of the almost dead. Crookedness, decay, a physical wearing out, the filthy accretions of usage—these are the recurrent themes not only of this passage but of a generation and more of Hebrew writers. The synagogue here, with its sunken ceiling, its inclining walls, its darkened windows, its atmosphere of heaviness, is a claustrophobic intimation of the grave. The compulsive redoubling of almost every image and phrase (an effect more pronounced in the original than in my translation) bespeaks both the emphasis of Brenner's feeling and his impulse to reproduce in prose something of the slow march of distichs and tristichs, single and double parallelisms, that distinguishes the biblical elegy.

This kind of writing is all the more disturbing because it is not satiric. Brenner finds in the much-extolled stronghold of Jewish faith only the abode of the dying and of death itself, but he also knows that it is his soul's intimate world, the one he is condemned to depict in painstaking detail with a sort of loving hatred. For he is equally aware that the new world (which in effect he has already joined) outside the tumbledown walls of the synagogue spells another kind of death for him—the denial of his ultimate identity, the betrayal of his people's history. "I have lost my old world," complains the hero of Feierberg's *Whither?* (1896), "and a new world I have not found." This general consciousness of anguished contradiction, of a lack of viable alternatives, attains its most intense, unflinching expression in the fiction of Brenner, where the protagonists desperately grope the walls of their moral prison for a "way out" (the title of one memorable story) and usually discover that the only route of escape is through madness or suicide.

The greatest Hebrew writer of the pre-Palestinian period responded to his own terrible vision of death within and death without in another way—through silence. Between 1900 and 1905 Haim Nahman Bialik had produced a sustained series of brilliant poems, both short lyric pieces and longer narrative verse, which in its concentrated achievement of genius recalls the creative outpouring of Keats in the months when he wrote all his odes. In a matter of three or four years, Bialik managed, I would say, to write more great Hebrew poetry than all the Hebrew poets combined since the death of Judah Halevi in the twelfth century. By 1907, however, the excitement had faded, Bialik's mood was saddened or embittered, and his poetic production had noticeably slowed; over the next nine years it became a trickle; and after 1916, when he was still only forty-three, he virtually stopped writing serious poetry with the exception of a solitary piece every few years when some experience particularly moved him. The paradoxical aspect of all this, what has made it a crux of criticism, is the fact that the poems written during the years of Bialik's "silence," whether we date it from 1916 or earlier, are palpably works of genius, so that his decision to stop writing cannot be attributed to a waning of powers. Bialik more than once alluded to his own poetic activity as the wielding of an ax by a hewer of wood, but what role, he began to wonder, could be played by poetry so conceived if the cleaving blade met only the soft insidious yielding of rottenness and decay? In other words, how could a poetry that spoke in the ringing tones of a tradition sustain itself when the tradition was dying, its divine authentication no longer believed, when the people who were the poet's audience gave only the most dubious evidence of spiritual, moral, or intellectual life?

Bialik lucidly perceived these reasons for his own eventual silence as early as 1904 in a poem called *Davar* ("Word," but in the sense here of "prophetic burden"), one of the first in what might be called his negative-prophetic mode. The poem begins with the shards of a broken altar among which the people scavenge like nasty rodents; the poet is then enjoined to pound his useless hammer into a shovel to dig a grave, after which the poem turns into a verbal symphony of negatives—the lines bristle with "not's" and "no's," with "emptiness," "impotence," "nothingness," and, especially, "chaos." "Let your word be bitter as death," the poet-prophet is commanded, "let it be death itself— / We shall hear it that we may know." The sardonic concluding lines of *Davar* summarize with biting succinctness the whole contradiction I have been describing between Hebrew literature as a mode of national renaissance and as a means of intimate, unpitying knowledge of the imminent end:

> Why should we fear death—when his angel rides
> our shoulders

His bit between our teeth?
So with a cry of rebirth on our lips, with the
   cheering of players
We skip to the grave.

After such words, little remains before the rest is silence.

The trouble with this entire picture of modern Hebrew literature is that it is misleadingly incomplete. Though it is true that the most honest and probing Hebrew works of this period often give voice to a stark, dead-end despair that is distinctive even in the rich gallery of despairs of modern Western literature, one can also find, sometimes in convincingly achieved writing, an antithetical imagination and an opposed set of themes. As the course of history in the past half-century has shown, the national renewal proclaimed by the new literature was not entirely illusory, however we may seek to qualify the concept of renewal or stress its problematic aspects: not only has a viable Jewish state been created, but within it flourishes a modern Hebrew culture that has powerful though often deeply ambiguous ties with the Jewish past. It is hardly surprising that the intimations of a genuine renewal, whether personal or national, should on occasion make themselves persuasively felt in imaginative works in Hebrew. This is the bright underside of the dark paradox we have been considering: if Hebrew literature in general touches a nadir of bleak depression remarkable among modern literatures, there are also impressive Hebrew works that preserve a mood of untrammeled joy and exuberance of a sort one scarcely finds in serious European writing since the Romantic movement.

Understandably, these joyous notes are sounded more often, more resonantly, in poetry than in prose, for the engagement of fiction in the description of actual milieux and institutions typically led to repeated confrontations with the sundry social pathologies of East-European Jewry. It is also worth noting that the poets who achieve the most convincing kind of joyfulness in their art are generally those who are also gripped by the characteristic Hebrew imagination of death and dissolution. The same Tchernichovsky who denounced his people as "walking corpses, the rot of human seed," could evoke them vividly in his long narrative idylls in all the teeming vitality of their life on the Russian steppes, all the bustling health of their birth and growth and marriage, their workdays and seasons of rejoicing. And Bialik, in the same period from 1900 to 1905 when he first struck the apocalyptic note of *Davar,* in the shadow of pogroms and the collapse of the old world-order, produced his remarkable series of poems on the theme of light, which convey a sense of sustained elation perhaps unmatched in the poetry of this century.

In some cases, however, elation came at a cost, or rather was the result of a self-conscious decision. Much Hebrew writing of the earlier twentieth century is not vital but vitalistic—which is virtually the opposite, the product not of an immediate intuition but of a willed choice to identify with a presumed flow of life-energy in the natural world and in mankind. One senses, for example, in some though not all of the paganizing poems of Tchernichovsky and Schneur that the primitive vitality of the ancient cults is not imaginatively felt, only programmatically declared as an ideological challenge to historical Judaism. A more complicated, perhaps more instructive, instance of this same ambiguity is the ecstatic poetry of the Palestinian pioneer period written by Avraham Shlonsky in the twenties. The excitement of these poems seems quite genuine, and in some of the short pieces it is beautifully realized, but much of the imagery looks forcibly devised to burst the shell of musty Jewish bookishness. Thus the earth is a pregnant black mare, the mountains of Gilboa are camels with bulging breasts (not udders) giving suck to the fields of Jezreel below, the June sun licks the wild-ass's skin which is the land, and so forth. The muscles of poetic invention visibly strain and bulge in such imagery; this may work to *épater les Juifs,* but it often seems the contrived equivalent of vitality rather than the direct experience of it. Shlonsky's poetry throughout his career has tended to vacillate between poles of joy and despair, and he is paradigmatically the Hebrew poet when, in the volume of verse after the Gilboa poems, he confesses that the happier tones seem perversely to elude him: "I too sought the drum for a song of exultation / But the craftsman made me a harp of weeping-willow wood."

What are probably the most fully realized moments of joy in this literature come in Bialik's poems of light, and even in them ecstasy can overtake the speaker only through extraordinary means. Here, for example, are the first lines in the concluding verse-paragraph of "Morning Creatures":

> O come to me, gleaming ones, pure morning
> creatures,
> Come under my brilliant white sheet!
> There let us wallow, let us wrestle till noontide;
> Dance over my skin and soft flesh.

"Come to," or "come into" (*bo el*) is the standard biblical idiom for sexual entry, and the lines that follow these, abounding in images of penetration and moving toward an ecstatic climax, make it still clearer that there is a play on the sexual meaning of the term. What is curious is that the male poet assumes the female role, eagerly waiting in bed for the morning light to caress his "soft flesh," to flood into him and possess him. This moment in Bialik is one remove from John Donne's prayer to be raped by God in the famous sonnet that begins, "Batter my heart, three-personed God." I mention Donne because of the instructive difference as well as the similarity. Donne's desire to be assaulted, violated, by a powerful male God bears witness to an agonized psychological distance from God, a desperate need to feel the impossible immediacy of the divine presence; it is just this tormented sense of separation that gives all of Donne's religious poems their peculiar taut energy. In Bialik, too, there is an inner distance from the sweet light he hungers for in his more typical poetic visions of grim deprivation. This, I would assume, is ultimately why both in "Morning Creatures" and in the longer poem "Splendor" he adopts the passivity of the woman's sexual role: brightness must take him by surprise, envelop him, overwhelm him. In contrast, however, to Donne's religious verse, the distance is crossed; the speaker in

Bialik's poems does not pray to be raped by light but rather welcomes its entrance as he is suddenly, exquisitely inundated. The poetry here, as the ripe sensuality of its language attests, is an experience of consummated rapture, in both the physical and the emotional sense.

The Israeli critic Dov Sadan has shrewdly observed that much of Bialik's poetry evokes in varying ways a single archetypal scene: a large, dark space in the midst of which is a candle, flickering and casting shadows. The candle flame in the darkness, Sadan suggests, is first the actual frail light Bialik knew as a boy in study-house and *yeshiva*, where he followed the traditional discipline of learning; then it is the altar flame of the long-destroyed temple, a central memory in classic Jewish consciousness at once historical and mythical; and, finally, as the poet draws near to the light, plunges into it, it becomes a wholly mythical substance, the "hidden light" of primal unity at life's beginnings to which Bialik's poetry—in this respect recalling Wordsworth's—strives to return. The same image of flickering light in sepulchral darkness appears elsewhere in Hebrew literary works of the period, but what is more important is that it is such an apt emblem of the Hebrew literary enterprise in modern Europe. There is, moreover, a nice correspondence between this representative image of Hebrew literature and the actual state of Jewish existence since the Emancipation—an existence that has been precarious, dubious, often hiding the face of dissolution beneath the mask of revival, but which also has afforded moments of genuine vitality, surprising explosions of light. The distinctive value of this new literature, then, which tries to refashion the language of tradition for a post-traditional world, is that it serves as a faithful instrument for taking the full measure of threatened extinction, and yet it can register sudden intimations of immortality, imaginative tracings of a bright renewal still possible to achieve.

1968

II *Four Writers*

SAUL BELLOW: A DISSENT FROM MODERNISM

It is hardly surprising that Saul Bellow's new novel, so clearly the culminating achievement of his career till now, should have evoked the kind of critical enthusiasm that it did in many circles. But it is interesting that some reviewers chose to praise *Herzog* in terms rarely applied to mere works of literature. More than one critic spoke of the novel as a "liberating" experience, and Julian Moynihan actually concluded his review in *The New York Times* by suggesting that, with the appearance of this book, things might be looking up for American civilization in general. However extravagant such praise may be, it has some relevance to Bellow and his rather special relationship to contemporary letters. We are now well into the seventh decade of our century, but—as so often is the case with changing eras— the literary world has needed a writer of vigorously independent vision to remind it that the first half of the twentieth century has in fact passed.

Bellow has been highly sensitive to the often hypnotic influence of the preceding age's great literature on the writers of our day. His own fiction, certainly from *Augie March* on, could be viewed as a sustained attempt to shake off that influence. We have by now made classics of the Western writers who created a new literature in the years before and after the First World War, but, paradoxically, we have also continued to insist on their strict spiritual contemporaneity with us. One important reason for this double relationship with the past— enshrining it, yet thinking of it as present—may be the uniquely revolutionary nature of the imaginative literature produced in the early decades of our century. In most respects, it represented such a violent break with the past, it was so startlingly *modern* in both its treatment of form and its attitudes toward life, that now to break with it in turn seems somehow counter-revolutionary, shirking, one might say, the agony of being modern. But, as Bellow sensibly observes, this very agony of being modern, once an immediate intuition of reality, has frozen into a fashionable posture and thus has become, even in a world where there is cause enough for agony, peculiarly irrelevant to life.

Bellow considered this question at length in a lecture delivered at the Library of Congress in January, 1963—significantly during the period when he was arduously working and reworking *Herzog*. The lecture in itself is an impressive document: it reveals even more transparently than his fiction the lucidity of mind and sane moral sensibility that give Bellow an intellectual distinction rare among American novelists. The task he set himself in the lecture presented problems of both tact and conceptual precision, but he handles all difficulties with unfaltering poise. If the word were not so solemn-sounding, one might describe the essential quality of the lecture (and of much of his fiction, too) as a kind of dignity; in the lecture, Bellow skillfully locates contemporary fiction in relation to the broad streams of twentieth-century social and intellectual history without a hint of pedantry or strain, while he judges his American literary colleagues rigorously but never jealously. One statement is especially worthy of attention because in it Bellow's critique of his fellow-novelists defines much of what he himself has attempted by contrast to achieve in his novels:

> Writers have inherited a tone of bitterness from the great poems and novels of this century, many of which lament the passing of a more stable and beautiful age demolished by the barbarous intrusion of an industrial and metropolitan society of masses or proles who will, after many upheavals, be tamed by bureaucrats and oligarchies in brave new worlds, human anthills. . . . There are modern novelists who take all of this for granted as fully proven and implicit in the human condition and who complain as steadily as they write, viewing mod-

ern life with a bitterness to which they themselves have not established clear title, and it is this unearned bitterness that I speak of. What is truly curious about it is that often the writer automatically scorns contemporary life. He bottles its stinks artistically. But, seemingly, he does not need to study it. It is enough for him that it does not allow his sensibilities to thrive, that it starves his instincts for nobility or for spiritual qualities.

A superficial glance at Bellow's own novels might lead one to conclude that the author of *The Victim* and *Dangling Man* belonged very much in the contemporary tradition of alienated writing which he here castigates. But even his earliest novels are quite distinct both in moral tone and in intellectual purview from that fashionable literature of alienation whose attitudes range from truculent resentment to anarchic rebellion. And while Bellow has built all six of his novels around victimized protagonists, what he had been attempting to do is to turn the clichés and conventions of victim literature inside out. In *Herzog*, this act of literary self-transcendence is at last fully achieved.

The writer's problem of relating to the immediate literary past, as Bellow poses it in his lecture, is a problem of moral outlook. But the characteristically modern sense of life translated itself into characteristically modern treatments of literary form, so the problem is also one of literary technique; and it may be helpful in trying to see Bellow's distinctiveness to consider first what he has done with form in the novel. Those great poems and novels of the earlier twentieth century which Bellow fears overshadow most writers today were, by and large, boldly experimental in their handling of form. The effect of this unprecedented period of formal innovation has been to preempt the whole field of literary experiment. After a work like *Finnegans Wake*, any experimental writing would seem to be left the alternatives of straining into willful unintelligibility or lapsing back into timid imitation.

And, roughly speaking, this is what has happened to much contemporary literature. More precisely, serious writing since World War II has generally followed one of three equally unsatisfactory alternatives. On the left is today's peculiar avant-garde, more like a rear guard, pronouncing the old slogans about modern breakdown of values, isolation of the individual, failure of communication, and so forth—simmering an overcooked brew of antinovels, absurd plays, and sundry solipsistic lucubrations, lyric, narrative, and dramatic. In the center one finds writers whose imaginative strengths are of a decidedly conventional sort, but who preserve a certain piety toward the great literary pioneers of this century, so that modern experiment flits through their work in a ghostly afterlife of modernistic gesturing. (A good example of this particular phenomenon is the National Book Award novel for 1963, John Updike's *The Centaur*. Updike writes perceptively about a father and son in a small Pennsylvania town, but the introduction of myth, instead of extending meanings and giving coherence to the details of the narrative, as it sometimes does in Joyce, merely calls attention to itself as a distracting stylistic trick and weakens our belief in the reality of the events narrated.) Finally, on the right we have those writers who do not seem to be interested at all in exploring the technical resources of the medium in which they work. They give us America of the sixties in a narrative envelope not strikingly different from the one, say, that novelists like Arnold Bennett and H. G. Wells used for Edwardian England. In sum, whether the great innovators in form of the immediate past are extravagantly outdone, mechanically reproduced, or simply ignored, the lack of an intelligent relationship with them contributes to keeping our literature, as Bellow complains, irrelevant to life.

In general, Bellow's handling of narrative method has been exploratory, tentative, but not obtrusively experimental. He has not been impelled to shatter traditional literary molds because, unlike the writers of the avant-garde, he has no orthodox belief about the nature of reality, such as a faith in the impossibility of meaning, which would serve as an imperative for an antitraditionalist program.

His first novel, *Dangling Man* (1944), is probably the least interesting from a formal point of view, though its thematic concerns are archetypal for Bellow's fiction: the Dangling Man will continue to swing through all the novels until he is finally set down on convincingly solid ground at the end of *Herzog*. The most obvious literary influence on the first novel is Dostoevski. The general plan of the book would seem to derive from *Notes from Underground*: Bellow's novel, like Dostoevski's, is presented as the journal-confession of a frustrated intellectual who focuses in himself the general condition of *anomie* suffered by individuals in modern society. The Dangling Man's dialogues with the Spirit of Alternatives also call to mind Ivan Karamazov's tortured colloquies with his own private Mephistopheles. In these and other respects, Bellow's first novel is more self-consciously literary than any of his later ones. The protagonist's journal, for example, is dated from December 15 to April 9; that is, from the winter solstice, the death of the year, to the time of annual rebirth—just as we witness in the journal a man's dying to his old self and then, at the end, a sharply ironic rebirth. In the subsequent novels, Bellow generally avoids this kind of neat symbolizing; it is clear that his imagination is most at home in the vivid creation of concrete situations, not in tracing timeless mythic patterns.

But *Dangling Man*, despite its penchant for schematizing and its relative sketchiness, reveals an important aptitude of Bellow's which contributes much to the imaginative richness of his later work. He demonstrates a high degree of responsiveness to the creative innovations of other writers and—in contrast to his use of Dostoevski—an unusual gift for assimilating them thoroughly into his own mechanism of sensibility without overt imitation. There is a striking passage, for example, in *Dangling Man*, which one suspects is ultimately inspired by Proust and his narrative use of present objects poignant with association as springboards into a personal past. But if the "source" of the passage is in any sense Proust, it is clear that the neurasthenic French devotee of aesthetic experiencing has suffered a deep seachange to be used at all by this American explorer of moral conditions whose sensibility is at once coarser and more vigorous:

This afternoon I emptied the closet of all its shoes and sat on the floor polishing them. Surrounded by rags, saddle soap, and brushes—the brown light of the street pressing in at the windows, and the sparrows bickering in the dead twigs—I felt tranquil for a while and, as I set Iva's shoes out in a row, I grew deeply satisfied. It was a borrowed satisfaction; it was something I had done as a child. In Montreal, on such afternoons as this, I often asked permission to spread a paper on the sitting-room floor and shine all the shoes in the house, including Aunt Dina's with their long tongues and scores of eyelets. When I thrust my arm into one of her shoes it reached well above the elbow and I could feel the brush against my arm through the soft leather. . . .

The diarist goes on to recall the brown fog in St. Dominique Street in Montreal, the glow of an old stove on his skin, and then a series of piercing memories of his poverty-stricken native quarter: cripples, beggars, a fallen horse in the snow, glimpses of the act of love made public by shadeless windows, a drunk after a fight bleeding a red trail behind him on the pavement. The present object—here part of a ritual reenactment and not an adventitious discovery as in Proust—launches the narrator upon a journey into himself which reveals to us much of what has made him the particular moral and psychological individual he is. In a lyric telescoping of great evocative power, we get a substantial sense of his formative encounters with cruelty, violence, lust, senseless suffering. This kind of to-and-fro movement between present and past through the eloquence of objects is certainly redolent of the twentieth-century literature that has been preoccupied to an unprecedented degree with representing states of consciousness. But as a narrative mode here and elsewhere in Bellow's novels, it differs from its use in flamboyantly "modern" writers like Proust, Joyce, Faulkner, Virginia Woolf, because it does not call attention to itself as a formal device.

The technique employed at this point in *Dangling Man* is much the same as the one used for Moses Herzog's extraordinarily suggestive backward glimpses into the world of his childhood. But *Herzog*, like Bellow's other books, is a complex novel without being a difficult one. Its imaginative revisiting of the past would seem to an unsophisticated reader to be merely an extended use of the technique of flashback that has been worked into bleary-eyed tedium by contemporary novelists. In point of fact, Herzog's flashbacks, unlike the popular device they appear to resemble, supply illumination in depth. They are as pregnant with meaning and at times as psychologically revealing as the impressive achievements by other writers in stream of consciousness or interior monologue. But, in contrast to these characteristically modern conventions, they do not stand out as part of an elaborate, pioneering discipline for the capture of consciousness, designed, as it were, to make the reader's way an arduous one.

And what is true in this particular matter of transcribing consciousness is largely true of Bellow's whole relationship with literary tradition and formal experiment. He shares many of the aims of the preeminently modern novelists, but he tries to realize them in forms that are not obtrusively modern. Despite the obvious thematic similarities, each of his novels is very different from the others because each represents a different kind of attempt to infuse fresh life into a traditional narrative form or novelistic sub-genre by using it in unexpected new ways. All his novels, with the partial exception of *Henderson the Rain King*, seem conventionally "realistic." But what Bellow has done—coming as he does after a great age of literary revolution—is to explore the possibilities of revitalizing prerevolutionary forms, putting to use, wherever appropriate, the awarenesses and technical resources made available by the major iconoclastic literature of the earlier twentieth century. The inventor of Augie March and Henderson is a master of literary combinations and permutations, or, to use a more appropriately organic metaphor, of the art of crossbreeding narrative genres. This is undoubtedly one of the reasons for the eager expectation with which many people of serious literary interests awaited the appearance of each new Bellow novel over the past decade. What, the cognoscenti wondered, was he going to try next?

Clearly, in such an adventurous approach to writing fiction, not every attempt would be wholly successful, but there would be new kinds of reading pleasures in each book. *The Victim* (1947) is not only a more fully realized novel than *Dangling Man* but also a very different sort of book. Two central characters instead of one generate a high tension of interrelationship not present in the first novel. Plot now is developed as a vehicle for carrying forward meanings, and the grimy New York setting is vivified by Bellow's rare lyric gift for rendering urban scenes as the background for urban souls.

The Victim gives the appearance of being a rather conventional novel—a story by a Jewish writer about a Jew and an anti-Semite, with familiar social or social-psychological implications. But there is something patently odd about Asa Leventhal's Jewishness. Compare it to the Jewishness of Herzog and it seems almost an abstraction. The ostensibly realistic novel is actually—as the epigraph from the *Thousand and One Nights* suggests—a moral fable, though it is told in terms of the nuanced relations, both emotional and social, between two particularized individuals. Leventhal's Jewishness (like the idea of being a Jew in Malamud's *The Assistant*) is not so much a given fact of personal history as a symbol of a general moral state: it is every man's susceptibility to victimhood, his dangerous but inescapable need always to be responsible for the implications of his actions, his befuddlement when confronted with the impermeable moral otherness of another human being. This parable of the ambiguities of moral life, while mainly following the narrative procedures of the socially realistic novel, also draws on resources of the folktale: Albee, the WASP victim and victimizer of Asa Leventhal, is for the Jew a disturbing kind of *dybbuk* figure, appearing and then reappearing like the spirit of one dead, refusing to be exorcised in his instance on the complicity shared by him and his enemy-brother.

In 1953, with *Augie March*, the book that established his national reputation, Bellow made his most ambitious attempt to exhume a traditional form of fiction—the picaresque novel—and make it serve the special needs of a twentieth-century writer. *Augie March* is remarkable both as an achievement in its own right and as an event in literary history, having fathered, as it did, over the past ten years, such a parti-colored brood of neo-, quasi-, and pseudo-picaresque novels. It is understandable that the picaresque image of an individual making his way adroitly through the interstices of society, observing it, taking advantage of it, but not wholly part of it, should appeal to contemporary writers. Bellow's picaro, incidentally, more closely resembles the traditional figure then do the heroes of Bellow's imitators because, like the original picaro, he is not really alienated from his surroundings, only detached. *Augie March* takes from the older picaresque novels a central emphasis on the endless and vivid variety of experience; it is, in fact, the thirst for and delight in such variety which dictate the unending string of episodes that is the inevitable picaresque narrative form.

During the first two-thirds of the novel, while Augie centers his dazzling variety of activities in Chicago, Bellow succeeds in a virtuoso re-creation of the classic picaresque novel. But once Augie exchanges the sharply drawn realities of his native city for a hazy Mexico of the imagination, signs of strain begin to appear. As I have argued in detail elsewhere,* the further Augie progresses in his adventures, the more a disparity makes itself felt between the picaresque form of the book and other novelistic ends Bellow was trying to achieve. The traditional picaresque hero seeks experience for its own sake, because it is pleasing or challenging or both. But by the last third of *Augie March*, it is apparent that experience for Augie is rather a means to an end—it is the medium for his relentless struggle to discover himself. The picaresque episodes, then, prove to be material for a *Bildungsroman*, a novelistic quest for authentic identity. The picaresque buoyancy and comedy of the book either diminish or become forced: intense Augie, very much a child of his times, cannot really participate in the traditional picaro's insouciance, his picaresque knack of adopting an untroubled attitude toward a very troubling world.

* *Rogue's Progress: Studies in the Picaresque Novel* (Cambridge: Harvard University Press, 1964), pp. 121–125.

But if *Augie March* is finally flawed, its imaginative successes largely compensate for the unconvincing sections, and it is hardly a book to condescend to, as some critics have done. Bellow, partly because of the independence of his literary aims, is not an easy novelist to pigeonhole, and peculiar judgments have been arrived at by insisting that he conform to critical expectations inappropriate to his work.

The obverse of the critical estimate of *Augie March* as a brilliant flop is the view of *Seize the Day* (1956) as Bellow's masterpiece. This general approach was illustrated recently and unfortunately in V. S. Pritchett's *New York Review* piece on *Herzog*. Mr. Pritchett formulates a kind of rule of all thumbs that when Bellow is brief, he is good, but when he spreads out, he "loses his theme"—or is it his reader? This sort of judgment is surprising from Mr. Pritchett, who has shown such a fine sympathy for the varying aims of an earlier age's expansive novels, but it is in keeping with the assumptions of many other critics today. There seems to be in some circles a vague unhappiness over Bellow's refusal to write novels tightly woven into a Jamesian perfection of form. Perfection in form, however, is something for which one usually pays a price. When the novelist restricts his own liberty to improvise, to give latitude to his narrative imagination, he also may restrict the scope of experience he can encompass.

One of the remarkable qualities of the novel, bulkiest of genres, is its capacity to absorb junk without serious detriment. Most of the great English novels—*Tom Jones, Clarissa, Vanity Fair, Middlemarch*, almost anything of the mature Dickens, *Ulysses*—are magnificent edifices with many splendid rooms piled high with junk. But one is willing to put up with the sentimentalism, the contrivance, the moralizing, the overwriting in such novels because they manage to take in so much life with such extraordinary penetration. It would appear that Bellow has something of this sense that it pays for a novelist to extend himself, to take chances. Now in his most substantial work, he has written a novel that is certainly not "perfect" in any Flaubertian-Jamesian sense, but the very freedom of association and invention in *Herzog* enables it to attempt more and say more than any American novel has done in recent years.

Seize the Day by contrast, is a remarkable short novel—perhaps, as some have claimed, nearly flawless—but it is also a limited book. This is, I suppose, Bellow's conscious effort to write a classical story—quite literally classical in its scrupulous preservation of the unities of time, place, and action, not to speak of the more modern unities of tone, theme, point of view. All this economy of means and compression of materials does have the effect of focusing our emotional response to the story, yet there is a concomitant paucity in the imagination of character and moral situation. Tommy Wilhelm is a memorable image of stunned, mouthless suffering, but set alongside Moses Herzog, whom he resembles in being a devoted father, an aging and tired man shaken by the failure of his marriage and career, the hero of *Seize the Day* does not seem very interesting. The point is not merely that he is no intellectual, that he lacks ideas, but that, in the restricted compass of the book, he lacks particularity of inner life and personal history. The catharsis at the end of the story in the rush of feeling from the numbed Wilhelm is not altogether satisfactory because we know so little about him. Has he learned anything? What really is he or might he become except a hapless, left-footed sufferer? These are questions the story raises without leaving itself enough room for the novelistic data to answer them adequately.

In Bellow's next book, on the other hand, he allowed free play to the quality of inventiveness which is one of his greatest assets as a novelist. *Henderson the Rain King* (1959) is his most ingenious and delightful reworking of a familiar form of the novel, and it brightly illustrates the appreciative distance he has put between himself and the dominant novelists of the two preceding generations. It almost succeeds in being—like *Don Quixote* or Fielding's *Joseph Andrews*—a perfect parody, both catching the outlandishness of its literary models and at the same time putting them to serious new uses that make it an independent imaginative entity. *Henderson* is a composite parody of all the memorable twentieth-century literature of personal or mythic quest into dark regions—Conrad's voyage into the heart of African darkness, Hemingway's safaris through the green lion-breeding hills of that same continent, D. H. Lawrence's pilgrimage to Mexican hinterlands where plumed serpents and other suitably phallic creatures throbbed with the intensity of primordial life-force. In an engaging reversal of the familiar pattern, Bellow has Henderson discover when he arrives at the savage heart of darkness—a Western-educated African intellectual, who combines his duties as native chief and stud to the royal harem with voracious reading and theorizing in the most brilliantly mad way about the relationship between mind and matter.

The reversal is, moreover, not merely a parodist's trick. It is significant that Henderson should find at the end of his long trek from the West a comic image of a consummately civilized man. For the great novelists of the recent past, whether moral pessimists or moral revolutionaries, the journey into dark continents was logically implied by the failure of Western civilization. Their fabulous voyagers discovered in the primal gloom of the jungle either how pitifully inadequate the civilizing process was to restrain man's chaotic instincts, or, on the other hand, how by turning to non-Western, primitive sources of renewal they could escape the withering of heart and mind that Western culture had become.

Bellow, in contrast, has never taken this dramatic but dangerous stance of giving up on our civilization. Henderson does not want to die to his past, he does not seek a new self in the jungles. Rather, he attempts—as truly civilized people have always done—to make rational sense of the self he has, to decipher the confused urgings of his heart so that he can put his life in order. King Dahfu, for all the unconventionality of his teaching methods, wants to convince Henderson of an ideal which Western thinkers and visionaries have dreamed about since the early Greeks and Hebrews: that man, using his intelligence, through a disciplined act of will, could change his own nature. The novel breaks down near the end only because the delightfully bizarre situation it has created is unable to bear this freight of serious statement very well. Henderson's spiritual calisthenics with Dahfu's lion do not suggest persuasively or particularly what, in fact, he is supposed to be learning about life. The very end of the novel, when Henderson cuddles an orphaned child, is in part an admission of this inadequacy: after the story itself has failed to say fully what it was intended to say, a conventional symbol of compassion, renewal, innocence, and so forth, is introduced to point the moral.

But despite the element of letdown in *Henderson's* concluding episodes, it offers many pleasures in reading—partly because, like Bellow's other books, it was written for readers and not primarily for the writer himself. Serious novelists in this century have not been distinguished by any great consideration for their readers, who have been expected as a matter of course to struggle with difficulties or to show infinite forbearance for *longueurs*. Serious fiction has in many instances come to be directed toward a devoted coterie, or, in extreme cases, an ideal reader-scholar-polymath with a lifetime for one book. Bellow, who enlivens the parody of mythic quest in *Henderson* with borrowings from the procedures of the popular novel of adventure, never willfully abandons the elemental task of the storyteller to keep his audience breathlessly with him, wondering what will happen next. This is true even in *Herzog*, where he manages to generate a kind of intellectual equivalent of suspense without the aid of anything like a plot.

The technical feat of the new novel is, of course, the way it revitalizes the convention of flashback narrative, just as the other books use other tired modes of novel-writing with vivid originality. Herzog's flashbacks, in contrast to the common handling of the convention, are fragmentary—and so from the first pages of the book we, the readers, are implicated in the tense process through which the hero tries to piece together the fragments of himself. Because Herzog, with his wry, satiric self-awareness, his irrepressible intellectuality, his capacity for uninhibited honest feeling, is such an attractive and interesting character, it is fascinating to learn continually more about him; the reader's traditional question about what happens next is replaced by our curiosity about what piece of Moses Herzog we will get next.

The fragmentary nature of the flashbacks, moreover, prevents the novel from bogging down in the past; it creates rather a sense that highly charged particles of past experience are constantly hurtling into the present. Equally important, the fragmenting of recollection allows the writer kaleidoscopic variety in the ways he can recapture the past. Herzog variously remembers: the sensuous nuances of a woman's physical presence near in time and place, a wrenching boyhood experience of his family's abjectness, a rapid series of truncated images recapitulating a stretch of months in the recent past, a summarized group of difficulties lived through that is more self-analysis than memory.

Nor does variety stop with the flashbacks. The scraps of messages Herzog writes to everyone from his mistresses to his analyst, from Eisenhower to Nietzsche, constitute one of Bellow's happiest inventions. One might even view this use of letters as a *reductio ad absurdum* of the epistolary convention with which the beginnings of the English novel are associated. In any case, it is hard to think of another technical device in a recent novel so successful in introducing ideas dramatically into a novel. Herzog, the intellectual historian, plays wildly and yet with desperate seriousness over a wide range of modern thought. The verbal slapstick to which he subjects some of the great thinkers is itself part of his seriousness; for thought—as Bellow has written elsewhere—is metaphor, it is the metaphor that makes the mind its captive; and what Herzog wants to do is to reestablish a meaningful connection with the world by breaking open the metaphoric capsules of thought to see what, if anything, is inside. Thus he writes a note to God near the end of the novel: "How my mind has struggled to make coherent sense. I have not been too good at it. But have desired to do your unknowable will, taking it, and you, without symbols."

The novel's flow of inventiveness extends also to the relationship between flashback and present action. In most novels, a series of long flashbacks is used to lead up to some crucial event in the present—most often, probably, to the protagonist's suicide or death by other means. In *Herzog*, the significant action occurs within the protagonist, while all he really "does" is to move nervously between points on the map. The inconclusive external experiences he fumbles through supply comic counterpoint or parallel to his inward reliving. Some of them parody the heightened action that commonly follows flashbacks in fiction, almost all laughably illustrate the farce Herzog has made of his life. One only has to recall Herzog, bare-legged before the mirror, in exuberant Madras jacket and summer straw hat; Herzog, stalking his wife and her lover with a pistol that both he and we know he could never use; Herzog welcoming Ramona, that tender aging goddess of the Sexual Revolution, as she emerges from the bathroom in nothing but spike-heeled shoes and black lace underpants.

In view of what Bellow has attempted to say in his novels, it is entirely appropriate that he should have turned from the formal models of iconoclastic modernism to transform and revitalize traditional modes of fiction in these various ways. The relationship of the great modern writers to the world has usually been one of retreat or attack—retreat from society to subjectivity, from politics ("in the Aristotelian sense," as Herzog puts it) to art or religion; attack upon bourgeois culture and industrialization, on all the institutional and individual forms of modern man's spiritual sterility. Such martial activity of the soul has often called for bold innovation in form, so that the writer could build his own bastion in literary structure or blow things apart with words.

Bellow, on the other hand, has sought in his fiction for ways to recover a civilized self, assuming that, for all that has gone wrong with our civilization, we can still learn within its context how to live decent, satisfying, really human lives. Significantly, Herzog's grandiose and unrealized ambition is to write a book "with a new angle on the modern condition, showing how life could be lived by renewing universal connections; overturning the last of the Romantic errors about the uniqueness of the Self; revising the old Western, Faustian ideology." Precisely revision, not rejection or revolution, has characterized the relationship of Bellow's fiction to both literary and moral traditions.

The moral pattern of all his work, first sketched out in *Dangling Man*, most vitally realized in *Herzog*, is clear enough. Perhaps the best résumé of that pattern is Bellow's play, *The Last Analysis*, which delightfully transposes virtually all the major themes of his fiction into a farcical key. Every one of Bellow's heroes suffers, like Bummidge in the play, from "humanitis"—which, as Bummidge's secretary explains, is "when the human condition gets to be too much for you." The term is appropriately mock-clinical: being human is a difficult business in Bellow's view, but he sees it as an evasion to paste down the difficulty with a quasi-scientific label like "neurosis" which implies that the problem can be handled by a professional, a therapist. Every man is his own analyst, Bummidge suggests, and this is pretty much the condition of each of Bellow's protagonists.

Each of the novels ingeniously develops its own secular equivalents for the cult of psychoanalysis. In one way or another, each of the central figures is engaged, like Bummidge, in recapitulating his own past so that he can make some sense out of his life. Herzog, with better intellectual equipment and more minute self-knowledge than any of the others, is the one who is able to bring the process to a successful conclusion. Beginning with *Augie March*, a series of guides or quasi-therapists is introduced into the novels, the people whom Herzog sardonically describes as "Reality Instructors." The Reality Instructors all claim to be, or at least know, the Way and the Truth. They are generally attractive figures, seductively so, and almost all are magnificent egotists, tinged or broadly streaked with madness. *Augie March* offers the most colorful gallery of Reality Instructors—the Napoleonic Einhorn, eagle-obsessed Thea, Mintouchian the worldly Armenian, the megalomaniac genius Basteshaw—but the later novels also abound with them—Queen Willatale and King Dahfu in *Henderson*, Dr. Tamkin in *Seize the Day*, Dr. Edvig and Valentine Gersbach in *Herzog*. With the exception of the figures in *Hender-*

son, the Reality Instructors are drawn more and more sharply as outrageous charlatans. Humanitis, the novels imply, is not a disease which can be cured by self-appointed professionals. Every human being must learn to handle his own case, putting on, as Bummidge does, his own dark glasses and Viennese accent, urging himself to go "deeper, deeper," in the words of Bummidge to the empty couch.

The point is not that Bellow has been carrying on in his writings a personal vendetta with psychoanalysis, though there may be some element of that. (The one character in *Herzog* even more drastically negative than Madeleine is Edvig, the analyst.) Psychoanalysis, as it is spoofed in Bellow's play and attacked in his most recent novel, is a dangerous delusion because it is the clearest instance of all the approaches to life which try to reduce solving human problems to a formula, a methodology, a technique. The Reality Instructors in the novels turn out to be fakes because reality is what Augie March calls a "multiverse," not a unified system in which fixed principles can be enunciated by those who know the system. There is a salubrious note of tentativeness in the moral self-exploration of all Bellow's heroes. This is probably the main reason for the relatively unsatisfactory endings of his novels until *Herzog*. Morally inevitable tentativeness of the sort Bellow imagines into his protagonists cannot really be brought to a resolution—it always implies more questioning, more self-discovery.

To describe this quality of tentativeness another way, one might say that there is a stubborn core of innocence in all Bellow's heroes. Each is a kind of Huck Finn with no faithful Jim to guide him, a person in some ways impressively knowing about the world, yet always looking at it with eyes of youthful wonder, insisting upon grasping it in his own way. The irrepressible desire for life, however deadening experience has been, which characterizes Bellow's protagonists, is the expression of this innocence, or, from another point of view, the means of preserving it. Henderson, in contrast to the typically modern voyagers to dark continents, is not jaded or defeated, only confused; and, as Willatale informs him, he has the gift of

Grun-tu-molani or "Man want to live," which is the talisman of his innocence and the motive force of his redemption.

The opposite of innocence as the word applies to Bellow's heroes is not worldliness or corruption but simply thinking you know what the score is. Bellow's innocents at home and abroad are always looking about in perplexity: there doesn't seem to be any scoreboard around. This is probably one important reason for the ring of authenticity in Herzog's sustained attack upon "the Wasteland outlook, the cheap mental stimulants of Alienation." Herzog does not attempt to replace the established Wasteland ideology with another one; his argument against it is based on his innocent—that is, tentative, personal—sense of life. To proclaim programmatically that life is good, that the Wasteland is mere fiction, would be another way of pretending to know the score. "We learn to be unfeeling toward ourselves and incurious," complained Joseph, the protagonist of *Dangling Man*. Herzog's ability to renounce what he calls the modern god of Death and to pull together the wreckage of his own life is the result of his resistance to this grim process of negative learning. He manages to remain genuinely curious about himself and to feel for himself; this is the ultimate source of his innocence, his ability to wonder. And if there are also elements of narcissism in his preoccupation with self, he is keenly aware of them and can turn them into redeeming comedy.

This redeeming comedy of Herzog's is clearly Jewish in tone and feeling, and that Jewishness in turn has a great deal to do with Herzog's particular kind of innocence. Irving Howe has pointed out that the influence of Yiddish on the prose of Bellow's new novel is profound and pervasive: instead of the usual nostalgic recall or working up of folk materials one finds in other Jewish writers, a real act of artistic transmutation, from one language to another, has taken place. But it is important to add that there is an inner connection between the Yiddish qualities of Herzog's prose—its rhythms, the tonal shifts of its ironies, its occasional stress on actual Yiddish or Hebrew phrases—and Herzog's rejection of the Wasteland outlook.

There has been so much talk about the Jew as the archetype of modern alienation that we sometimes forget that, traditionally, Jews rarely thought of themselves in such terms. They were not alienated from themselves or from a large world of unfolding purpose; they were merely considered aliens by people whom they tended to look down upon in any case. Jews, by and large, did not revel in suffering; they lived on terms of contemptuous familiarity with it. But—in contrast to fashionably modern views of *Angst*, existential despair, and the like—suffering was not generally thought of as a means of fulfillment or a condition indispensable to human life.

Herzog at several key points emphasizes that, because he is a Jew, he looks at the world with different eyes. "I, a Jew . . . would never grasp the Christian and Faustian world idea." He preserves the mental habit of his forebears particularly in being unwilling to concede the absurdity of an apparently absurd universe. "Convinced that the extent of universal space does not destroy value, that the realm of facts and that of ideas are not eternally separated. And the peculiar idea entered my (Jewish) mind that we'd see about this!" Against the looming abstractions of the philosophical spokesmen of alienation, he counterpoises a very Jewish sense of the particularities of ordinary life—"the strength of a man's virtue or spiritual capacity measured by his ordinary life."

The snatches of Yiddish and Hebrew in the novel sometimes are used merely to give the text authentic coloring, but, more often, they catch up in themselves the underlying attitudes with which Hezog takes his ultimate stand on life. This is certainly true of the bits of High Holiday liturgy he recalls—those desperate pleas for mercy directed to a hiding God. And it is evident in the use of Yiddish at moments like the one when Herzog reflects on his father's death: ". . . he died, and that vivid blood of his turned to soil, in all the shrunken passages of his body. And then the body, too—ah, God!—wastes away and leaves its bones, and even the bones at last wear away and crumble to dust in that shallow place of deposit. And thus humanized, this planet in its galaxy of stars and worlds goes from void to void, infinitesimal, aching with its unrelated significance. *Unrelated?* Herzog, with one of his Jewish shrugs, whispered, '*Nu, maile*. . . .' Be that as it may." The untranslatable verbal shrug, after the dizzying vision of mortality and cosmic emptiness, focuses perfectly the Jewishness of Herzog's wry, skeptical, worldly, almost disarming, faith in life. One of the impressive achievements of the novel as a whole is its success on a larger scale, through the mind of its central character, in creating translations for such untranslatables.

There is, then, a serious imaginative logic in the fact that Herzog, toward the end of the novel, as he arrives at a new self-acceptance, invokes a biblical word fraught with associations: "Here I am. *Hineni!* How marvelously beautiful it is today." *Hineni* is the word of answer used in the Bible by Abraham, Moses, and others to the imperative call of God: it is an affirmation of identity and readiness to serve before the ultimate source of reality, and so Herzog's repetition of the word here constitutes a rediscovery of existential trust against the background of an age-old tradition.

One other obvious way in which Herzog's Jewishness is felt is in the distinctive tone and strength of his family instincts, his capacity for unabashed affection. This, too, is tied up with his innocence: a corollary of being able to care for oneself with the humanly vital solicitude that Bellow's heroes possess is the ability—and need—to care for others. Herzog is a loving man, one of the few really convincing ones in modern literature. But Bellow never makes illegitimate capital of abstract ideas like the idea of loving. Love in *Herzog* is not that tired god from the machine which so many "positive" writers dutifully lower into their final scenes. Herzog cannot live without loving, but it clearly does not solve his problems. For nothing in Bellow's fiction, whether affirmation or negation, is reduced to a simple formula. Perhaps that finally is why he is one of the few American novelists today who seem to write for grown-up people.

At the end of his Library of Congress lecture, Bellow tries to indicate something of what he feels should be the attitude of the novelist toward his eternal subject, human nature. Again, his criticism of his contemporaries suggests by contrast much of his own distinctive achievement:

> Undeniably the human being is not what he commonly thought a century ago. The question nevertheless remains. He is something. What is he? And this question, it seems to me, modern writers have answered poorly. They have told us, indignantly or nihilistically or comically, how great our error is but for the rest they have offered us thin fare. The fact is that modern writers sin when they suppose that they *know*, as they conceive that physics *knows* or that history *knows*. The subject of the novelist is not knowable in any such way. The mystery increases, it does not grow less as types of literature wear out.

Throughout his own career, Bellow has managed to resist all the subtle seductions that draw a novelist into thinking of his subject as something known. In the latest achievement of his artistic maturity, he has also succeeded in creating a character whose tonal and intellectual complexity and imaginative concreteness powerfully suggest, as no recent figure in fiction has done, the mystery of being a man. *Herzog* is in so many ways the full realization of aims Bellow attempted to carry out in all his earlier novels that it would seem as though he has now written this vein out. One might guess that, like Herzog, Bellow's victimized, floundering, self-redeeming heroes have "no messages for anyone" after this book. What he may try to do next is hard to predict. But, as always, it will be intriguing to see.

1964

BERNARD MALAMUD: JEWISHNESS AS METAPHOR

From his earliest stories in the fifties, the relationship between Bernard Malamud's literary imagination and his Jewish background has been a peculiar one. For the most part, it has proved to be a remarkably creative relationship, though there are a few points in his work where the wedding of Jewish materials and fictional invention seems largely a shotgun affair, performed to legitimize imaginative offspring that ought to have validated themselves without benefit of skull-capped clergy. Now, American Jewish novelists, from Abraham Cahan and Ludwig Lewisohn to Philip Roth, have, quite understandably, often written about Jews, as the kind of people they have known best; and since the novel as a rule tries to reconstruct the social matrices of individual character, this has generally meant writing about Jewish milieux, first in the ghetto, more recently in suburbia. The concentration on Jewish social environments has not, however, led to anything like a distinctively Jewish mode of imaginative writing. Henry Roth's *Call It Sleep*, for example, still probably the most fully achieved work of fiction by an American writer of Jewish descent, is a novel of immigrant experience, using Joycean methods for the lyric rendering of consciousness; the principal characters happen to be Jews, but I see nothing in the conception or execution of this extraordinary book that could not be readily transferred to a novel about a family from some other immigrant group.

In Malamud's work, on the other hand, the immigrant experience is at once more peripheral and more central than in writers of comparable background. Although most of his protagonists are avowedly Jewish, he has never really written *about* Jews, in the manner of other American Jewish novelists. Especially revealing in this connection is the fact that nowhere does he attempt to represent a Jewish milieu, that a Jewish community never enters into his books, except as the shadow of a vestige of a specter. What literary sense, then, does Malamud make of the emphatic, vividly elaborated ethnic identity of his characters—those whitefish-eating, Yiddish-accented isolates in a bleak, generalized world of harsh necessity? He clearly means Jewishness to function as an ethical symbol; it is, as Theodore Solotaroff has written, "a type of metaphor . . . both for the tragic dimension of anyone's life and for a code of personal morality." I have had occasion to observe elsewhere that such symbolism (as in the relationship between Morris Bober and Frank Alpine in Malamud's *The Assistant*) can become uncomfortable; when a writer assigns a set of abstract moral values to the representatives of a particular group, the connection thus insisted on may strike a reader as arbitrary, an artistic confusion of actualities and ideals. The symbolic use Malamud makes of Jewishness deserves more detailed attention, but before we consider that, it is worth noting another, more organic, way in which Jewish experience enters into his writing.

Malamud is, to the best of my knowledge, the first important American writer to shape out of his early experiences in the immigrant milieu a whole distinctive style of imagination and, to a lesser degree, a distinctive technique of fiction as well. He is by no means a "folk" artist, but his ear for the rhythms of speech and the tonalities of implication, his eye for the shadings of attitude and feeling, of Jewish folk culture, have helped make the fictional world he has created uniquely his own. Though such influences are hard to prove, I suspect that the piquant juxtaposition in his fiction of tough, ground-gripping realism and high-flying fantasy ultimately derives from the paradoxical conjoining of those same qualities that has often characterized Jewish folklore.

To put this another way, it would seem as though the homespun Jewishness of Malamud's characters affords him a means of anchoring his brilliant fantasies in reality, for the dreariness of daily privation and frustration familiar to him through the ghetto are his indicators of what the real world is like, reminding him of the gritty, harsh-grained texture of ordinary human experience. It is significant that the only book he has written in which there are no identifiable Jews, his first novel, *The Natural*, is also the only one in which the underpinnings of reality are finally pulled away by the powerful tug of fantasy. *The Natural* is a spectacular performance, a sort of *Parzival* on the ball field that combines serious moral fable with pointed comedy, superbly sustained suspense, and sheer wish-fulfillment, zestfully imagined; but in the end the novel entertains more than it convinces because too much of the world as we know it has been rearranged in the service of imaginative play.

The Jewish folk figure on which Malamud has modeled most of his protagonists is, of course, the *shlemiel*, the well-meaning bungler, compounded with the *shilmazel*, the hapless soul who is invariably at the wrong end of the bungling. The way he handles this doubly ill-starred figure illuminates his whole artistic relationship to his Jewishness. The *shlemiel* is, we hardly need to be reminded, often an engaging kind of character, and Malamud treats him—most memorably, in the Fidelman stories—with a very special quality of amused sympathy modified by satiric awareness. The spirit of wry folk humor that Malamud has caught in his personages is nicely expressed in the Yiddish joke about the man who comes to a doctor to complain that he talks to himself all the time: when the doctor answers that he, too, talks to himself and that it is really nothing to worry about, the man objects, "But, Doctor, you have no idea what a *nudnik* I am!" Malamud's protagonists are frequently just this: *shlemiels* who talk to themselves, who repeatedly engage in self-confrontation, shrewdly but futilely aware of their own limitations, like Fidelman, "self-confessed failures" caught in the trap of themselves and rankling over their predicament, though just a little amused by it, too.

The *shlemiel-shlimazel*, however, is not merely a source of colorfulness in Malamud's fiction, the stock comic property that the type has become in so much American Jewish fiction. To be a *shlemiel*—which, for Malamud, is almost interchangeable with the idea of being a Jew—means to assume a moral stance, virtually the only possible moral stance in his fictional world. For if circumstances are at best indifferent to this individual, if human beings are so complicated, varied, and confused that to be truly open to another person means to get mixed up with and by him, even hurt by him, the very act of wholehearted commitment to the world of men means being a blunderer and a victim. The only clearly visible alternative to the stance of the *shlemiel* in Malamud's fiction (and this is, of course, a boldly foreshortened version of reality, one good reason why it works better in the short stories than in the novels) is the stance of the manipulator. Gus the Gambler and the sinister club-owner, the Judge, in *The Natural*; Karp, the "lucky" liquor-store neighbor of inveterately luckless Morris Bober in *The Assistant*; Gerald Gilley, the Cascadia professor scheming for the departmental chairmanship in *A New Life*—all these are characters who in varying degrees take a sharply instrumental view of humanity, who manage to stay on top of circumstances and people by being detached from them so that they can merely use them. Gerald Gilley's physical sterility is emblematic of the general condition of moral withdrawal shared by all the manipulators: he can "enjoy" his wife sexually, but, in her expression, "he has no seeds," he cannot give of himself what is ultimately a man's to give a woman in the most intimate of shared experiences. By contrast, S. Levin, the novel's hero, can and does give all to Pauline Gilley, even when he scarcely intends it, so that his openness to the world and his commitment to accept the consequences of his own acts brings him, inevitably, to a *shlemiel*'s fate—ousted from the profession of his choice, burdened with a family he didn't bargain for, and a woman he loves only as a matter of principle, rolling westward in his overheating jalopy toward a horizon full of pitfalls.

The *shlemiel*, it should be said, lends himself much more readily to revelation in a short story than to development in a

novel, perhaps because his comic victimhood invites the suddenness and externality of slapstick; when that technique is
merely multiplied in being transferred to a novel—where we
expect more subtlety and innerness, a more discursive and
analytic treatment of character—the comedy becomes a little
tedious. Thus, in the first hundred pages or so of A New Life,
S. Levin has a casserole spilled in his lap, is pissed on by a three-
year-old, steps into a cow pie, walks in to teach his first class with
(of course) his fly open, slips in front of his school building
with an armful of books, is interrupted on two separate occasions at the point of sexual entry. Even when he tries to scale a
stone across a pond on a walk with a girl, it sinks! All this is
funny up to a point, but after so much repetition it begins to
look like sheer reflex on the writer's part, and it is not particularly helpful in establishing the inner life of an anguished
intellectual struggling against both his own weakness and the
resistance of the world around him to make himself a new man.
The accumulated calamities, however, of S. Levin—whose Jewish identity is mentioned only once in the novel, at the very
end—suggest why Malamud's symbolic Jews must be *shlemiels*,
for, as we shall see, Malamud's central metaphor for Jewishness
is imprisonment, and even when no actual enclosing walls are
present, his Jews remain manacled and hobbled to their own
scapegrace ineptitude.

The central development of the idea of Jewishness as
imprisonment occurs in *The Assistant*. That novel is suffused
with images of claustrophobic containment, and Morris Bober's
grocery, which is the symbolic locus of being a Jew with all the
hard responsibilities entailed thereby, is frequently referred to
as a prison. "What kind of man did you have to be," wonders
Frank Alpine, "to be born to shut yourself in an overgrown
coffin? . . . You had to be a Jew. They were born prisoners."
Later, Frank reads some Jewish history, and his understanding
of it (Malamud's, too, it would appear) is much of a piece with
his vision of Bober in the store: "He . . . read about the
ghettos, where the half-starved, bearded prisoners spent their
lives trying to figure it out why they were the Chosen People."

Frank himself is from the outset an ideal proselyte in being a kind of Italianate *shlemiel* on his own way into a tight prison: "With me one wrong thing leads to another and it ends in a trap." The real symbol of his conversion to Judaism is his clumsy act of toppling onto Morris Bober's coffin as it is being lowered into the grave; the subsequent circumcision merely pays obeisance to the institutional forms. In this respect, the curve of Frank's experience is paralleled by that of Arthur Fidelman—from the frustrations of a bungler ("The Last Mohican") through the captivity of sexual bewitchment ("Still Life") to the iron jaws of imprisonment ("Naked Nude," where Fidelman is held prisoner by gangsters in a whorehouse, at one point chained hand and foot to his bed).

Claustrophobic images of Jewish experience are hardly Malamud's invention—they recur frequently, for example, in Hebrew writers of the late nineteenth and early twentieth century who rebelled against all that was stifling in the life of the *shtetl*. But the way such images function in Malamud's work is quite new. Since his Jews are, after all, more metaphoric than literal, the imagery of imprisonment turns out to be the symbolic representation of an already symbolic state. This is made explicit in the case of S. Levin, where the prison motif is invoked for the first time at the end of the novel, to elucidate the denouement. Levin, we learn, was originally accepted for the teaching position that led to his comic-disastrous entanglement with the Gilleys because Pauline Gilley happened to spot his picture in a stack of applications and was attracted by his Jewish face—thus capricious fate selects its victims, hardly intending them as victims, and we see how the Jew-as-*shlemiel* is, in the most ironic sense, "chosen" for his destiny. After hearing this story, Levin ponders his future with Pauline Gilley:

> His doubts were the bricks of a windowless prison he was in. . . . The prison was really himself, flawed edifice of failures, each locking up tight the one before. . . . Unless the true prison was to stick it out chained to her ribs. He would look like a free man but whoever peered into his eyes would see the lines of a brick wall.

Imprisonment, like the condition of being a Jew with which it is elsewhere identified, is seen here as a general image for the moral life with all its imponderable obstacles to spontaneous self-fulfillment: it is living in concern for the state of one's soul, which means knowing with an awful lucidity how circumscribed the will is in its ability to effect significant change, how recalcitrant and cowardly it can be, and shouldering the terrible onus of responsibility for one's acts, especially as they are implicated in the lives of others. The prison, like the *shlemiel* who is usually its chief inmate, is Malamud's way of suggesting that to be fully a man is to accept the most painful limitations; those who escape these limitations achieve only an illusory, self-negating kind of freedom, for they become less than responsible human beings. One does not have to be a Jew to be thus enmeshed in the endless untidiness of moral experience—witness the protagonist of "The Prisoner," an Italian in a candy store instead of a Jew in a grocery—but, as the saying goes, it helps, for the Jew, at least as Malamud sees him, has undergone the kind of history that made it difficult for him to delude himself about his defeats and humiliations, that forced him to accept the worst conditions because he had no alternative while trying to preserve his essential human dignity. Malamud sees, moreover, in the collective Jewish experience of the past a model not only of suffering and confinement but also of a very limited yet precious possibility of triumph in defeat, freedom in imprisonment. His reading of Jewish history is clearly undertaken from a rather special angle, and with perhaps less than adequate information—European Jewry, even in the ghettos, often was, and felt itself to be, much more than a trapped group of "half-starved, bearded prisoners." Historical accuracy, however, is beside the point, for what is relevant to Malamud's literary achievement is that an aspect of Jewish experience, isolated and magnified, has afforded him the means of focusing in an image his own vision of the human condition.

Against this whole background, Malamud's new novel, *The Fixer*, emerges as a far less radical departure from his earlier fiction than one might initially conclude. The surface differences, to be sure, between this book and his previous work are abundant and striking. Malamud has always written about spheres of experience with which he was personally familiar; here he sets his novel in Kiev, toward the end of the Czarist regime. Except in a few of his comic fantasies, he has always written about everyday people in a world whose most basic quality is uneventfulness; here his subject is a lurid murder case and an incredible conspiracy against justice. Suffering in his novels and stories has generally been a matter of humiliated egos or the gnawing fears of poverty; in *The Fixer* the central action is a process of suffering through violence, torture by inches, complete with the obscene inventions of a jailer's sadism, an attempted poisoning, a suicide, even Dostoevskian hallucinations, including one where a frantic-eyed horse is beaten over the head with a log. Malamud has always known the art of counterpointing a flat, understated style with flights of whimsy and poetic invention, but never before has he written such taut, vigorous prose—as, for example, in this prisoner's nightmare, with its staccato parade of short declarative sentences and sharply-etched physical images that give fantasy the weight and tactile hardness of palpable fact:

> The wind wailed mutely in the prison yard. His heart was like a rusted chain, his muscles taut, as though each had been bound with wire. Even in the cold he sweated. Amid the darkly luminous prisoners he saw spies waiting to kill him. One was the grayhaired warden with a gleaming two-headed ax. He tried to hide his crossed eye behind his hand but it shone like a jewel through his fingers. The Deputy Warden, his fly open, held a black bullwhip behind his back. And though the Tsar wore a white mask over his face and another on the back of his head, Yakov recognized him standing in the far corner of the cell, dropping green drops into a glass of hot milk.

Perhaps the greatest external difference between *The Fixer* and Malamud's earlier work is the relationship in it between fiction and actual events. The novel is very closely based on the Beiliss Case, the last conspicuous occasion after the Middle Ages when a Jew was actually brought to trial on the charge of ritual murder. By an odd but happy coincidence, Malamud's novel appears in print almost simultaneously with Maurice Samuel's *Blood Accusation*, an elaborate, painstaking, yet eminently readable account of the complicated details of the Beiliss Case. Many readers of Malamud's novel will want to consult Samuel's book, out of simple historical curiosity, which the novel rouses but of course cannot satisfy, and because of the readily available opportunity to see, through a comparison with the facts, how a novelist has transmuted history into art. On the whole, Malamud has altered very few of the basic facts of the case. His protagonist, Yakov Bok, is, like Mendel Beiliss, the overseer in a Kiev brick factory, a simple man, not much of an observant Jew, who one early spring day in 1911 finds himself to his utter amazement arrested for the murder of a Christian boy whose body has been found in a cave near the brickyard, stabbed many times with a sharp instrument, in a manner, say the accusers, which indicates that the blood was slowly drained to be collected for use in *matzos*. Bok, like Beiliss, is incarcerated for more than two years while the investigating magistrates, in collusion with the most fanatical forces of reaction, trump up a case against him for a murder they more or less know has been committed by a stunningly brazen Russian woman (in the novel, the boy's mother, in fact, the mother of a friend) together with a gang of her habitual partners in theft and orgy.

Malamud's novel follows the train of events from the discovery of the body to the point at which the accused is brought out of prison to be tried. The actual trial ended on an appropriate note of muddled ambiguity, the jury at once acquitting Mendel Beiliss and concluding that the murder had occurred in the brickworks, not in the apartment of the Cheberyak woman where the clearest evidence placed it, and that the child's blood had been methodically drained for unspecified purposes. Malamud rearranges some details of the Beiliss affair in the interests of necessary simplification or even credibility— the Czarist government's case against Beiliss, for instance, was based on such a shabby patchwork of anti-Semitic fantasies that

Malamud, in order not to violate novelistic probability, had to invent some shreds of circumstantial evidence for his prosecution to grasp at. Other changes in the actual circumstances are made in order to emphasize themes; to a few of these we shall have occasion to return.

Why should the Beiliss Case attract a serious contemporary novelist and why in particular should Malamud find it a congenial subject? The first half of this question is answered in part by Maurice Samuel in the suggestive, though regrettably brief, Epilogue to his account of the case. The significance of these events, Samuel argues, extends far beyond the historical question of anti-Semitism. The case was really "a crude preview of the possibilities of the twentieth century," one of the early instances of the use by a government of the big lie, through which a powerful bureaucracy totally subverts the moral sense of its individual members and, as Samuel aptly puts it, "makes its assertions with brazen disregard for what is known . . . , seeks, by immense clamor, by vast rhythmic repetition, to make thinking impossible." To translate Samuel's observation from politics to the viewpoint of individual experience, the Beiliss Case is one of the first striking public occasions in this century when Kafka's fiction of arbitrary arraignment, of a reality which is governed by an insane, inscrutably perverse logic, became historical fact.

One often feels in *The Fixer* that for Malamud 1911 is 1943 in small compass and sharp focus, and 1966 writ large. The Beiliss Case gives him, to begin with, a way of approaching the European Holocaust on a scale that is imaginable, susceptible of fictional representation. For the Beiliss Case transparently holds within it the core of the cultural sickness around which the Nazi madness grew, representing as it does a symptomatic junction of the medieval demonological conception of the Jew as satanic enemy to Christ and mankind, and the modern phobic vision of an international Jewish conspiracy, manipulated through commerce and politics and underworld activity by the sinister Elders of Zion. (Murky hints of genocide actually crept into some of the verbal attacks on the Jews during the

Beiliss affair, as when they were characterized in the reactionary
Russian press, quoted by Samuel, as "an exclusively criminal
class which brings death to any wholesome society.") Malamud
seems quite conscious of this aspect of his subject, but I would
assume that the blood libel and false arrest are even more
important to him as an extreme paradigm for the condition of
impotence in a mad world that all people today share, whether
they live under absolutist regimes or in the mass societies of
that part of the world which ritualistically calls itself free. The
credo of Bibikov, the one sympathetic government investigator,
confided to Yakov Bok in his cell, is substantially the implicit
credo of Malamud's earlier fiction, where the settings are
contemporary, but it is an affirmation spoken from the heart of
a tensely dramatic situation that gives a new kind of stark and
bold concreteness to its moral abstractions:

> One often feels helpless in the face of the confusion of these
> times, such a mass of apparently uncontrollable events and ex-
> periences to live through, attempt to understand, and if at
> all possible, give order to; but one must not withdraw from
> the task if he has some small thing to offer—he does so at
> the risk of diminishing his humanity.

The Fixer is clearly Malamud's most powerful novel—and,
it seems to me, his first wholly successful one. An important
reason for its tight artistic unity is the identity in it between
central metaphor and literal fact: the Malamudian prison is
here not merely an analogy, a moral and metaphysical state, but
has real, clammy, stone walls, excretory stenches, heavy-fisted
jailers, dank unheated cells, lice. Similarly, Malamud's symbolic
Jew is much more believable here than in his last two novels
because the character's symbolic implications flow naturally
from the literal fact of his Jewishness which is, after all, the real
reason for his arrest. Though to be a Jew in this novel does
imply a general moral stance, it also means being involved in
the fate of a particular people, actively identifying with its
history—in contrast, for example, to Morris Bober, for whom

the meaning of Jewishness is exhausted in "to do what is right, to be honest, to be good."

In this connection, one difference between Yakov Bok and Mendel Beiliss is revealing. The brickworks in which Beiliss was employed were in a section of Kiev forbidden for Jewish residence, except to certain classes of Jews who could obtain special permits. Mendel Beiliss had such a permit and lived at the brickworks openly, with his wife and children, on terms of respect and cordiality with his fellow workers. Yakov Bok has no residence permit: he lives alone at the brickworks, under a Gentile name, suspected as a Jew by his fellow workers and thoroughly hated by them. His masquerading as a Russian is the beginning of his troubles when he is arrested, and it is the one crime he freely confesses: "He had stupidly pretended to be somebody he wasn't, hoping it would create 'opportunities,' had learned otherwise—the wrong opportunities—and was paying for learning." (Malamud once before touched on this idea, in a somewhat lighter mood, in "The Lady of the Lake," where Henry Levin-Freeman loses the girl of his dreams by pretending to be a Gentile and thus dissociating himself from the Jewish fate in which she has been tragically involved and to which she is committed.)

Circumstances force Yakov Bok, who sought to escape from the *shtetl* to a new world of possibilities in the big city, into being a Jew despite himself. And he becomes, of course, a Jew in Malamud's special sense, a prisoner placed in progressively restricting confinement—from communal cell to solitary confinement to being shackled to the wall hand and foot—who is mangled physically and mentally by his imprisonment but never lets himself surrender his integrity because of it. Emblems of membership in the traditional community of Jews are thrust on him by his jailers, and he accepts them, with a kind of ironic gratitude, because he has no choice. He is thrown a prayer shawl and phylacteries—the phylacteries he puts aside, the prayer shawl he wraps about him because it gives him warmth. A fistful of bloodstained pages from a Hebrew Bible is flung into his cell—he pieces them together and reads them over and over, fitting the verses to his own fate and hopes, though the God that speaks through the ancient words, in Whom he does not believe, alternately angers him and stirs his pity. Forced in this and related ways to summon up all his inner resources of survival in order to stay sane and alive in solitary confinement, Bok in his cell recapitulates the darkest, most heroic aspects of Jewish existence in the diaspora.

The quality of his character, moreover, makes him admirably suited to the task of survival and to his larger symbolic role in the novel. Though the vividly comic aspects of the type are naturally muted, Bok is another of Malamud's plain, earthy Jews, the first of these figures, so happily used in the short stories, to work effectively as a major character in a novel. There is a touch of the knowing *shlemiel* in him—"If there's a mistake to make," he thinks, "I'll make it"—which leads him to expect calamity and ruefully resolve to hold up under it. Meagerly self-taught, he is not a subtle man but is shrewd and straight-thinking. His speech and reflections are laced with the salt of wry Yiddish irony, and his skepticism is tough-minded and unpretentious: "Take my word for it," he tells his pious father-in-law, who tries to convince him that faith in God can sustain him in his sufferings, "it's not easy to be a freethinker, especially in this terrible cell." Perhaps Mendel Beiliss was not so different from this: he laughed out loud just once at his trial, Maurice Samuel reports, when the prosecution solemnly averred that he had the reputation among his fellow workers of being a *tzaddik*, a Hasidic wonder-rabbi.

There is, furthermore, a special thematic appropriateness in the fact that the hero of *The Fixer* is a simple man. Yakov Bok has no desire to become involved in history; at the beginning of the novel, we see him as someone who has led a deprived, unhappy life and who merely wants to find a better existence for himself, in that vague and rather pathetic way in which so many of Malamud's protagonists long for "something more worthwhile." But history seizes him by the collar, and at first all he can do is wonder, stunned, why it should all be happening to him—again, Malamud's previous protagonists repeatedly ask themselves much the same question about their misfortunes— "What was a poor harmless fixer doing in prison?" The obvious answer is that he is in prison because he is a Jew. Bok soon arrives at the generalization that "being born a Jew meant being vulnerable to history, including its worst errors." This has largely been true of Jews collectively during two thousand years of exile, and Bok now finds it to bear just as directly and heavily on his own life. Confronted with such awful vulnerability, a man may want to rebel or opt out, seeking to escape the inescapable, but the only alternative for Yakov Bok that will allow him to retain his self-respect is to accept the entanglement in the worst of history together with the responsibility for those who are similarly entangled, making a "covenant with himself," since he can't make one with God, that he will not betray his fellow Jews, that if necessary he will die rather than assent, even through the most oblique compromise, to the lie that would deny their humanity.

The lesson that Bok learns, in short, is Malamud's familiar lesson of the necessity for moral involvement, with all its painful, awkward, humiliating consequences, though the idea emerges from Bok's anguish with greater force than anywhere in the earlier fiction. At the very end of his two-year ordeal of incarceration, as he is carried through the streets of Kiev to the courthouse, surrounded by a mob of faces, some curious or hostile, some even compassionate, he summarizes what he has gradually made clear to himself: "One thing I've learned . . . there's no such thing as an unpolitical man, especially a Jew."

This last sentence nicely states the relationship between particular and universal in this novel and in Malamud's work as a whole. The speaker is undeniably a Jew in all the distinctive qualities of his mental and physical being, his wasted flesh and aching bones. The Jew, however, is conceived by the writer not as a creature *sui generis* but as an extreme and therefore pellucid instance of all men's inevitable exposure to the caprice of circumstance and the insidious snarl of history: all people are in this way "chosen," Jews only more transparently than others.

The Jew as Everyman is a kind of literary symbol that is likely to wear thin very quickly; it is a tribute to Malamud's resourcefulness as a writer that he has been able to make the symbolic equation succeed to the extent he has in his stories and novels. In his most recent book, he gives new imaginative weight to his conception of Jewishness by adding to it the crucially important dimension of history, and in so doing he manages to transform his recurrent symbol into the stuff of an urgent, tautly controlled novel that firmly engages the emotions and the intellect as well.

1966

Good Ending

S. Y. AGNON: THE ALPHABET OF HOLINESS

The Jews of Galicia are proverbially noted for wiliness, at least among other European Jews, and Hebrew readers of Shmuel Yosef Agnon are not likely to forget his origins in that eastern province of what was then the Austro-Hungarian Empire. Agnon's Galician hometown of Buczacz, which he left in 1907 at the age of eighteen, figures directly or obliquely in the greater part of his fiction. It plays an important role in all three of his major novels, serving a triple function in them and elsewhere in his work as an image of the undisturbed piety of premodern Jewish life, as a point of convergence for forces of cultural and spiritual dissolution (he sometimes gives Buczacz the fictional name Szybuscz, suggesting "breakdown" or "corruption" in Hebrew), and, finally, as a broken, twisted testimony to the brutal destructiveness of twentieth-century history.

But the way Agnon uses his Buczacz background is also one of many indications that he has more than a generous share of the alleged Galician wile. The image of himself which he likes to project to the general public in interviews and to his readers through his narrating persona is that of a simple, pious, retiring man—indeed, a kind of archetypal Young Man from the Provinces, like the naïve Galician hero of his long novel, *Just Yesterday*—who is astonished to find himself proclaimed an important literary figure.

As a rule, Agnon chooses to give the impression that he is much more withdrawn from the modern world than he is in fact. Since 1927 he has lived in the quiet neighborhood of Talpiot in the southeastern corner of the New City of Jeru-

salem, where his house at the end of a secluded street looks out
through a grove of evergreens toward the Temple Mount. A
man with no political involvements or commitments to public
life, Agnon often presents himself as an isolated artist, standing
at his lectern—a relic of the talmudic academies which he
prefers to a writing desk—inscribing Hebrew characters in his
minute hand with the painstaking care of an old-world craftsman, his ears closed to the stridencies of the contemporary
reality around him. This image does faithfully represent one
aspect of Agnon the man and the writer, but no more than
that.

In point of fact, Agnon has an avid interest in his immediate social surroundings, in the lives of the people he encounters,
and in the broader world of modern culture. It is true that from
his earliest years he has steeped himself in the literature of
Jewish religious tradition, and he has no formal secular education, but since his youth he has been reading his way through
European literature with the zest and energy of a classic auto-
didact. He knows German literature intimately and extensively
—he lived in Germany from 1913 to 1924—and in German
translation he has also studied the major Russian, French, and
Scandinavian writers. Agnon, who in general tends to be reticent
about what he has read, is occasionally vehement in denying
influences, but this is hardly surprising, for a kind of provoca-
tive elusiveness is an essential part of his whole artistic method.

Over the past two decades, as the awareness gradually
dawned on Hebrew readers that Agnon was a bold modernist,
not merely a pious teller of tales, critics have quite naturally
looked for influences from the outside, and the one that has
been insisted upon most frequently is the one that annoys
Agnon most—Franz Kafka. In characteristic fashion, Agnon
professed in one interview a thorough distaste for Kafka, of
whom he had "barely read two books"—Kafka of course barely
wrote three—though he also admitted that his wife happened
to admire the German writer and kept a complete set of Kafka
in *her* library. There is, moreover, even a personal link between
Agnon and Kafka in Max Brod, Kafka's friend, biographer, and

literary executor, who has been an acquaintance and admirer of the Hebrew author since the twenties; interestingly, Brod was persuaded to give Schocken Books the rights to the publication in German of Kafka's works at the same period in the twenties when Schocken became Agnon's exclusive publisher in Hebrew.

Yet I think that by and large Agnon is right in minimizing the importance of modern literary influences on him, for he is both a peculiarly original writer and one who derives from peculiar literary traditions, so that the qualities that make him remarkable are most likely to be found not in resemblances to European writers but, on the contrary, in the characteristics unique to him as an individual artist, as a user of the Hebrew language, and as a Jew.

Influences from the outside, however, or even coincidental similarities with the outside, are obviously not altogether irrelevant to criticism. A collection of stories like Agnon's *Book of Deeds* (1951) reflects certain affinities with Kafka so pronounced that they can hardly be overlooked. *The Book of Deeds*, in the manner of Kafka, introduces its readers to a dreamlike world where the ordinary laws of time and place, of logical sequence and causality, seem to be suspended. Although Agnon has little of the neurotic intensity that distinguishes Kafka's writing, although the discontinuities in his stories seem more diffuse, less violently jarring, than Kafka's, he possesses something of the same sense of a world where terrible things are waiting to spring out from the shadows of experience. Moreover, while Agnon rarely seeks the shocking visual effects one sometimes finds in Kafka, his Hebrew has much the same carefully understated, deliberately restrained tone as Kafka's German, and achieves a very convincing Kafkaesque *frisson*, often through the imagery of sounds. Here is a characteristic passage from the story "A Whole Loaf":

> Again the clock rang out. My ears ached with tiredness and the lamp smoked and a black stillness filled the room. In the midst of the silence, I heard the scraping of a key in the lock, like the sound of a nail being driven into flesh, and I realized that they had locked me in and forgotten me.

Agnon seldom offers elaborate visual images of the action he describes, but his quiet, orderly, almost detached contemplation of horror creates a strange and disturbing effect by the very contrast between the manner and matter of narration. The same character who finds himself shut up for the night in an empty restaurant goes on to tell what happens after the final turn of the key in the lock.

> I heard a kind of rustling and saw a rat that had jumped up on the table and was nibbling at the left-over bones. Now he's feeding on the bones, I told myself. Afterwards he'll chew up the tablecloth, then the chair I'm sitting on. Afterwards he'll start on me. First he'll chew up my shoes, then my socks, then my feet, then my calves, and finally the whole body. I fixed my eyes on the wall and saw the clock. I waited for it to ring again, hoping it would frighten away the rat before he got me. A cat appeared and I thought I was saved. But the rat ignored the cat and the cat ignored the rat. The two of them crouched there and gnawed away.

The narrator of this story, like most of the protagonists in both Agnon and Kafka, is a wholly passive figure, at the mercy of demonic or at least enigmatic forces that mock him or threaten to destroy him. And the Hebrew writer, like the German, is repeatedly concerned with the theme of judgment. His characters often find themselves peremptorily summoned before some sort of tribunal; their crucial experiences are set characteristically on the eve of the Jewish New Year or on the Day of Atonement, when Jews place themselves under the scrutiny of divine judgment. In all this nightmare world, moreover, Agnon's surrogates, like Kafka's, discover the greatest horror in the reality of their own selves. For example, the short novel *Till Now* (1952) is set in the Germany of World War I that the author knew firsthand, and examines the dislocating and dehumanizing effects of the war; the dramatic and moral interest of the book, however, is characteristically built up around the private experience of the self:

> I dreamt that a great war had come upon the world, and they called me up to fight. I swore a solemn vow to God that

if I returned from the war unharmed, whoever came out of my house to greet me when I returned I would offer up as a sacrifice. I returned to my house unharmed, and it was I myself who came out to greet me.

Agnon's earliest stories are largely artistic reworkings of themes drawn from folktales and pious tradition. But one of the folktale themes that attracted him from the start was that of the fatal mistake and its inescapable consequences, one which also preoccupied Kafka. *Agunot* ("Mateless Souls"), the first story he published after his arrival in Palestine in 1907 and the one from which he took his name, begins, significantly, with an image of disrupted moral order. God is described weaving a beautiful prayer shawl from the threads of loving-kindness in the actions of the people of Israel. But sometimes a mishap occurs: a thread is broken off, the fabric begins to unravel, evil winds pierce it and rip it to pieces. "At once men are seized by a feeling of shame and they know that they are naked." These last words, of course, echo the description in Genesis of the shame of Adam and Eve. And though some of Agnon's artful folktales, both early and late, present Edens of ideal harmony and piety, his imagination is more usually drawn to situations where the serpent's counsel has been followed, and there is no way of revoking its disruptive and evil consequences. In "Mateless Souls" a father contracts the wrong marriage for his daughter; in the long story, "And the Crooked Shall Be Straight," a storekeeper squanders his family's savings and then abandons his wife; in "The Outcast" a proud aristocrat calls down a holy man's curse on his house—and in each case the protagonists are caught up in an irreversible stream of circumstances that carries them to their ruin. In his later work, Agnon no longer presents this situation in the traditional terms of inexorable fate, but he places his characters in the same predicament of being subject to inscrutable forces over which they have no control.

A similar kind of helplessness is discernible in the heroes of those later novels by Agnon which have realistic social backgrounds. As in Kafka, this helplessness frequently expresses

itself in the passivity of male figures vis-à-vis the domineering
and sometimes demonic females who enter their lives. Herschel
Hurwitz, the hero of A Simple Story (1935), a novel about life
in Buczacz at the turn of the century, is controlled first by his
mother and then by the woman to whom he is married against
his will. Yitzhak Kummer, the protagonist of Just Yesterday
(1945), which is set in Palestine in the years before the out-
break of World War I, is buffeted between two women—
Sonya, the "emancipated woman" in the new settlement at
Jaffa, and the pious daughter Shifra in old Jerusalem. Manfred
Herbst, the central figure in the unfinished novel Shira (chapters appeared from 1951 to 1954), is a university professor in
the Jerusalem of the late thirties, a man with a dangerous habit
of passivity both in his career and in his private life. He allows
himself to be seduced by the hard-mannered, sensual nurse,
Shira, at the very moment when his wife is giving birth to their
child in the hospital where Shira works.

Though such points of resemblance to Kafka may in some
ways be instructive, Agnon, the distinctive artist, is, it need
hardly be said, much more than a Hebrew Kafka. Even his
"Kafkaesque" stories bear the unmistakable marks of Agnon's
own special vision; in any case, they constitute only one seg-
ment of his varied literary production over more than half a
century. But beyond all similarities, there is one radical difference between the two writers: while Kafka exemplifies the
distress of rootlessness that has characterized so many Jews in
modern times, Agnon's uniqueness derives from the fact that he
is so deeply rooted in a tradition. Agnon is in many ways the
most profoundly Jewish writer to have appeared in modern
Hebrew literature, and it is in his role as heir to a Jewish religious and cultural heritage that much of his artistic distinctiveness is to be sought. During the same period in the early thirties
when he was conceiving the first stories of The Book of Deeds,
Agnon published a charming little anecdotal essay, "The Sense
of Smell," which includes a short section entitled "The Secret
of Writing Stories." Here he discloses the religious impulse of
his fiction and the peculiar imagination of history behind it:

Out of affection for our language and love of the holy, I burn midnight oil over the teachings of the Torah and deny myself food for the words of our sages that I may store them up within me to be ready upon my lips. If the Temple were still standing, I would take my place on the platform with my fellow choristers [Agnon traces his ancestry to the tribe of Levi] and would recite each day the song that the Levites used to say in the Holy Temple. But since the Temple is destroyed and we have neither Priests in their service nor Levites in their chorus and song, I devote myself to the Torah, the Prophets, the latter Scriptures, the Mishnah, Halakhah and Agadah, the Tosefta, rabbinical commentaries and textual glosses. When I look at their words and see that of all our precious possessions in ancient times only the memory is left us, I am filled with sorrow. And that sorrow makes my heart tremble. And from that trembling I write stories, like a man banished from his father's palace who builds himself a small shelter and sits there telling the glory of his ancestral home.

The passage suggests not only Agnon's religious conception of his role but also the inborn need of a poet to sing, in one way or another, which has motivated him since boyhood. The years around the turn of the century, when the young Agnon was learning Talmud in his native town of Buczacz, were part of a period when one might often discover a copy of Euclid or Spinoza hidden inside a *yeshiva* student's bulky Talmud folio. But if anything were found slipped in between the pages of the youthful Agnon's Aramaic text, it would probably have been a sample of his own Hebrew verse. Unlike the surreptitious pamphlets of mathemathics and philosophy, his verses were directly and closely related to much of what was printed on the pages of the Talmud, and when Agnon left the traditional study-house to venture out into the world of belles-lettres, he did not leave the Talmud behind, as did his contemporaries from the *yeshivot* when they made their entrance into European culture. The common opposition, in fact, between traditional Jewish life and modern secular culture played no significant part in Agnon's formation. Though the home he grew up in was solidly Ortho-

dox in faith, his mother was well read in German literature, his
father had even tried his hand at Hebrew verse, and the whole
family viewed with pride rather than pious dismay the poems
and stories that Agnon began to publish in Hebrew and
Yiddish journals in Galicia while he was still in his mid-teens.

Agnon has devoted his whole life to writing—and with a
permanent annual stipend from Schocken Books, he is probably
the only Hebrew writer ever to make a comfortable living from
his writing alone. But he has also devoted his life to the study of
Torah. On Agnon's worktable in his home in Talpiot, one
might conceivably find a copy of James Joyce (in translation) or
Rilke, but one is more likely to see some yellowed, flaking
volume that proves to be an obscure eighth-century homiletical
commentary on the Pentateuch, or a collection of Hasidic
parables, or perhaps a late medieval mystical treatise. In this
respect, Agnon continues the tradition of the illustrious rabbinic line from which he is descended, and possesses a volumi-
nous knowledge of traditional Hebrew and Aramaic source
materials—the Bible with all its rabbinic commentaries, the
Talmud, the Midrash, Maimonides and the medieval Jewish
philosophers, legal codifiers, and poets, the Kabbalah, the literature of the *Musar* movement and of the Hasidic tradition of
more modern times.

While all this Jewish erudition has served as an inexhaust-
ible mine of materials—both verbal and conceptual—from
which Agnon has fashioned his creative vision, the relation
between Agnon the author and Agnon the learned and pious
Jew is to some extent ambivalent. There are times when he
looks ironically on his own role as writer (or *sofer,* which in
traditional Hebrew meant Torah scribe, and in modern usage
generally means author); a Jew, he implies, ought to be an in-
scriber of holy scrolls, not someone who simply tries to write
pretty things. In at least two of his stories he attempts to resolve
this conflict by imagining himself as a *sofer* in both senses of
the word—a writer whose stories and novels form one long
Torah scroll.

The image that Agnon draws of himself as the craftsman of

a holy book in which the people will read and God's name will be sanctified is instructive, but it is not an altogether faithful self-portrait. It is true, on the one hand, that Agnon's work often gives evidence of a writer who has a sense of himself not merely as the artist before his audience, but as the artist-member of a people standing before God. There are stories that he uses from beginning to end as vehicles for "telling the glory of his ancestral home." When he depicts the greatness of a Jewish past —which means for him the traces of God's working, or the lives of godly men, in the ancient or recent past—his role as artist does not differ substantially from that of the creative imaginations in the early Middle Ages that produced the Midrash, or of the half-forgotten medieval poets who produced the ornamental liturgical verse of the *piyyutim*. One senses, however, that such stories are the work of a virtuoso ventriloquist, not direct expressions of the world in which the writer really sees himself. In any case, it is also true that a large part of Agnon's work is intensely personal, even confessional, in nature. The *sofer* who has mastered the calligraphy of sacred scrolls is no less a modern writer struggling with his own individual problems and with his own needs for expression. The banished son attempting to recall the splendors of his father's house cannot shelter himself from the world around him with its visions of destruction and uprooting, its dream demons and their twisted Jephthah-vows.

Thus at times there is a perceptible tension between the artist and the traditionalist in Agnon; but what is most remarkable about him is the way he has absorbed Jewish tradition, made it part of himself in making himself part of it, so that he has been able to build upon it a distinctive and highly personal artistic vision. Agnon's creative adaptation of traditional materials can best be examined in terms of the language and the motifs and symbols he employs. At the same time, his use of language and symbol discloses the recurrent ideas and concerns of Jewish tradition that appear in his writing.

When Agnon chose to reveal to his readers the secret of writing stories, he mentioned first his affection for language, and it is certainly true that his painstaking concern for words plays a large part in the originality of his art. During a conversation with Agnon in Jerusalem in 1960, I mentioned to him the often unpredictable struggle with the medium of words that Virginia Woolf speaks of in A *Writer's Diary*. Agnon nodded, then told me about a short story he had written over forty years earlier called "The Outcast." It had begun, he explained, as a full-scale tetralogy, but the more he worked it, the more the scheme shrank, until he finished with just sixty pages of Hebrew print. "I couldn't carry out the original plan," Agnon concluded, "because at that time my language wasn't adequate for the task." If language in general tends to be a clumsy instrument for the demanding requirements of human expression, modern Hebrew, as a language that has barely advanced beyond the stage of its own rebirth, is clumsier than most. What Agnon has done through the years is to create a Hebrew of his own that has come to fit his particular needs of expression with extraordinary precision. It is about as different from the Hebrew spoken in Israel today as Elizabethan English from modern colloquial American—though one is likely now to hear occasional archaic turns of speech among literate Israelis which, one suspects, have come straight out of Agnon.

In a satire written in the forties on the politics and bureaucracy of the new state, Agnon apologized for not representing the speeches of the state's leaders in their own special shade of purple prose. "[Instead] I've put down their words in my own language, an easy and simple language, the language of the generations that came before us and of the generations that will come after us as well." Agnon's use of an older Hebrew comes largely from his desire to avoid the provincialism in time from which so much of modern culture—and particularly Israeli culture—suffers. A writer of immense ambition, Agnon quite seriously means his work to take its place with the great Hebrew literature of the ages, and so he uses the language in which a hundred generations of pious Jews studied, wrote, gave shape to their inner world. Though he has fashioned his style from many sources, with spoken Yiddish and the language of relatively recent devotional literature playing important roles, the Hebrew he writes has a predominantly medieval flavor, frequently recalling the Hebrew of the Mishnah, and even more, of the Midrash—that is, of the earliest compilations of rabbinic law and homiletic commentary, respectively.

The term "medieval" may give the wrong impression to an American or European reader because there is really no analogue among the Western languages to the body of Hebrew upon which Agnon draws. One tends to think, for example, of older literary English, at least since the later Middle Ages, as more ornate, more rhetorically elaborate and consciously artificial, than its modern counterpart, while Old English has for most of us the roughhewn look of a less developed language. The Hebrew of the Midrash, on the other hand, does not suffer from either old-fashioned ornateness or from even the appearance of crudeness. The style of this great medieval collection of homiletic and legendary variations on biblical themes is simple, even-toned, quietly modulated (and consequently Agnon's own style can be deceptively "easy and simple"), but it possesses a peculiar lyric grace, and its flexibility of syntax and breadth of vocabulary make it capable of representing minute details of action and fine nuances of feeling.

Midrashic Hebrew is, moreover, much closer to the modern Hebrew reader than its history of nearly two thousand years would suggest. The source books in which it is used have been traditionally studied from childhood on with the sort of application that would make them as familiar to the cultivated reader of Hebrew as, say, *Pilgrim's Progress* once was to English schoolchildren. Agnon's Hebrew stands with the readers for whom it is intended on a footing of old and intimate acquaintance, in all its archaic accouterment. It has a distinctive poetic charm that necessarily disappears in translation, and because of the deliberate simplicity of the style, Agnon in a Western language is likely to look rather wan and anemic.

Throughout his long career, Agnon has had the perfectionist's passion for polishing and repolishing style which is associated in European literature with figures like Flaubert and Joyce. Agnon may write a story, lock it up in a drawer, and let it sit for ten or fifteen years until he is ready, then take it out, rework it, and finally publish it. At present he has nearly four hundred pages of two different novels that have appeared in progress in various periodicals over the past decade; there is no way of knowing whether he has actually finished either book or when he will decide to let any more chapters get into print. Today, at the age of seventy-three, he continues to follow an active work schedule, is still a vigorous experimenter, and even now he will on occasion make stylistic revisions of stories he published more than thirty years ago.

But Agnon is no more a Hebrew Flaubert than he is a Hebrew Kafka. In his own concern for language there is one major distinguishing element: the Hebrew he writes is for him not merely a language (*lashon*) but the Holy Language (*l'shon ha-kodesh*). In explaining "The Secret of Writing Stories," he naturally connects affection for the language with love of the holy; for, like generations of Jews before him, Agnon regards Hebrew as the Jew's indispensable means of entrance into the sphere of sanctity. His stylistic perfectionism partly derives from his feeling that as a Hebrew writer he is a kind of guardian of sacred vessels who must protect them from every possible contamination. It is through the direct continuity which he preserves in his style with the Hebrew of the past that he is able to maintain a grip on the spiritual vision of the past. Even in the darkest corners of his nightmare world, the language he uses becomes a safeguard of sanity, a constant though sometimes ambiguous testimony of the continuing strength of traditional values.

In a volume of his stories published in 1952, there is a striking account of a father and daughter who are forced to flee their home after anonymous enemies have destroyed their house and all their possessions. The father asks the little daughter (who in Agnon's symbolic scheme represents the soul) if she knows what the Hebrew letters *aleph bet* spell. She answers correctly that they form the word *av* ("father"). The father then tells her: "You see, my darling, two little letters stand in the prayerbook as if they were all alone; they come together and make *av*. And not only these letters, but all the letters when they are joined make words, and the words form prayers, and the prayers rise up before our Father in heaven who gives ear and listens to the voice of our supplication." For Agnon this alphabet alone—the Hebrew of tradition in which he writes—is the alphabet of holiness. It was the instrument through which the sanctity of the past was expressed and preserved; it is what enables him to hold on to a sense of that sanctity and to re-create it in his writing, even when he is most intensely aware of the chaotic and threatening aspects of the world he lives in.

Together with the words of tradition, Agnon has adopted for his own uses a wide variety of motifs and symbols from this religious—and often highly poetic—literature. In effect he has found in it one solution to a problem that has typically concerned modern writers beginning with Yeats, Eliot, and Joyce: the need for a living body of mythology from which the artist can draw symbols meaningful to his audience to use in his own work. Agnon discovered a virtually untapped reservoir of symbolic richness in Jewish tradition, and, most particularly, in the Midrash. His development of traditional motifs endows his vision with an unusual poetic coherence, even over the apparently ambling stretches of some of his longer novels. A novel by Agnon is likely to prove to be, among other things, an extended variation on several symbolic themes, frequently themes he has taken from the Midrash.

A well-known midrashic legend, for example, represents the people of Israel in exile as a prince (that is, God's son) who has been transformed by sorcery into a dog and who must suffer in this state until a redeemer will restore him to his original regal figure. Agnon's major novel, *A Guest for the Night* (1939), which deals with the physical and spiritual destruction of East-European Jewry, elaborates on this theme with great effectiveness. At the very beginning of the book, the narrator sees a plaque upon which the name of a Polish king had been inscribed in gold; the plaque is now broken, the letters are tarnished, and blood-red weeds have sprung up over them.

Everywhere the vestiges of majesty are trampled on or cast under the shadow of death. The inhabitants of the war-ruined Galician town in which the story takes place stubbornly refuse to regard themselves as anything better than animals—and rather pitiful animals at that. "The greatest of all evils," reflects the narrator, "is when a prince forgets he is a prince." And so the theme is reiterated and developed throughout the novel.

To cite a somewhat different use of symbolic source material, an apparently formless piece like the expressionistic story called "The Orchestra" achieves a poetic unity through the manipulation of contrasting imagery of light and darkness. On its narrative surface, the story looks like nothing but a series of broken zigzags: the narrator sits down to write letters on the eve of the New Year, gets up to bathe for the holiday but is frustrated in his attempt to enter the bath awaiting him at his grandfather's house (which presumably exists in another time and place); he goes home as the sun sets and then finds himself wandering into a bizarre concert at which the conductor remains invisible. Verbally and visually, however, the story has considerable coherence. Several key references (which someone reading the story in the original would be more likely to notice) are to verses in Psalms: the associations made by the Psalmist of light-God-salvation and darkness-trouble-death are recalled at critical points. The little girl in the story who longs to go to the concert has a Hebrew name that means light, while the Russian name of the old woman at the grandfather's house suggests darkness. As soon as the little girl leaves the narrator, the old woman approaches. The narrator's daughter calls out "Light" plaintively as darkness falls on this Day of Judgment, and the story concludes with a vision in the light of bright stars against a dark sky. It is possible that, in addition to the light-imagery from Psalms, Agnon may have had in mind the symbolic use of light in the lore of the Kabbalah, where human existence is conceived as a struggle to redeem the scattered sparks of the broken divine effulgence from the envelopes of darkness in which they are imprisoned.

In some cases, Agnon's knowledge of Jewish tradition has

served merely as a source for his own symbolic imagination, and he brings his final creative product very far indeed from its literary antecedents. The remarkable story "Forevermore,"* about a scholarly investigator of an ancient culture who renounces prospects of worldly glory to enter a leper colony, seems to reflect such a process in operation. The germinal idea for the story's symbolic use of the lepers is in all probability a passage in the Midrash Bereshit Rabba commenting on the verse from Psalms, "Make me not the reproach of the base." The Midrash explains the verse as a plea to God by the Jews that He keep the other peoples from singling them out in their exile with the reproach, "Are you not a nation of lepers?" But in the story Agnon develops an original and self-sufficient fantasy from the image of the Jews as a people of lepers. I say fantasy, because the writer has gone out of his way to stress the quality of bizarreness and in this way to remind us that the reality of the story is a product of the imagination. He achieves this effect through the willfully bizarre details of the ancient Scroll of Gumlidata, and, more generally, through the peculiar impression he creates by beginning all proper names in the story with one of two letters. The Hebrew consonants *ayin* and *gimel* are the first two letters of Agnon's own last name, so the exclusion of all names that begin with other letters is a means of asserting that the events of the story exist peculiarly within the domain of its author's imagination. But what is most remarkable about "Forevermore" is the way its central symbol embodies in a single image the two contradictory elements of a highly paradoxical attitude toward Judaism. On the one hand, the lepers are prisoners of a living death. Their parchment book that tells the glory and destruction of an ancient city is befouled by the suppurations of its diseased readers. Yet it is only among the lepers and from their book that Adiel Amzeh finds the truth.

"Forevermore" is a striking illustration of Agnon's artistic distinctiveness in still another way, because it combines the most deadly seriousness with a studied, playful coyness about

* Available in English in *Israeli Stories*, ed. Joel Blocker (New York: Schocken Books, 1962).

revealing meanings. One is tempted to associate the *ayin*-people of the story with a sphere of commitment and the *gimel*-people with a sphere of empty worldliness: the numerical value of *ayin* is seventy, the decade of sevens sanctified by Jewish tradition, and *gimel* is three, the first incomplete number after unity and balanced duality. But if Agnon encourages us—here and elsewhere—to play such interpretative games, he discourages us from thinking we have won them. The characters of "Forevermore" almost fall into the neat polarity I have suggested, but there are enough ambiguous cases, possible exceptions, to leave us wondering about the adequacy of the scheme. And the Scroll of Gumlidata uncovered at the end of the story, with its parade of brilliantly fantastic details—a mantle woven with bands of calves' eyes, a princess giving suck to asses, and more of the like—invites the interpreter to go to work while defying him to be satisfied with his efforts.

It is indicative of Agnon's originality as an artist that he has drawn from so many sources and yet managed to avoid making his work into a literary pastiche. A sound creative insight led him to choose from the tradition what was most appropriate for his personal needs of expression. For example, in an autobiographical story entitled "The Kerchief," Agnon creates a memorable portrait of family love and moral coming of age by building on a single comment of Rashi's on a verse in the Book of Lamentations. The verse is, "How is she [Jerusalem] become as a widow!" Rashi points out that Scripture does not say "a widow" but "as a widow"—"like a woman whose husband has gone to some far-off place but with the intention of returning to her." The absence of the boy's father is identified with the absence of God from the Land of Israel. The mother sits at the window waiting for her husband's return like Jerusalem waiting for its redeemer, and the boy has childish imaginings about the advent of the Messiah. Every night he tries to fall asleep with one ear open in case the ram's horn of redemption should sound before morning. But the boy has to discover that a genuine sense of the Messiah's coming—like the feeling of the family when the father finally arrives home—is only to be had by learning to face the most repellent sufferings of humanity in the unredeemed world.

When, by contrast, Agnon takes youthful love as his theme in "Nights"—his stay in Jaffa from 1907 to 1913 is the background for his story—he adopts a rich lyric prose filled with reminiscences of the language of the Song of Songs. This haunting love story is a kind of extended prose-poem, luxuriant with the floral imagery of the Bible's great love poem. Agnon can even adopt so unlikely a form as the moralistic parable and turn it to his own artistic purposes. One of the recurrent concerns of his writing is the struggle—and the general failure—of the individual conscience to carry out its own moral responsibilities. He dramatizes this struggle with great effectiveness in a parable called "The Garment"—the story of a tailor who postpones making a garment commissioned by a great lord, stains the fabric while eating at his worktable, and finally drowns when he tries to wash the ruined material in the river. "The lord has many garments and he can afford to do without one of them. But the tailor who spoiled the garment made with material from the lord's workshop—what will he answer and what will he say when they ask him where is the garment?" Agnon does with the parable what the great Hasidic teachers might have done if they had been masters of Hebrew prose.

Of all his achievements in adapting the materials of Jewish tradition to his own fictional modes of expression, the most important has been his remarkable success in weaving the legendary tapestry of the medieval Midrash into the texture of the twentieth-century world lived in and experienced by Shmuel Yosef Agnon. One significant instance of this process is his treatment of the theme of the house. Perhaps the greatest single concern in Agnon's writings is the problem of modern man who, spiritually, finds himself with no place to live. Though this theme is almost everywhere in Agnon's fiction, it receives its most extensive and resonant expression in *A Guest for the Night*: the very title of that novel suggests the uneasy fate of transience to which most of his central characters are condemned, and the main action is the futile, finally self-deceiving attempt of the protagonist, who has returned from Jerusalem to his native Szybuscz, to revive there the old study-house, the key educational and religious institution that in fact had been the sheltering spiritual "home" for East-European Jewry in recent centuries. The comment made by the hero of Agnon's short novel *Till Now* might serve as an epigraph for the author's collected works. "I'll tell you the story of a man who has neither house nor room, who left the place he did have and lost the one he found. And so he goes from one place to another, looking for a place for himself."

By a strange double coincidence, Agnon has had two experiences in his own life paradigmatic of the violent destruction of order which has been such an important element in the history of our times. In 1924, when the Hebrew writer was living in Hamburg, his house burned down, and everything he owned went up in the flames, including his library of four thousand books and the manuscript of an autobiographical novel (which he never attempted to begin again). The suddenness and totality of the loss shocked Agnon profoundly. Within five years, the same thing was to happen to him again. This time it was his home in Jerusalem that was ravaged, and the agents of destruction were the Arab rioters in the Palestine pogroms of 1929: once again, significantly, a valuable library of rare books and manuscripts was lost.

There is evidence enough in Agnon's work that he has brooded ever since over this twice-experienced archetypal event of destruction. In any case, the typical subject of his stories since the thirties is the dispossessed—the physically, culturally, and most important, spiritually dispossessed. Typically, the enemy has destroyed a man's house. In one story we may encounter him on the road, running away. Or, in others, he may be on a bus or train or ship that will not take him where he wants to go. There are no vacancies when he looks for an apartment, or he is unable to find the address he wants, or the house is locked and he has no way of getting in. The house he once lived in—the ordered structure of an older way of life—has been knocked to pieces, and he finds himself a radically displaced person in a world without homes.

This subject is hardly a unique one in twentieth-century fiction, but Agnon's conception of the dispossessed is distinctive because it connects the image of homeless man with the complex of symbols and ideas bound up in the idea of *galut* (exile) enunciated in the literature of Jewish tradition. The Midrash characteristically portrays *galut* as the banishing of a prince from his father's palace (the Land of Israel) to live in a series of makeshift huts. (For this reason Agnon, the would-have-been Levite, builds himself a "small shelter" to recall the glory of his father's house.) The creators of the Midrash intended to instill in their audience a deep realization that any house until the time of redemption was only a temporary and flimsy shelter. *Galut* is not simply a matter of geographical displacement. When the people of Israel went into exile, the Divine Presence was said to have gone into exile as well. The notion of *galut*, in other words, involves a cosmic as well as a historical event, implying the idea of a whole world-order out of kilter, with even God out of his appropriate place. Or as the Kabbalists poignantly put it, not Israel alone was in *galut*, it was the whole world that was in *galut*, and the world had to be redeemed if Israel was to be redeemed.

The Midrash in this way gives Agnon not only the language and images with which to represent the state of homelessness of modern man, but also a way to interpret this distressing phenomenon. Jewish tradition always opposes to the hut of exile the image of the house that was, which is also the image of the house that will be; the dark reality of exile is confronted in the unswerving belief in a redemption to follow the exile. There are many moments in Agnon's stories when his dispossessed protagonists seem on the point of being wholly submerged by the forces that threaten them, but what ultimately distinguishes Agnon from an uprooted Jew like Kafka is the fact that at times he can honestly envisage a restoration of the shattered order, a rebuilding of the ruined house. To be sure, it is often difficult to know quite how to take Agnon: even his occasional images of hope flicker ambiguously, are gravely threatened by the world of shadows around them, but they possess an imaginative reality that cannot be entirely discounted.

Agnon has in his varied literary enterprise confronted some of the most disturbing aspects of the contemporary world, and he is too shrewd, too tough-minded an observer to be capable of deceiving himself about the way things are. Yet by remaining constantly in touch—both in his art and in his private life—with the spiritual wholeness of the past, he has preserved the conviction that such wholeness of spirit is both indispensable and still possible to achieve, however unreachable it may now seem. Agnon is sometimes able, then, to conclude his visions of disaster on a note of affirmation. It is not a loud or insistent note: it seems to waver somewhere between the reliance of faith and the devout, even desperate, hope of prayer. But the occasional affirming voice has the ring of authenticity, and in these "war days," as Agnon often designates the last half-century, it is a rare and precious sound.

1961

ELIE WIESEL: BETWEEN
HANGMAN AND VICTIM

The novels of Elie Wiesel strike me as a singularly impressive instance of how the creative imagination can surprise our expectations of what its limits should be. It is natural enough to wonder whether it is really possible to write about the Holocaust, to use the written word, which by its very nature is committed to order, as a means of representing and assessing absolute moral chaos. With this awesome difficulty in mind, the British critic, A. Alvarez, has suggested that any adequate writing on the Holocaust must be in some way antirealistic, fracturing reality into jumbled splinters, as in fact the Nazi horror fractured the moral world which people used to imagine. The suggestion is plausible, and Alvarez offers one persuasive example for his thesis in the patterned madness of *Blood from the Sky*, a novel by another East-European Jew writing in French, Piotr Rawicz.

The achievement, however, of Elie Wiesel's five published books reminds us of the danger in issuing prescriptions about things of the spirit. He has managed to realize the terrible past imaginatively with growing artistic strength in a narrative form that is consecutive, coherent, and, at least on the surface, realistic, in a taut prose that is a model of lucidity and precision. Yet by the very nature of his subject, what we might want to describe as the "realism" of his technique constantly transcends itself, as we are made to feel the pitiful inadequacy of all our commonsense categories of reality. Thus, when the young prisoner in *Night* arrives at Auschwitz, the report he gives us of a flaming ditch filled with the bodies of burning babies is of an event that actually happened at a particular point in history, in our lifetimes. Before the fact of the Holocaust, perhaps only a great visionary poet like Dante could thoroughly imagine such a gruesome reality; after the fact, it still requires a peculiar imaginative courage to abandon all the defenses of common sense in order to remember and reconstitute in language such a reality. It is ultimately this imaginative courage that endows Wiesel's factually precise writing with a hallucinated more-than-realism: he is able to confront the horror with a nakedly self-exposed honesty rare even among writers who went through the same ordeal.

Wiesel's relation both to his subject and to his craft required that, before he could invent fiction, he should starkly record fact, and so his first book, *Night,* is a terse and terrifying account of the concentration-camp experiences that made him an agonized witness to the death of his innocence, his human self-respect, his father, his God. His innocence, of course, was irrevocably destroyed, like his flesh-and-blood father, but what Wiesel has done in the fiction after *Night* is to try to rediscover grounds for human self-respect, to struggle to imagine a God who is neither dead nor insane, using the same tightly compressed style and the same narrative of ultimate confrontations which were inevitable for that initial record of his actual experiences. Here, for example, is the way his first novel, *Dawn,* begins:

> Somewhere a child began to cry. In the house across the way an old woman closed the shutters. It was hot with all the heat of an autumn evening in Palestine.
> Standing near the window I looked out at the transparent twilight whose descent made the city seem silent, motionless, unreal, and very far away. Tomorrow, I thought for the hundredth time, I shall kill a man, and I wondered if the crying child and the woman across the way knew.

There is nothing in this world but the prospect of terrible confrontation, together with the natural reminders of its imminence (sunset, pointing toward the fixed hour of death at dawn) and the symbolic resonators of its implications (the child crying). The closest literary analogy I can think of for Wiesel's imaginative landscapes is the kind of lyric love poetry where all existence is focused in the presence of the lover and the beloved (as in Donne's famous lines, "She's all states, and all princes, I, / Nothing else is."). In Wiesel's case, the world seems to contain only three classes of people, each with its own kind of guilt of complicity: executioners, victims, and spectators at the execution.

If this drastic selectivity in some ways foreshortens the view of reality in his novels, it also generates an extraordinary degree of intensity, at once dramatic and moral. The imponderable keys of life and death are placed in the hands of each of Wiesel's protagonists with the imperative to decide how they should be used: the hero of *Dawn* is a terrorist who has orders to execute a British hostage; in *The Accident,* the protagonist lies in a hospital, hovering—almost, choosing—between life and death; *The Town Beyond the Wall* is the story of a man under torture by secret police, trying to save his friend's life; and *The Gates of the Forest* recounts three wartime episodes in which the hero must save his life—twice while a comrade dies—by hiding or disguise, then a fourth incident, after the war, in which he goes on with the struggle begun in the terror of the war to save his soul.

To describe this focus on finalities in another way, Wiesel's novels, for all the vividness with which they render certain contemporary situations, are more theological parable than realistic fiction: they are written for and about Abrahams on the mountain, Isaacs under the slaughtering knife, and a God who watches but no longer sends His messenger to stay the descending blade. In this kind of parabolic novel our expectations of what people will say, do, or even think are very different from what they would normally be. It is as natural, say, for the patient in *The Accident* to ask his doctor, "Do you believe in God?" as it would be in a more conventional novel for one character to ask another, "Do you smoke?" The protagonist of *The Gates of the Forest,* after meeting a madman, perhaps a divine messenger, in his cave hideout, says to himself, "I think I have lived only for this encounter and this night." And the imagined figure of his grandfather replies, "That, my child, is true of all encounters, of every night." It is a strange truth we are made to feel almost everywhere in Wiesel's fiction of ultimate confrontations.

Since most of the action and thought in Wiesel's novels take place on the broadest level of philosophical or theological generalization, it is entirely appropriate that the argument of the books should repeatedly crystallize in wisdom-statements, whether by one of the characters or by the narrator himself. Sometimes these take the form of extended and impassioned expositions. More often they are memorable aphorisms: about man—"The just man has a thousand truths, and that's his tragedy; the murderer has one alone, and that's his strength"; about God—"The lack of hate between executioner and victim, perhaps this is God"; and their interrelation—"The Jews resemble their God; they're always hiding: the world's not only *Jüdenrein,* it's *Gottrein* as well."

I suspect the fact that Wiesel works in French makes this sententious method of writing fiction much more natural for him than it could be for an American or British novelist. In this connection, it is interesting to speculate about the reasons for his decision to write his novels in French, a language he did not begin to learn until the age of sixteen, rather than in his native Yiddish or in Hebrew, both of which he writes fluently and eloquently. Perhaps he was motivated in part by the desire to bring his urgent message to a larger audience, but he may also have been attracted to French because of its readily available heritage of stylistic classicism that makes possible the expression of serious emotion with a chaste conciseness quite unlike the effects of pathos and effusion to which Hebrew and Yiddish easily lend themselves. There is a long tradition of aphorism as a major mode of expression in French that goes back to Pascal and La Rochefoucauld and that blends into the novel with some of the nineteenth-century masters, so that the aphoristic style of Wiesel's fiction has ample precedents in the language he has chosen to use. In our own time, moreover, Sartre, Camus, and Malraux have demonstrated in different ways how the French novel could be used to test out or illuminate perplexing and urgent philosophical questions. To these French traditions Wiesel brings a rich knowledge of midrashic, talmudic, and, above all, Hasidic lore, in which aphorism is also very important and where the concise tale is typically used as a revelation of spiritual truth.

The imaginative logic, then, of Wiesel's literary and religious backgrounds explains much of the centrality given not only to the aphorism but also to the figure of the Teacher in his novels. The wisdom taught by the Teacher in his books is, of course, always "existential," never academic, because the figure for Wiesel always derives from the Hasidic spiritual guide—more particularly, from a kabbalistic master of his own childhood whose message was one of redemption, involving the secret knowledge through which man could learn to loose the chains in which the Messiah is bound.

The Teacher first appears in the novels as Kalman the Mystic, but after the Nazis have reduced Kalman to ghastly smoke, his presence returns in a dozen unlikely faces—an eccentric painter, a philosophic smuggler, a soulful partisan, a passionate terrorist. *The Gates of the Forest,* in fact, has at least one teacher for each of its four sections. But is there anything these guides can possibly teach to the Eliezer of *Night* who remains, after all, the protagonist of all the novels—a young man possessed by death, feeling that "To live is to betray the dead"? Wiesel's protagonist is pursued everywhere by the unbearable starkness of dead or deathly eyes—his own eyes as dehumanized victim (the end of *Night*), or as victimizer (the end of *Dawn*) the eyes of the slaughtered kin that were brutally torn from the light (*The Accident* and elsewhere). What the Teachers attempt to do is to exorcise these paralyzing visions without committing the spiritual folly of suggesting that they be forgotten, and this act has general, not merely personal, significance because all of us, to the extent that we have courage to think about the recent past, must be haunted in some way, however intermittently, by these same specters.

The point is worth emphasizing. Some may find it tempting to think of Wiesel simply as a man who has gone through unspeakable horrors and, by means of his writing, is trying to "work it all out," as we like to say in clinical condescension. For Wiesel, however, Auschwitz was not just a personal trauma but a dark revelation of what man, God, and history were all about. He recurs to the broad implications of this revelation again and again in his work; in an essay called "In Defense of the Dead" he states the grim meaning of the death camps with eloquent succinctness: "At Auschwitz not only man died but the idea of man. It wasn't worth much to live in a world where there was nothing else, where the hangman acted as God and judge. For it was its own heart that the world burned at Auschwitz."* We are all part of that incendiary world, and Wiesel's writing is intended to remind us repeatedly, painfully, of this fact. Let me hasten to add, though, that his fiction is more than a literary exercise in the infliction of punishment. Although all four of his novels deal with victims and refugees of the Holocaust, the books are all set—with the partial exception of *The Gates of the Forest*—in the aftermath of the war, for Wiesel's principal concern is to imagine a humanly possible aftermath, for himself, for all of us. The exorcism he attempts of the demons of the past is one that all men now urgently need to carry out, for after all that has happened since 1933 it is not easy to reconceive humanity in any configuration other than the fatal triangle of executioner, victim, and spectator.

It is almost misleading to try to paraphrase the terms in which this exorcism is undertaken in the novels because any possible "message" in Wiesel's fiction is meant—like the charismatic teaching of the Hasidic masters—to be experienced as much as it is comprehended, through the tensions and flexions of particular personalities pounded and wrenched by particular

* In this one instance, the translation from the French is mine.

experiences. This is why the aphorisms carry conviction, and this is why, I think, as Wiesel has moved toward a kind of affirmation in his two most recent novels, he has also needed a more elaborate fictional strategy, a fuller world of people and events, to give weight and credibility to whatever affirmations are intimated.

The positive statement of the last two novels is memorably summed up by Pedro, the principal Teacher in *The Town Beyond the Wall*: "To say, 'I suffer, therefore I am' is to become the enemy of man. What you must say is, 'I suffer, therefore you are.'" Out of context, this may sound a little like the familiar formula of love and the brotherhood of man that is offered as an easy anodyne for all the world's ills by certain contemporary writers. Wiesel's novel, however, concludes with a harrowing illustration of the awful difficulties in applying Pedro's maxim to harsh reality. The hero of the novel is locked in a prison cell for an indefinite period with a completely brutalized, mute idiot boy. (The cell here, like the cave at the beginning of *The Gates of the Forest* and the cellar in *Dawn*, becomes the whole world.) The protagonist determines to defy the utter hopelessness of his imprisonment by devoting all his energies to an attempt to teach the brutalized idiot some semblance of a human response. The Talmud speaks of man's partnership with God in the work of creation, but here the prisoner must pray to God not to be against him "this time" as he himself, with his pitiful human powers, "resumes the creation of the world from the void."

This is not only courageous, Wiesel makes clear; it is also mad. The idiot continues to stare blankly while his fellow prisoner shouts, cajoles, pleads, exhorts, prophesies of the time when this maimed creature will enter into the wholeness of community with other men. The entire scene is absurd, outrageous, and very moving. In the kind of world we live in, the novel suggests, one has to be mad in order to be truly sane; if God has betrayed His creation, man has to be crazy enough to assume God's responsibilities, even with the knowledge that he is only man.

The same notion of a fateful exchange of roles between man and God is expressed with further complications in Wiesel's most recent novel, *The Gates of the Forest*. Since this book is in a sense a culmination, even a kind of tentative, uneasy resolution, of his earlier work, an account of its general imaginative scheme may reveal something of the spiritual enterprise his writing represents. The book's theme is role-playing in the most deadly serious sense: the struggle over and with the names—in the Bible this term implies "essential nature"—that man attaches to himself, the words he assigns himself to speak. In the epidemic madness of Final Solutions, Wiesel suggests, words themselves have been twisted into a hideous reversal of their primary function as instruments of creation: "Words kill. At the beginning there is always the word. *Fire!* a lieutenant was calling out somewhere, and a line of men and women tumbled into a ditch." In the sinister jumble of such a world, man no longer knows who he is or who God is, and so Wiesel's protagonist begins, like Jacob in Genesis, by struggling with a mysterious stranger for his name.

But his predicament differs in one crucial respect from that of the biblical figure: the stranger has deliberately abandoned his name in the war, and the protagonist, instead of winning a name from his adversary and friend, ends by giving him his own—Gavriel, which signifies "man of God." The ambiguity of this transference is the central one of the novel. Does the man of God really exist, wonders the hero who now takes the Gentile name Gregor, or has Gavriel been only a creature of his own naming, his own creation? The entire relationship between divine and human has become profoundly confused. Late in the novel, when the Jacob motif is recalled in another wrestling of souls, between Gregor and a Hasidic rabbi, Gregor asks, "Which one of us is Jacob, and which the angel?" and the rabbi himself must answer, "I don't know." Perhaps, the novel argues, man has to be able to exchange roles with God, if God has so completely abdicated His responsibilities; perhaps men must become, individually, the Messiah, if the

Messiah has so failed to live up to the name of Consoler that tradition assigns him.

The Gates of the Forest establishes an impressive narrative equivalent for this sense of reversed positions and dubious identities by presenting much of its most critical action under the aspect of conscious playacting. In the background of Gregor's personal ordeal, while he hides out from the Fascists in the Transylvanian hill country, European history is seen in glimpses as an incredible, unreal play in which machine gunners, given their cues by comic-opera officers, methodically topple line after line of human beings like bizarre dolls. In the foreground, Gregor's two central experiences in the war after his initial encounter with Gavriel both involve playing a part until the actor becomes the part. The first of these episodes concludes in a stunning dramatic action: Gregor, pretending to be a deaf-mute Christian, is made to play the role of Judas in a passion play put on by the schoolchildren of a little Hungarian village. At the climax of the play, audience and actors merge in an orgy of no longer pretended hatred for the betrayer of Christ, and the dumb sufferer saves his life only at the last moment by prostrating his attackers with sudden speech, a terrible indictment after silence kept too long.

If role-playing of this sort, in which murderous history is reenacted, can invite man to be less than human, there are other parts to be played which—however ambiguously—may teach him to become more fittingly himself. In Gregor's next experience, he and a girl named Clara enter a Hungarian town, pretending to be innocent young lovers, in order to spy for a band of partisans. Gregor's acted love soon becomes quite genuine, but Clara has other attachments; ironically, when they finally marry after the war, she will undermine his affection for her by making him play in her mind the role of her dead lover, Leib.

By means of these dramatizations, these repeated revelations of the fluctuating gap between part and player, action and identity, Wiesel has managed to create a fictional world in which both the terrifying traps and the slender possibilities for hope in life after the Holocaust are sharply illuminated. His arresting aphorisms resonate more fully here than in his earlier novels because they have greater reverberations in the pattern of the action itself. "What, then, is man?" asks the narrator, echoing the Psalmist, but also echoing Gregor's whole relentless struggle with an elusive man whom he has given a name— "Hope turned to dust. But . . . the opposite is equally true. What is man? Dust turned to hope."

This striking summary of ultimate contradictions, which expresses so much of Wiesel's spiritual world, is reminiscent of a teaching of the Hasidic master, Simha Bunam of Pzhysha, who used to say that every man should have two pockets, one in which to put a slip of paper with the rabbinic dictum, "For my sake the world was created," and the other to carry Abraham's confession of humility before God, "I am dust and ashes." The transmutation that occurs in Wiesel's restatement of the paradox is instructive. In the Hasidic teaching, both man's awesome importance and his nothingness are conceived in terms of his stance before the Creator. In Wiesel, on the other hand, the theological center has shifted to the human spirit: it is pathetically finite man who is the source of miraculous aspiration, of regeneration, in a world where all life is inevitably transient. We may tend to be suspicious of affirmations, for it is often in their affirmative moments that even writers of considerable integrity yield to the temptation of offering a facile and superficial counterfeit of wisdom. In Wiesel, however, one senses that the affirmations are hard-earned, and, indeed, by incorporating as they do their own threatened negations, they may even be hard to assimilate. What is true of the affirmations is true of Wiesel's books in general, which are easy to read but difficult to assimilate. For they are the stages of his own way both from and toward faith, and, at this point in history, that way could not be easy, either to walk or to imagine.

1966

III *The Israeli Scene*

CONFRONTING THE HOLOCAUST

Most people in our time have the face of Lot's wife, turned toward the Holocaust and yet always escaping.—Yehuda Amichai

With all the restless probing into the implications of the Holocaust that continues to go on in Jewish intellectual forums in this country, and at a time when there has been such an abundance of novels—even some good novels—by American Jews, it gives one pause to note how rarely American-Jewish fiction has attempted to come to terms in any serious way with the European catastrophe. Alfred Kazin, among others, has argued that no one can really write an imaginative work about the Nazi terror because art implies meaning, and Hitler's whole regime represented an organized annihilation of meaning. It would in any case be an act of spiritual presumption for someone other than a survivor to try to reconstruct the hideousness of the experience from within. But, even standing outside what actually happened, we all have to live with this irruption of utter meaninglessness into history, which implies, finally, that we have to make some kind of sense of it. This is what historians, social commentators, literary intellectuals, and others over the past two decades have tried to do in introspective or even argumentative essays; it is just this that the more serious American-Jewish novelists have been unwilling or unable to do in their creative work. Two possible explanations for this disparity in response suggest themselves. It may be easier to reason discursively about the inconceivable, to box it in with words, than to assimilate it imaginatively; and, for a variety of reasons, American writers in recent years often seem to have found that the essay, not the novel, has offered the most dependable and penetrating kind of illumination into the dark areas of their inner life and the deepest perplexities of their moral world.

Although in Israel the reflective essay does not have this kind of ascendancy over the imaginative genres, there have been other reasons why Hebrew fiction, at least until fairly recently, has done almost as little as American fiction in the way of looking into the wound of consciousness left by the destruction of European Jewry. (Survivors of the Holocaust living in Israel and writing in Hebrew must of course be excepted from this and all that follows.) Israeli writers, to begin with, have all been participants in a very different kind of major historical event—the rebirth through armed struggle of an independent Jewish state. It was not only that this latter event was more immediate, more palpable, more humanly comprehensible than the grim events in Europe that preceded it, but also that those terrible events raised certain disturbing questions about the values and the very existence of the Jewish state which, at least for a time, Israeli writers were not prepared to confront. During the fifties, Hebrew fiction came to be more and more a medium for wrestling with problems, both personal and cultural, but not this particular problem. In a purely descriptive sense, I would say that there is something strikingly adolescent about Israeli fiction of the fifties. In a number of the important Hebrew novels of this period, the major characters are all, in fact, adolescents; plot and dialogue serve as means for the characters (and the writer) to work out identity crises in a sustained effort consciously to come of age. As one might expect, these adolescent heroes and their retrospectively adolescent authors have little interest in anything that is outside the immediate circumambience of a self struggling for definition, anything beyond the youth movement, the army, the party, Papa and Mama's bourgeois staidness or old-fashioned Zionism, sweet Dalia or Shula and that moonlit night of first nakedness on the shore of Lake Tiberias.

I am not completely sure whether Israeli fiction of the sixties is getting significantly better (though I suspect that it is), but it has clearly gone beyond this stage. Israeli writers now more typically turn to the adult society in which they actually live, where the problems of self-definition are set in the complicating context of urban existence, professional responsibilities, and married life, where the characters have lived through enough to realize that what is most profoundly relevant to them is not always identical with what immediately impinges on them. Even the retrospective novel of adolescence, as we shall see, is now able to imagine its subject in circumstances that more firmly engage it in a complex historical reality.

As the Israeli writer in recent years has been better able to see his own condition entangled in a broad network of social, cultural, historical particulars, both the passage of time and the pressure of public events have pushed the European experience more toward the center of his awareness. The Israeli-Arab war seems to have been a kind of collective trauma for many sensitive young Israelis. Several of the most serious Hebrew novels of the fifties tried to work out the terror of an experience in which the sons of the pioneer-conquerors of desert and swamp were called upon to fight people, to kill in the name of the state. But as the sharpness of this experience now gradually fades, the raw edges of the deeper, darker trauma that preceded it begin to be exposed. At the same time, the events of the past four or five years have repeatedly focused attention on Israel's morally problematic relationship with Germany. The imminent end of reparations made many people in Israel aware of the extent to which the country's economy was dependent on these payments from Germany for the horrors inflicted upon European Jews. The arms deal with Bonn pointed to an even more grimly ironic dependence of Jew on German for instruments of destruction. The prospect of diplomatic relations with Germany, finally realized in 1965, introduced a note of inescapable conclusiveness to the official acceptance by the Jewish state of postwar Germany. And looming behind all these events in the early sixties is the figure of the mass murderer in his glass cage in Jerusalem, with all the storm of worldwide debate, moral and legal, about him, about his being there, about what he represented.

It is against this general background that, in 1963, the first important novel by an Israeli dealing with the Holocaust appeared, Yehuda Amichai's *Not of This Time, Not of This Place*.* For the sake of accuracy, I should say that Amichai was born in Germany, from where he was brought to Palestine in 1936 at the age of twelve. The fact of his German childhood, his awareness of kin and earliest friends murdered by the Nazis, clearly determines the broad direction of the sections of his novel set in Germany, and yet the general attempt of the book to make moral contact with the destruction and its perpetrators is eminently that of an Israeli beyond the experience, not of a European Jew actually torn by it. Indeed, the peculiar structure of the novel—a brilliant but not fully worked out invention of Amichai's—provides a kind of diagrammatic illustration of the difficulties Israeli writers have in trying to imagine this ultimate catastrophe and how one can live with the knowledge of it.

The hero of Amichai's novel is a young archaeologist at the Hebrew University—quite obviously, a man dedicated to digging up buried layers of the past. Like the protagonist of virtually every Hebrew novel of consequence over the last ten years, he has gradually fallen into an unsettling sense of aimless drift after the challenging years immediately before and after Israel's independence. At the beginning of the book, we find him wondering whether he ought to stay in Jerusalem for the vacation and perhaps find some great, intoxicating love (he is married and vaguely loyal to his wife), or spend the summer in Germany confronting the murderers of his childhood companion, Ruth. The wife of a friend—we afterward discover that she is about to be committed to an asylum—tells him that he must do both these things at once. And so he does. That is, the novel splits into two alternating narratives, one continuing in the third person to report a summer of sensual abandon in Jerusalem with an American woman named Patricia, the other switching to the first person to tell the story of the same character's return to his native city of Weinberg for the purpose of

---

* Available in an English translation published by Harper and Row (New York, 1968). Since the translation is from a version revised and slightly abridged by the author, not all details which I cite from the original Hebrew edition will be found in it.

"wreaking vengeance," as he dimly and grandiosely puts it, on the Nazi murderers. The hero of the novel, to cite a mythic parallel that Amichai alludes to obliquely, is a kind of bifurcated Odysseus: he descends into the underworld in hope of encountering the spirits of the dead and learning from them his own future, and, simultaneously, he lolls in the paradisiac bed of Calypso, the alien goddess who keeps him from the responsibilities of home and people.

Amichai clearly means to suggest that both experiences— eros in the city of Jerusalem, thanatos in the town of Weinberg—must be exhausted to enable his hero to find some new point of anchorage for his life. But what actually happens in the novel is that the Jerusalem sequence is vividly and convincingly realized, while the German episodes, despite many arresting moments, occur in a hazy twilight region between memory and fantasy, history and self-dramatization. This attempt of the novelistic imagination to immerse itself in the aftermath of the horror ends up being a kind of earnest exercise in synthesizing the literature of nightmare—dramatic situations from Kafka; motifs from Rilke; and from Agnon, style (the aphorisms of the abyss), narrative technique (the expressionism of Agnon's *Book of Deeds*), and even symbolic plot outline (Agnon's *A Guest for the Night*, also about a man from Jerusalem who returns to a destroyed European hometown in a futile search for the world of his childhood). Amichai intends his protagonist to discover both the old and the new Germany, but in fact his archaeologist of the self wanders about in a Germany compounded of symbols through which historical actualities are only intermittently glimpsed. One gets the uneasy sense that events happen only in order to be available as symbols: there is a roller-skating competition in Weinberg, to serve as the occasion for reflections on the pointless way our lives go round and round in the postwar era; a little German girl is named Sybil, to trigger a meditation on pagan prophecy and apocalypse; a cynical Indian appears in Weinberg solely to gather material for a book about Despair, and to pronounce bleak epigrams on that subject.

The Jerusalem sections of the novel also reflect Amichai's

fondness for symbols, but in this case the unique city he knows so intimately affords him a very natural symbolic landscape. No one else has caught with such sharpness the bizarre, slightly mad life of the intelligentsia in Jerusalem, with its serious academic types, its bohemian poets and artists, its drifting cultists from home and abroad, sundry amateurs of Yoga, Zen, vegetarianism, and the Kabbalah. No one else has been so imaginatively alive to the uncanny suggestiveness of Jerusalem's stark location at the borders of the desert, the sky, and the enemy.

> Joel walked along, carrying the bundle of Patricia's dress under his arm. With great happiness he felt the dress and with great happiness he felt the city, its houses and empty lots, and the no-man's land beyond them. He felt the shards and rubble, the rusting oil drums, and the barbed-wire fences in which flying pieces of paper were caught as the wind shifted. No-man's land served as a kind of strainer. A strainer of hatred, of the past, of distant history. It was also the place of mines, the maps for which had been lost, so that no one knew where they were buried. And behind all the hubbub, the buildings and the walls, with no transition, the desert stretched out. All at once a desert of many hills rising in heavy, silent folds all the way to the mountains of Moab.

In passages like this, Amichai does not have to "work up" his symbols because they are already there in his city: the freight of meaning in landscape and objects is as immediately *felt* as the palpable burden of clothing imbued with Patricia's physical presence. But it is significant that the sense of reality radiates out from an object associated with sensuality; this explains much of the disparity between the two halves of the novel and, as I shall try to show, is an orientation explicitly shared by other Israeli writers in attempting to create a credible world against the unthinkable background of the Holocaust. Where horror has deadened the nerve of response to reality, made it difficult to believe in the real world, it seems as though there is a natural movement toward the primal act through which the body affirms life, in an effort to recapture the sheer sense of being alive. "They wanted to stretch out over reality," Amichai writes of his lovers, fusing the act of love with Elisha's miraculous resuscitation of the dead child in the biblical story, "eye to eye, mouth to mouth, and to give it life again with their own breath." But the miracle is not achieved, and Amichai's hero comes at some points to feel that the only fully credible reality is a purely sexual one: "The whole world seemed to Joel to be emptied, and covered over with canvas and tin and flimsy boards, like the world of stalls and stands in a fair. The last and only thing actual to him was Patricia's body. Not even her speech, but the sinking into her."

This sexual submergence, however, means forgetting both personal and collective history. Early in the novel, we are introduced to one of the protagonist's friends, a survivor of the death camps who has had the tattoo of a mermaid superimposed upon the tattooed number on his arm—not in order to obliterate the grim blue figures but to leave them just barely perceptible through the lines of the mythological female form. As the image of the ambiguous tattoo floats in and out like an apparition through both halves of the narrative, Patricia is associated with the mermaid and the sea: she is seen as a bowsprit figure on an old ship, her favorite skirt is made of sailcloth, the pitch of ecstatic fulfillment to which she brings her lover makes him think of "waves, waves" Amichai finally turns her into a mythic embodiment of all the allurements of otherness for his protagonist (with a redeeming touch of playfulness, since he seems aware of the comic aspects of our modern penchant for mythicizing experience). Patricia is American and Christian, she is imagined by her lover as a sort of female Davy Crockett, a creature of the Wild West, half lizard and half mare; she is Venice, the sea-city that is the antithesis of mountainous Jerusalem, or, alternately, she is the Jerusalem of no-man's-land (the Hebrew equivalent literally means "area of abandonment"). The sea, however, remains the chief mythic sphere with which Patricia is associated, a sea at once attractive and potentially destructive to the man whose calling is to delve into the parched earth covering the dead past. As a physician friend dabbling in Kabbalah pointedly tells Joel, "Lilith comes from the sea."

The thematic complement to this absorption of life by erotic experience in Jerusalem is the fantasy of sexlessness in the German half of the novel. The narrator dreams of becoming an "angel" (the Hebrew *malakh* also suggests "messenger," a being with a single, appointed purpose) in order to carry out unswervingly his schemes of revenge. He looks at the display in a toy-shop window and compares the hesitancy of flesh and blood with the implacable fixity of the manufactured object: "All dolls, even the most perfect ones, have no sexual organs; they are angels." The opposition between this fantasy in the town of Weinberg and the sexual actuality in Jerusalem sets up a dilemma that the resolution of the novel cannot cope with. Amichai's attempt at a denouement is to arrange for the destruction of the Jerusalem-Joel while the Weinberg-Joel comes home, having undergone some undefined catharsis, ready to resume his life, though tentative about himself and unsure of the future. The thematic development of the novel, however, suggests that there is no way out for this self divided by love and death. The only means by which Amichai's protagonist can enter into active relation with the European past, that grisly realm of mass-produced death, is to divest himself of his humanity, and this is no more possible for him than it is really desirable. But the other self, the one that revives its humanity by obliterating past and future in the sweet intensity of the sexual present, is also living a lie. The dark revelations of history from 1933 to 1945 are too radical in implication to be forgotten with impunity. This, in any case, would seem to be what is suggested by the incident with which the Jerusalem plot concludes: the dangerous buried residue of the past—an unmarked mine from another war—explodes beneath the neglectful archaeologist as he tries to untangle the knot of conflicts in his love for his mistress and his love for his wife.

During the year 1965, two more Israeli novels of unusual interest that attempt to deal with the Holocaust appeared,

Haim Gouri's *The Chocolate Deal* and Hanoch Bartov's *Wounds of Maturity.** Each of the two novels is remarkably different from Amichai's, neither could be said to be "influenced" by the earlier book, but the extent to which Gouri and Bartov share Amichai's moral problematics is equally remarkable. The authors of the two more recent novels are both native Israelis about the same age as Amichai: Bartov served in Europe with the Palestinian unit of the British Army at the end of World War II; Gouri is the author of a book-length account of the Eichmann trial and has translated Elie Wiesel into Hebrew. Of the two, Gouri is closer to Amichai in his technical handling of the European experience, possibly because he, like Amichai, is a poet writing his first novel; the strategies he adopts to get a hold on his intractable subject are more typically poetic than novelistic.

The Chocolate Deal is set in the rubble of a large German city (Berlin?) in the months immediately following the war. Rubi Kraus and Mordi Neuberg, two old friends who in their separate paths of flight have managed to survive the Nazis, meet by chance in a dreary railroad station. Rubi has schemes of establishing himself through the help of a rich uncle, one of the prominent lawyers of the city; Mordi, knowing that the uncle and his family were sent to the death camps, tries to dissuade his friend from going in search of his relatives. It does not take us long to realize that the sketchy action of the novel constitutes a parable about the moral ambiguities of survival. Of the two returned refugees, Mordi is unfluctuating in his loyalty to his slaughtered fellow Jews, but this loyalty proves to be, necessarily, a relationship impregnated with death. "There is no future in me," says Mordi (whose name may even unconsciously pun on the French *mort*). Living for him means the necessity for joining hands with the murderers and their accomplices—nature itself, the birds in the sky and the spring rain, seem to him silent collaborators with the planners of the

* Both novels were published in English translation in 1968 by Holt, Rinehart, and Winston, the Bartov book happily retitled as *The Brigade*.

Final Solution. Mordi dies mysteriously and symbolically about halfway through the book, just at the moment when Rubi is in bed with a German woman, the first woman he has had since the war. When the lights come on and the plot unfolds, she turns out to be his old mistress and former servant of his uncle's; during the war she had apparently been a kind of Gestapo camp follower, and she is now doubling as a street-walker and as a servant to the German doctor who has usurped the house of Rubi's uncle.

Because Rubi wants money, he conceives a plan of black-mailing this German doctor into issuing false medical statements to influence the price of surplus chocolate that the American occupation forces have been dumping on the local market. His course of action clearly illustrates the other half of the dilemma of survival raised by his friend Mordi. The only way to keep one's loyalty to the dead uncontaminated is to die. A Jew who wants to go on living in a world of murderers must end up cashing in somehow on the murderers' guilt—one thinks of Israel and the reparations issue—and thus must become implicated in the guilt himself. The weakness of Gouri's formulation of the moral quandary generated by the Holocaust is apparent: like most parabolic fiction, his novel states moral alternatives too sharply, not leaving a sufficient middle ground of possibilities between the extremes.

The Chocolate Deal does, however, handle its subject with an imaginative richness scarcely suggested by this abstract of its moral argument. Gouri has used his resources as a poet—in a more calculated fashion, I think, than Amichai—to create a world in which the metaphysical implications of the Holocaust will be everywhere manifest. The sense of time, after the break-down of history, is dulled, confused; time speeds up, skids along erratically, stops dead, allowing no meaningful progression. Action itself then becomes arbitrary: one act will do as well as another; fantasy, accident, and choice are indifferent alternatives; the narrated event becomes (as in Amichai) the sketching out of mere possibility, not the report of accomplished fictional fact. In this *univers concentrationnaire*, place, too, is emptied of

its distinctiveness so that one gray setting is almost interchangeable with another; and, finally, individuality is blurred, a character may have several, simultaneous identities (like Rubi's
mistress) or may be a mere counter to which some future
identity could be assigned. The bleakly elegiac prose and the
disorienting generality of descriptive viewpoint in the following
passage typify much of the novel:

> Slowly, slowly, the ways turn to meet. Time passes, false healer,
> giving to the suffering the potion of forgetfulness to quiet them,
> to take them further away. Sending the lost to sleep the very
> extended sleep, till the last trumpet. A gap yawns wider and
> wider between the rememberers and those who are remem-
> bered, and there the rivers flow, and there are the seasons of the
> year, and there the cities dark-gray in the snows, cities of marble
> and gold in the sun. In the purple conflagrations. And there
> the privilege of those who move to demur to the silence, to
> dream, to go onward.

In this world of flattened dimensions where roads, rivers,
seasons, and time all run together on the same plane of occur-
rence, even a hint of affirmation—"those who move to demur
to the silence"—is partly withheld through a kind of syntactic
reticence. A more precise syntax would imply an explicit and
coherent ordering of existence in which Gouri is unable to believe. His most distinctive stylistic trait is the verb followed
directly by an infinitive, with the logical connection between
the two suppressed, as at the beginning and end of this passage,
or in sentences like "This time is dying away to be finished."
The disjuncture here between the process and the end product
of the process, between the happening in time marked by the
temporal verb and the absolute state marked by the infinite
verb, is the quintessential expression of Gouri's post-Holocaust
world—a present which scarcely dares think of the past or hope
for the future, where one empty now crumbles into another,
ceaselessly, to the unimaginable end of time, "the last trumpet."

The Chocolate Deal suggests two ways out of this bleak
prison of the present. The first, and more convincingly realized,
avenue of escape is sexuality. Gouri's protagonist, like Ami-

chai's, plunges into the sphere of sensual otherness of an alien woman in order to revive the sense of life in himself, though the symbolic retreat from Jewish selfhood involved in the act is stated more extremely here than in Amichai because the woman in this case is directly connected with the murderers. But where Amichai imagines the act of love contracting life into the present, Gouri sees in it a moment that partakes of past and even future—always, however, in a personal or mythic sense, never historically: "On the other side of the emptied space [between their bodies] is his own private messianic era. . . . And now he is about to perform an act ancient as death, surviving beyond him." It is significant that the one moment in the novel when memory comes fully alive is Rubi's recollection of a distant night of pleasure with his uncle's maid. At other points the past is caught obliquely in confusing fragments, or, in the one case of Mordi's account of his war years, it is rehearsed consecutively in the deadened, somnambulistic voice of the present. By contrast, the details of Rubi's sensual memory are unaffected by the passage of time: the glint of the August moon through the blinds, the chill touch of the brass doorknob that turned to the left, the suntanned body against the white sheets—through these sensuous particulars the past for once becomes present.

The other gateway from the present, but this time to a historical, not merely personal, past, is through an acceptance of the terrible paradoxes of survival while actively engaging heart and mind in the fate of those who were murdered and also of those who managed to escape. It is here that Gouri is most reticent of all, perhaps because, with the kind of integrity he has, he is afraid that any affirmation of "the tragic necessity for commitment" may quickly degenerate into a slogan. This is clearly the alternative that it is most important to imagine and most difficult to imagine honestly. Though Gouri concludes his novel on a note of commitment to the martyred ones, he manages no more than a thinly symbolic gesture. Earlier in the book, Mordi had told of meeting a certain Mr. Schecter at the end of the war. Mr. Schecter, a watchsmith (obviously, the man who is to remind his fellow Jews of time and history), was genuinely concerned for Mordi, acted vaguely to tie him to his prewar past. At the end of the novel, as Rubi stands over Mordi's grave—the whole Chocolate Deal, we suddenly realize, has been a projected possibility, not an action carried out—someone calls to him, portentously, "Reuben Kraus? Mr. Schecter is looking for you." The intention here is surely admirable, but Mr. Schecter has been only a shadowy figure in the book, and I do not think this is one of those moments of achieved art that help us see into the dark places of our existential quandaries.

Hanoch Bartov's *Wounds of Maturity* is less original in technique than the other two novels, but it succeeds in throwing into sharper focus the perplexed problems of national values involved in an Israeli's attempt to relate to the grim past. Bartov's first-person narrator, the eighteen-year-old Elisha Kruk, begins his story with the words, "About the surrender." He has enlisted in the Palestinian Regiment of the British Army in hopes of redeeming his self-respect as a Jew by participating actively in the battle against his people's enemy. But his unit has not yet made contact with the German forces in Italy when the Nazi surrender is announced. This pattern of frustrated intention recurs in a series of memorable variations through the remainder of the novel. The company of Palestinian soldiers goes rolling north toward Germany, with the chalk-scrawled menace of *Die Juden kommen!* on the tarpaulin sides of their transport trucks—only to be halted at the border, where they are stationed in a small Italian town. After a delay of almost two months, the Palestinians get orders to move into Germany, but on the last night in Italy, their campsite is inundated by a flashflood, and when the self-styled avengers cross the German border, this is the figure they cut: "Along the sides of our vehicles we had stretched out lines and belts and had hung up our clothes to dry, and our bodies we covered with whatever had been rescued from the water. We looked like a traveling camp of gypsies."

This is, of course, an old story in war fiction: it goes all the way back to the farcical frustrations of Fabrice del Dongo, Stendhal's aspirant to heroism at the tail end of the Napoleonic Wars. But the familiar antiheroic theme assumes a special gravity and morally problematic nature when it is associated with an Israeli's relation to the destruction of European Jewry. Bartov's novel makes one point particularly clear: the Holocaust raises larger questions for an Israeli than for an American Jew because it casts a long shadow of doubt on the new vision of Jewish identity implicit in the creation of a modern Jewish state. If the new Jew is, ideally, a kind of reincarnation of the rebuilder of Jerusalem in Nehemiah, "one hand performing the work, the other holding his weapon," what is such a figure to make of six million of his people allowing themselves to be led off to the slaughter, and what good is his own brave posture of armed self-assertion as a response to Nazi monstrosities, for which any conceivable retribution through violence could be only the nightmare of a maniac? The point of the novel's vaguely melodramatic title (which puns ironically on an Israeli idiom for "acne") is that the young Palestinian begins to discover through his encounter with both the survivors and the perpetrators of the Holocaust who he is—that whoever he may be, he is not the man on the Zionist poster out of Nehemiah, and not so different, perhaps, from Jews in other lands.

Bartov has an extraordinary gift for inventing dramatic situations that bring into high relief the contrast between what his Palestinian soldiers really can be and what they are expected to be, by others and also by themselves. The first of these scenes takes place in a pizzeria in Bologna, where Elisha Kruk finds himself hauled into the victory celebration of a group of wildly drunken Negro soldiers. When they finally understand that he comes from Palestine, one of them hails him in the style of an evangelist preacher as "the youth from the city of Bethlehem, the birthplace of Lord Jesus our Savior." Kruk, drunk himself, is prodded into a dizzying speech on the miraculous splendors of the holy city of Bethlehem, in fact a dirty little Arab town. The tipsy hallelujah cries that punctuate Kruk's fantastic oration set the keynote for the role of the Jewish soldiers as spurious redeemers. Later, Kruk and three of his friends will come upon their first actual refugees from the camps—a group of pious Hungarian tailors sitting in a basement at their Sabbath meal, singing the traditional table-hymns about the coming of the Messiah. At the entrance of the soldiers, the tailors leap up from their places, clutch the young men to make sure of their reality; they are ready to pack, in the middle of the Sabbath, and to be led by these Jewish men of war across the sea to the Promised Land. The Palestinians, of course, can only respond lamely—the authorities will arrange these matters, one must be patient and wait for official procedures—and so the tailors' cries of enthusiasm die in their throats.

Still more disturbing for the soldiers are the encounters in which their own image of themselves as a bold new breed of Jews is threatened. Kruk and his friends meet a handful of deported Ukrainian women, sitting by the roadside cooking their morning *kasha*. The soldiers are unable to convince the women that they are members of the "Jewish Army." The women, in a kind of obscene coquetry, take this claim as some obscurely ribald joke and answer with a knowing wink: "We've seen the Jewish armies; in chariots of flame they went up to heaven, in columns of smoke." The ambiguous question of kinship with European Jewry becomes most agonizing when Kruk discovers an actual cousin in a refugee camp. His initial eagerness is dissipated in a moment as his cousin tells him nonchalantly, almost proudly, how he managed to survive by working in a crematorium. "More than anything else," Kruk says of himself, "I was filled with the terror of belonging to him. More than the shock, more than the disgust." Such inability to face the survivor, twisted as he may be by his experience, is clearly a more immediate problem for the Israeli than for the American because in Israel the survivor is everywhere.

The most crucial inadequacy, however, in the Hebrew soldiers' attempt to take hold of this unmanageable historical reality, is revealed in the fantasies of revenge to which a few of them give voice. The logical consequence of a Jew's learning to fight for himself, as others do, would seem to be that he should take bloody vengeance for himself, as others do. What will we say, wonder the angrier of the young men, when our children ask us someday why we failed to use this one possible moment of history to pay back a little for all the horrors that were done to us? "We are here as blood-redeemers. For one wild Jewish vengeance. Just once like the Tartars, like the Ukrainians, like the Germans." Or, as the chief advocate for the course of revenge puts the case with more intellectual subtlety, possibly thinking in the Nietzschean idiom of Jabotinsky's Revisionist Zionist ideology, "One can free oneself from the fear of the bestial crime only by means of bestial retribution."

But any retribution the young soldiers try to take is hesitant, bungling, and, of course, grotesquely inadequate. The one attempt at vengeance, moreover, almost carried out in the novel, provides the culmination to that series of revelatory scenes begun in the pizzeria through which the Palestinians are forced to face their own inner weakness, the uncertainty of their ideals. Elisha Kruk and his cynical (European-born) friend Brotsky have billeted themselves in the home of an SS officer who has fled, leaving behind his wife and grown daughter. From their room upstairs, Kruk and Brotsky hear two other Jewish soldiers break into the kitchen and attack the women. Brotsky sits listening intently to the struggle below with a "glassy smile." Kruk, frightened by the reflection of himself that he sees in Brotsky's expression and unnerved by the women's shrieks, seizes his rifle, rushes downstairs, and angrily orders the would-be rapists out of the house. Bartov makes it clear that Kruk's deliverance of the German women is *not* a moral act—it proceeds from weakness, just as to join the rapists would have confessed to a different kind of weakness. Kruk, like Isaac Babel's Jewish soldier, might well dream of having "the simplest of proficiencies—the ability to kill my fellow-men"; but he knows, perhaps better than the Babel character, that he is compelled by his nature and upbringing to remain achingly human in a world that is for the most part callously inhuman. "In a single moment," he comments on his response to the quaking vulnerability of the assaulted women, "all the anthems of hate were wiped away and I was once more Papa's son. Wallowing in purity. A human being. A crapped up human being. Now I know, that's what we are, condemned to go around with the divine image on our forehead like the mark of Cain."

Bartov's protagonist, like Amichai's and Gouri's, is at least temporarily pulled away from the world of harsh moral confrontations by an alien woman, in his case a sensually generous, high-class Venetian whore, appropriately named Felicia. She nearly succeeds in keeping him with her in Venice just when his company is receiving orders to move into Germany; and, later, when he tries to focus his hatred for the Germans, the memory of her vivid body intervenes and confuses him. It is clear that to luxuriate with Felicia and to violate the women of Germany are simply two different alternatives of alienation from self for the young Palestinian: he literally flees from Felicia's sun-drenched bedroom as he psychologically flees from the bestial darkness of the rape. In the end, Elisha Kruk has no choice but to go on with his old Jewish self, understanding now its terrible inadequacies, its confusions and cowardice—and, just possibly, its potential for moral sensitivity. Bartov concludes his novel by recalling, as does Amichai, the image of Lot's wife in order to suggest his protagonist's relationship with the Holocaust: " 'I will never turn my face back there,' I whisper like an incantation over the bleeding memory, but my thoughts turn into pillars of salt."

All these novels, Bartov's most explicitly, suggest the moral purpose that Hebrew fiction on the Holocaust is trying to fulfill: the writers do not seek to scare themselves or their readers with horror stories, but, recognizing the necessity to exist now in the presence of the ultimate horror, they want to see by its baleful light what a Jew can discover about himself, how he can go on with the difficult business of living unillusioned and yet responsible. The novel is an ambiguously potent means to this end. Because it creates its own world, it can place us at the nexus of time, place, and event where a dilemma raised by history is totally felt, in this way overcoming the distance of abstraction and analysis inherent in discursive treatments of the same dilemma. But because the novel necessarily manipulates the elements of its own world, it may inadvertently contrive reality, reducing it to an overly simple scheme. Both the inherent advantage in the novelistic approach to moral issues and its potential weakness are present in the three novels we have been considering, but the general effect of each of the books is clearly to bring us a little closer to the imponderable realities of recent history and to the problems of identity raised by that history. It is not easy to think of another area of contemporary Jewish culture, either in Israel or in America, where the written word and the imagined act have been used with such self-critical intentness, such freedom from moral posturing and institutional cant, or where such an unflinching effort has been made to look into the abysses flung open by the Holocaust in both the individual and the collective lives of Jews.

1966

THE ISRAELI NOVEL
1. *"The Two Generations"* (1962)

Every country is endowed with a characteristic feature by which you can easily identify it. Russia has its steppes, Italy has its gondolas. But what is the distinctive feature of this country? Perhaps there is nothing really authentic about you or the life you lead; perhaps it is an unreal life. . . . —Yitzhak Shenhar, "Country Town."

The recent American reissue of *A Whole Loaf,** Sholom J. Kahn's anthology of Israeli fiction, raises a number of questions about the kind of literature that is being created in Israel. The most obvious fact about this collection of stories—and about the Israeli literary scene as well—is that it is not a whole loaf at all, but two loaves so different from each other that they hardly seem to have been baked in the same oven. The organization of material in the Kahn collection is itself partly a concession to the profound disparity that exists between two broad modes of fiction practiced in Israel today. The first half of the anthology is devoted to "Wars and Independence" and mainly represents the younger generation of Israeli writers, that is, writers still under the age of forty when the volume was originally published in Tel Aviv in 1957. The second half of the book, entitled "Backgrounds," is, with one exception, the work of the older literary generation. It is ironically appropriate that this second section should be bracketed with two stories by S. Y. Agnon. For though the seventy-four-year-old master of Hebrew fiction was nurtured in roughly the same cultural environment as the other writers of his generation, his moral and artistic concerns and his technical virtuosity lead him both further back

* *A Whole Loaf: Stories from Israel,* edited by Sholom J. Kahn (New York: Vanguard Press, 1962).

and further forward than his close contemporaries; he is at once more distant than they and closer to the younger writers.

Every literature, of course, has more or less recognizable literary generations, usually defined by the inevitable movement of rebellion by the younger writers against the tastes, standards, and objectives of their immediate predecessors. But the literary situation in Israel is in some respects unique. To get an idea of the position in which a young Israeli novelist finds himself, one must imagine writers with the interests, say, of Malamud, Bellow, or Styron, setting out to create their novels of moral quest when their older contemporaries are people like Fielding, Smollett, and Goldsmith.

Though some qualification would have to be made, it is not misleading to think of the Hebrew literary generation now in its sixties as deriving from the same world as Peretz, Sholem Aleichem, and certainly Isaac Bashevis Singer. The typical Sabra writer, on the other hand, has grown up in Mandatory Palestine in a socialist youth movement, worked for a while on a kibbutz, fought in the Israeli Army and perhaps earlier in the British Army, supported himself with a variety of odd jobs ranging from manual labor to journalism and high-school teaching. The limiting pressures of his native milieu thrust against—but do not mold—the contours of his personality: in most cases he has outgrown the Sabra's pose of toughness, his strident self-assertiveness, and is self-consciously attempting to overcome his provincialism as well. The writer's attitude toward the traditional Jewish life that used to exist in the diaspora is not necessarily negative—as is often claimed—but is certainly unconcerned. East-European Jewry, by and large, is simply beyond the horizons of his own life. The language he writes in is the language he has always spoken—a new Hebrew whose vocabulary, grammar, syntax, and idioms are often determined by its present-day speakers and whatever languages they have brought with them to Hebrew. This modern Hebrew, of course, takes advantage of linguistic resources from the Bible, the Talmud, the Midrash, even the prayer book, but a novelist who writes in it is as far away from the older stylists who model their language on tradition as Malamud's prose is from Fielding's.

A *Whole Loaf* gives a reasonably fair idea of the relative success or failure of Israeli writers in representing Israeli life, though some details of the picture suggested by the fifteen stories will have to be corrected. Except for certain peripheral areas the older writers are quite incapable of capturing the new accents and rhythms, the distinctive nuances in feeling and thought that characterize the contemporary Israeli scene. The younger writers, on the other hand, continue to fumble—with considerable intentness—for ways to bring their awareness of themselves and their culture into sharp literary focus.

Flipping through the "Backgrounds" section of A *Whole Loaf*, and thinking back over the novels located in Israel written by the older Hebrew writers (Agnon always excepted), I am led to propose the following rule of thumb: when an older Hebrew writer sets his narrative in Israel, he either succeeds by selecting an enclave of life in Israel which is not Israeli and therefore is in some sense familiar ground to him, or he fails by writing a story with such a thin social texture that it could fit almost anywhere, but nowhere in particular. The latter alternative is seductive to the many derivative writers in contemporary Hebrew letters; their imaginations seem principally engaged in imitating a literary model—or more often, an amalgam of models—rather than in transcribing real human problems in real human situations. Two painfully clear examples in the Kahn anthology are the stories by Yehuda Yaari and Yisrael Zarchi; though both are set in Jerusalem, the only detectable local atmosphere is a certain odor of pulp magazines compounded with a mustiness of late nineteenth-century continental fiction.

The success of the other strategy is attested by several stories of the older writers in A *Whole Loaf*. Pieces like Haim Hazaz' "The Lord Have Mercy," Yaakov Churgin's "Reb Shmelke of Safed," and Yehoshua Bar-Yosef's "The Lateborn" have a distinctive warmth and charm which should be familiar to anyone even casually acquainted with Yiddish literature. Like so many Yiddish stories, these examples of "Israeli" fiction have little plot, no tight structure, no crisis, moral or otherwise; they seem to stand apart from any main tradition of Western fiction. The stories are pleasantly ambling sketches of colorful folk types—and the types themselves are familiar from Yiddish literature: the long-suffering pure-hearted simpleton, the quixotic ne'er-do-well, the genuinely loving couple constantly at swords' ends. A writer does not have to have grown up in Eastern Europe in order to go in for this kind of old-world art. As a matter of fact, both Churgin and Bar-Yosef are native Palestinians; but Churgin was born at the turn of the century and Bar-Yosef, a decade younger, was raised in the old Orthodox community of Safed. There are abundant pockets of old-world life in Israel: whether they derive from Galicia or Lithuania or Yemen, they all have the same appeal of quaintness for the practicing "folk" artists and literary ethnologists among Hebrew writers.

The career of Haim Hazaz, generally considered the most important of the older writers after Agnon, illustrates with paradigmatic clarity how the novelists oriented toward the Old World have responded to the challenge of Israeli reality. Hazaz is a writer with great gifts for lyric description, for bold caricature, and for lively characterization. A good part of his earlier work concerns itself with the portrayal of colorful figures from the East-European *shtetl*. Later, as a resident of Palestine and Israel, Hazaz began to devote his abundant energies to his portraits—the word is inevitable with such a writer—of Yemenite Jewry, both in Yemen (the *Yaish* trilogy) and in Israel (*Mori Said*, available in an English translation by Ben Halpern). The transition, of course, was not from diaspora to Israel, but from one kind of Jewish folk-material to another. When Hazaz tries to deal with the more characteristic aspects of modern Israel (as in the volume of stories, A *Belt of Constellations*, published in 1958), his work is much flatter and suffers more obviously from ideological tendentiousness. Hebrew critics like to praise Hazaz for his "vivid depiction of the life of the Yemenites." To an American critic this is likely to seem a rather limited and anachronistic achievement in the middle of the twentieth century. To a young Israeli writer, it is likely to seem that way, too. In any case, the older writers who spend their energies on quaint and loving portraits of quaint and lovable types can teach the young novelist nothing about how to render his own problematic world.

A young Israeli setting out to be a writer is confronted with a further difficulty—or at least annoyance—from which creative artists in the West are comparatively free. While he is doing his best simply to probe with honesty and intelligence the reality in which he finds himself, something more is often expected from him—by many critics, by older writers, by the press, by educators, by his party (if he has one), by the regime. Modern Hebrew literature, from its beginnings in Central and Eastern Europe, was to a great extent publicistic in nature; by the latter half of the nineteenth century, it had become the handmaiden of nationalism for many Jews: Ahad Ha-am in the Odessa of the nineties could feel justified in rejecting for publication in his *Ha-Shiloakh* some fine lyric poems by Bialik because they did nothing to heighten national consciousness. It is hardly surprising that in an Israel of the Age of Ideology there are circles—often the product, in fact, of Ahad Ha-am's cultural nationalism—that preserve this quasi-propagandistic notion of the function of literature. The whole notion derives, I suppose, from a European and especially Russian conception of the political responsibilities of literature, but if this helps explain the phenomenon historically, it hardly justifies it.

The persistence of such an attitude was made extremely clear by the furor raised over the publication in 1958 of S. Yizhar's long novel about the Israeli-Arab War, *The Days of Ziklag*. Though Yizhar's book suffers from some artistic uncertainty and too much verbiage, it is a strikingly revealing moral document. Yizhar's young soldiers, both in their interior monologues and in their lengthy discussions, lay bare all the pained questionings and radical self-doubts of sensitive Israeli youth: about the significance of statehood, about their Jewishness and their cultural future, about the existence of any certain values by which they can live. While the novel had many enthusiastic defenders, particularly among the younger intellectuals, it was

denounced by most of the older critics as "cynical" or "nihilistic," and it was turned down for the coveted Bialik Prize largely
because, as one of the judges asserted, it "betrayed" the brave
Israeli youth that had fought in the War of Independence.

There is, moreover, little indication that this demand for
good Zionists and good Jews in Hebrew literature has relented
since 1958. In April, 1962, at the festive twentieth convention
of the Hebrew Writers' Association, the younger novelists and
poets found themselves assaulted from two sides. The convention began with a message from Ben-Gurion which sharply
criticized Hebrew writers for their lack of social responsibility,
for their indifference to the great national effort of Israel's Ingathering of Exiles. Then Haim Hazaz, in the opening address,
castigated with equal vehemence both the younger writers for
turning their backs on the riches of Jewish tradition and the
Israeli public for its lack of interest in Hebrew books.

It is true that literature in Israel must struggle to keep its
own footing in the tide of translated culture that floods its
relatively tiny reading audience. But it is also true that the
indigenous literature of Israel often seems pale and uninterest-
ing not because its writers have failed to be loyally Israeli or
authentically Jewish, but because they have not yet found
adequate ways to be themselves in literature. The problem is not
that "there is nothing really authentic about you or the life you
lead," in the words of the protagonist of one story in A *Whole
Loaf*, but that the younger Israeli writers are only beginning to
discover coherent literary forms for their lives.

One fact that is clear about the novels and stories of this
younger generation is that their authors are honestly trying to
find what they can or should expect of themselves instead of
attempting to write what others may expect of them. For example, there is not the slightest echo of patriotic drumbeating
among their stories in A *Whole Loaf*. In the "Wars and Independence" section, each of the younger writers finds that war
tests traditional values and brings moral ambivalences or con-
flicting allegiances into high tension; and much the same moral
tenor is found in their authors' longer works. One finds the

characteristic tone in the battle-hour reflections of the protagonist in "The Living and the Dead," an excerpt from S. Yizhar's first novel, *The Grove on the Hill:*

> . . . you remember that there are others like you and they haven't forgotten you, and the job you're doing and your own life are part and parcel of the big undertaking, and so on and so forth; and yet for some reason these are only fine phrases that are far from the truth. For the heart feels sour, so sour, far beyond any supposed deeds of daring, beyond sacrifice or all kinds of things; and you have to hide this well, because you're among people who believe in and look up to you. . . .

The passage illustrates both the moral integrity and the artistic weakness which characterize the work of Yizhar and his close contemporaries. One often has the feeling that these writers—particularly when they move beyond the short story to the novel—are unable yet to establish a necessary distance between themselves and their narrative. In their intent desire to grapple with their own moral problems, they frequently neglect the artistic demands of fiction, so that instead of structured novels with individualized characters and realized social settings, they are likely to end up with long, amorphous dialogues or monologues in which faceless voices crying out in a void discuss the moral dilemmas which beset the writers. Yizhar, who is probably the most talented and is certainly the most ambitious of the younger novelists, still suffers from this tendency to slide into formlessness; eleven years after *The Grove on the Hill*, it persists as the chief weakness of *The Days of Ziklag*, despite the strands of leitmotif with which he tries to hold together the twelve hundred pages of his later novel.

It is worth noting in this respect that of the fiction included in *A Whole Loaf*, Yizhar's piece is the only one—again with the exception of Agnon's stories—that shows any experimenting with literary form. While it would be silly to want or expect Israeli fiction to be particularly avant-garde, the timidity or indifference of the younger writers in exploring the medium in which they work often results in a failure on their part to develop an original style. That is to say, none of these writers has adequately reproduced in language the distinctive texture of the world around him. Yizhar comes closest, but as the passage quoted from "The Living and the Dead" indicates, he does not seem to have really worked out what he wants to do technically with the stream-of-consciousness form, or rather, with the rough approximation of it which he uses. The presumable justification for his blurring of syntactical connections, his redundancies, his sprawling, ungainly sentences, is that this is the way people think. But, in fact, Yizhar's sentences are far too conversational, too much like slack monologue.

The Days of Ziklag, impressive a book as it is for what it has to say, similarly put off many intelligent readers in Israel by its awkward manner. The long interior monologues are sometimes so amorphous, and so undifferentiated from one character to the next, that one has to look back to the beginning of the chapter to recall who is supposed to be thinking. Yizhar is particularly effective in reproducing the impact of fear and the weight of boredom upon a soldier's awareness, and he shows real virtuosity in his detailed lyric descriptions of natural settings. However, he will have to develop a more disciplined and resourceful technique to carry out his intentions as a novelist.

Two names of the younger generation often mentioned with—or after—Yizhar's are Moshe Shamir and Natan Shaham. Each is represented in A Whole Loaf by a well-told war story, though Shamir's piece is flawed at points by melodramatic clichés. In their longer narratives, both Shamir and Shaham have suffered from the typical failure to achieve sufficient artistic distance from what they were writing. That You Are Naked (1958), one of the most recent novels of the prolific Shamir, illustrates this general weakness with great clarity. The novel is meant to present a young Israeli trying to define himself as an individual against the pressures of a group—in this case, his youth movement. Like a number of novels by the younger writers in Israel (including Yizhar's major work), all the principal characters are adolescents: they are precisely at the age of confused seeking for values and for an acceptable definition of self. The hero of That You Are Naked is the most thinly veiled autobiographical figure: his name is Moshe Avni (both *Shamir* and *Avni* suggest "stone" in Hebrew); he was born in the same year as Shamir; like his author, he has grown up in Tel Aviv and is a member of a left-wing youth movement. Moshe Avni, moreover, takes frequent pains to remind the reader what his story is all about: "With desperate persistence we are searching for ourselves, as though we were seeking a sanction for our existence, as though without some sanction we would be thrown out into the cold." This slow-moving, repetitious book reads more like a personal declaration of independence than a novel; there is little evidence that the novelist has made as yet the subtle but crucial distinction between life and literature.

The Poor Man's Wisdom (1960), Natan Shaham's latest novel, offers a somewhat different illustration of precisely the same failing. There is nothing obviously autobiographical about Shaham's novel, but again the writer is bent on the pursuit of his own existential problems to the manifest neglect of the novelistic demands of his book. The protagonist of *The Poor Man's Wisdom* is a Polish Jew who has devoted his life to the Communist Party. Finally disillusioned with the party, he escapes to Israel in the hours of grace in 1956 and goes to live on a kibbutz. Through a long series of unwieldy flashbacks, through repeated discussion and debate with his old party friends and with the kibbutzniks, he ponders the problem of individual conscience within a party discipline, the difficulty of the intellectual in adapting to communal life and manual labor, the force of moral obligations outside the sphere of political activity. In all this earnest but somewhat tedious dialectic, elements like plot and character receive only the most perfunctory attention, and again one feels that the book is not quite a novel.

One might expect that the younger Israeli writers would turn for help in their technical difficulties to the one major creative figure of the older generation, S. Y. Agnon. Yet the fact is that Agnon, at least until very recently, has had no appreciable impact upon them. The reasons for his lack of influence are clear. However profound his artistic vision may be, it is also highly idiosyncratic, intimately connected with his own background and personality. Agnon's stylized, traditional Hebrew is, moreover, centuries removed from the language of the Sabras, and his imagination was nourished in a Galician study-house, not on a collective farm in the Negev or in a war against the Arabs.

Nevertheless, there are some significant points of contact between Agnon's world and that of the native Israeli writers. Like them, he is essentially concerned with moral issues; that is to say, at the center of his work stands an individual who is continually faced with critical choices or imperatives. And Agnon, for all his attachment to tradition, often reveals a disturbed sense of ambivalence toward values about which tradition or society claims to be sure. His great theme of radical homelessness even provides a specific parallel to the sense of disinheritance and moral isolation which makes itself felt in much of the writing of the younger generation. Yitzhak Kummer, the doomed outsider torn apart between two worlds in Agnon's *Just Yesterday*, is no less an Isaac bound for a meaningless immolation than the soldiers in *The Days of Ziklag* or the young socialists in *That You Are Naked*. (All three novels use the Binding of Isaac as a central motif.)

Even apart from his affinities in outlook, it seems almost inevitable that Agnon's fertile symbolic imagination and fine control of tone and style would eventually tempt younger Hebrew writers to borrow and even to imitate. Three recent pieces of Hebrew fiction suggest the possibility that Agnon's influence may prove to be more fruitful than one would have initially supposed. Yehuda Amichai's *In This Terrible Wind* (1961), Yoram Kaniuk's *The Acrophile* (published in English in 1961—the Hebrew original has not yet appeared), and Aharon Meged's *Fortunes of a Fool** (1959) make use in varying degree of Agnonesque effects and techniques, particularly those that come from the rich antirealist and symbolic vein of Agnon's work.

* An English translation was published by Random House in 1962.

In This Terrible Wind is the most radically experimental
and also by far the most uneven of the three books. Amichai,
who has acquired considerable reputation as a poet in the last
few years, attempts in this volume of stories to apply some of
the methods of poetry to first-person narrative. Many of the
longer stories wander unsteadily through a plotless, characterless
vacuum, but a few of the shorter pieces are quite striking. One
is tempted to describe Amichai's world as surrealistic, but it
would be more accurate to say that reality is essentially meta-
phorical for him: people become metaphors and metaphors
become people, every element of experience demands a symbolic reading. Amichai diligently explores the possibilities of
each passing comparison: "[When the war was over] we scattered like papers after the elections, in every direction. Only the
dead were cast into the dark ballot box, only they influenced
what would be." And he finds tongues in trees, sermons in
stones, and, generally, gloom in everything.

> When I drew near [the sickbed], I heard the great oxygen
> bomb whispering. It used to be that an angel stood by the
> beds of the sick. Now there are bombs filled with whispering
> oxygen. Divers and pilots are also given oxygen tanks. Where
> will my father go? Maybe he'll dive, maybe he'll climb. Any-
> way, he'll leave us.

This sort of brooding over the mysteries of metaphor sometimes
occurs in Agnon, though it is certainly never given such free
rein. Be that as it may, the entire dreamlike mode of narration
of *In This Terrible Wind* is in some degree inspired by the
expressionistic stories of Agnon's *Book of Deeds*. Though Amichai's touch is often unsure, he has made a brave attempt to
create a new kind of story which can serve as an artistically
coherent expression of his own inner world.

Yoram Kaniuk, on the other hand, has a firmer grasp of his
method: *The Acrophile* is a spare but skillfully managed novel.
It also gives evidence of considerable technical indebtedness to
Agnon. Kaniuk's tone is often reminiscent of the older writer's:
it has many of the same resonances, even much the same pace,

the same quiet control, ranging from wry humor to muted lyricism. This, for example, is the way Kaniuk conveys the pain of separateness of a couple who will soon be divorced.

> Mira remained silent. I put my arms around her and tried to kiss her. She was cold. I let her go, feeling like a fool. Two strangers, we walked together through the morning chill, the play of wind and trees, the game of the yellow leaves on the sidewalk.

And this is how Agnon, in "Metamorphosis," one of the stories included in A *Whole Loaf*, presents the same emotion in a couple who have just been divorced.

> The sun was about to set. In the fields the wheat swayed silently, and the sunflowers gazed one-eyed out of their darkening yellow faces. Hartmann stretched his hand out into the vacant air and caressed Toni's shadow.

Some of the situations and symbols in *The Acrophile* also distinctly call Agnon to mind. The protagonist of *The Acrophile* is involved in the symbolically significant work of piecing together "the language of the black cave people," just as Adiel Amzeh in Agnon's "Forevermore" is trying to reconstruct the ancient civilization of Gumlidata, and just as Dr. Ginath in Agnon's longer story, "Edo and Enam," unearths the two archaic languages which provide the link "between the very beginnings of history and what preceded." Or again, when Kaniuk's Daan locks himself out of his apartment on his wedding day and all circumstances conspire against his getting back in, readers of Agnon will recall a whole series of closely similar situations in *The Book of Deeds*. With all this, I do not mean to imply that Kaniuk is a derivative writer, merely that he appears to have borrowed a little and learned a great deal from the older Hebrew novelist.

Agnon's influence on Aharon Meged is more tangential, perhaps no more than awakening him to the possibilities of adapting a Kafkaesque narrative to Hebrew fiction and Israeli reality. In any case, *Fortunes of a Fool* derives much more clearly from Kafka than from Agnon. The presence of the

German writer in fact makes itself felt with awkward obtrusive-
ness in the first section of Meged's novel. The nameless protagonist is invited by somebody called "B." to a meeting of the
Society of Evildoers; after he has been laughed out of the meeting for claiming he has a conscience, he tries desperately to win
acceptance from the Society, but his efforts end in a shattering
fiasco when he tumbles from the lofty scaffolding where he was
to give a speech on the Society's behalf. As Meged works further into his novel, the symbolic machinery creaks less, and the
protagonist who began as a pawn in a Kafkaesque chess game
turns out to be a rather believable *homme moyen moral* involved in an absorbing struggle against both the pressures of
conformity from without and the limpness of his own timidity.

It is significant that Meged, in following Kafka's conception of the novel as a moral fable, manages in the end to get
across a much sharper sense than his more conventional colleagues of the distinctive reality of present-day Israel. Perhaps
he owes part of his success to the entrenched bureaucratic way
of life in modern socialist Israel. Kafka, of course, was himself a
bureaucrat (as is the hero of *Fortunes of a Fool*), and the kind
of novel he created reflects in many ways the peculiar character
of this experience. In a bureaucracy, people have initials instead of names. In a bureaucracy—as anyone who has ever
dealt with Israeli officialdom certainly knows—the individual
is at the mercy of a madly confused machine in which no part
accepts ultimate responsibility and from which on occasion
inscrutable decrees are issued without warning or possibility of
revocation. For an Israeli, there could be no more appropriate
image for Judgment Day than the one offered by Meged's
novel: an obdurate tax-examiner, clutching the dossier that con-
tains the protagonist's entire adult life, seems quite literally to
hold the hero's fate in his unrelenting hands.

The case of *Fortunes of a Fool* could be particularly instructive to the writers we have been considering. While bor-
rowing generously from a European writer, Meged has not been
solely imitative and, in fact, has managed to invoke and explore
his own national climate with considerable fidelity. The small

strip of Hebrew-speaking culture at the east end of the Mediterranean does not have to be engulfed by the imposing cultural blocs of the West. At the present, there are at least a few hopeful indications that the new Israeli fiction may be developing its own distinctive voices.

1962

2. *"Language and Realism"* (1966)

In order to make any sense of what is happening to the novel in Israel, one must take full account of the stubborn and peculiar fact that Israeli novels are written in Hebrew. Because of the unique history of the language and the unique process of revival which it is still undergoing, this has rather more complicated implications than, say, the fact that American novels are written in English. The anomalies of the Hebrew writer's linguistic situation play an important role in determining his relationship with other generations of writers in his own literature, the lines of influence from the outside that are open or largely closed to him, and even, to some extent, the particular modes of fiction he will adopt. To understand why this should be so, it will be helpful to review a few essential facts of Hebrew literary history.

The East-European intellectuals who formed the nucleus of modern Jewish immigration to Palestine more than half a century ago did not arrive in the new pioneering community and then as a result begin to write fiction in Hebrew. Almost the opposite is true: it is partly as a result of Hebrew literary activity in nineteenth-century Russia and Poland that the fantastic idea was conceived of reestablishing a Hebrew-speaking culture on the soil of Palestine. Short Hebrew fiction of a crude sort was being written in Galicia by the 1820's, and the first identifiable Hebrew novel was published in 1854, decades before people dreamed that anywhere in the world toddlers would be prattling, cabbies cursing, professors lecturing, in Hebrew. By the first decade of the twentieth century, Hebrew literary centers in Odessa, Vilna, Warsaw, and elsewhere had produced a surprising variety of writers of fiction—most of them, intent, imitative, and imaginatively limited, but among them one novelist of real stature, a number of sensitive short-story writers, and even a serious experimenter in a kind of stream-of-consciousness fiction. All of this creative work took place, it must be remembered, in a milieu where the common spoken language was Yiddish, not Hebrew.

The whole development, then, of the Hebrew novel, from its beginnings until the 1940's, went against the linguistic grain that has been one of the generic distinctions of the novel. For the general movement of the novel, as we are often reminded, has been to narrow the gap between literary language and the language of everyday experience: that is why the genre typically begins with, and frequently recurs to, fictional memoirs, letters, journals, "true histories," fiction presented in the vocabulary and form of documentary fact. The earlier Hebrew novelists, on the other hand, were forced to work in exactly the opposite direction: by writing in Hebrew about people whose language was in fact Yiddish, or, occasionally, Russian, Polish, German, they had to produce what was manifestly no more than an "as-if reality," in the phrase of the Israeli critic, Dov Sadan. Where the European novel often tended to camouflage its own status as invented literature, the Hebrew novel had little choice but to flaunt its literary nature, to find ways of converting its obtrusive literariness into an artistic resource. It is understandable, then, that the first Hebrew novel, Avraham Mapu's *Love of Zion*, is historical—an involuted and improbable romance set in Jerusalem in the time of Isaiah, written in a style that is a sort of impassioned pastiche of biblical phrases. Mapu's language was hardly a suitable instrument for rendering contemporary realities with minute particularity, and when the Hebrew novel came of age toward the end of the century in the work of Mendele Mocher Seforim ("Mendele the Bookseller," pen name for S. Y. Abramowitz), it was through a recapitulation of the whole range of Hebrew literary history, a bold synthesis of the language of the Bible, the Talmud, rabbinic legend, of the medieval exegetes and philosophers, of the prayer book and later liturgical poetry, of moral tracts and legal codes, even of communal records. Using all these materials, Mendele was able to re-create with remarkable sensuous particularity the world of Russian Jewry in which he lived, peopling his books with Dickensian caricatures vividly and lovingly rendered down to the last bristling wart on the nose and the last grease spot on the hem of the kaftan. But Mendele was always highly conscious that the components of his style were traditional and literary, and his practice and achievement fully established the peculiar central tradition of the Hebrew novel in which the principal rhetorical device is literary allusion.

The novel in general has, quite obviously, taken as its subject the new problematic look assumed by the human condition in a secularized world where traditional ideals, religious or otherwise, no longer obtain. What sets the Hebrew novel apart is that its language, until fairly recently, has been to a large extent the language of piety, suffused with the associations of a religious tradition, so that, typically, a continual tension—usually a pointedly ironic tension—is set up between the reminiscence of lofty spiritual ideals in the language and the fallen nature of the world which the language describes. Now, this allusive mode of fiction is rapidly disappearing from the novel in Israel as an increasing proportion of the writers are native Israelis, who have acquired their Hebrew naturally as a spoken language; the transition is itself one of the problematic aspects of the Israeli literary scene. Writers now in their forties or younger make only occasional and fragmentary use of the old allusive mode, while it continues to be a standard practice of the elder novelists still active, who, for the most part, are European-born and so have learned their Hebrew first from sacred texts. The result is that by and large there is no common artistic language shared by literary generations in Israel, and as the younger writers have come to dominate the scene during the last two decades, they have found themselves in the unenviable position of initiating, tentatively and unsurely, their own "tradition" of the Hebrew novel, every five years or so.* This disparity is heightened by the fact that the older generation includes one figure who is indisputably a great novelist— the seventy-eight-year-old Shmuel Yosef Agnon—while the younger group has so far produced no more than some very interesting possibilities and uneven achievements.

Agnon, who was raised in a pious and scholarly household in a small town in Galicia, has a masterly knowledge of the varied literature of Jewish tradition, legal and legendary, moral and mystic, and his highly stylized language, with its predominantly medieval coloration, represents the consummate achievement of the allusive mode in Hebrew fiction. For this very reason, his books tantalize, exasperate, and finally defy translation; if the words can be more or less translated, their complex allusiveness must be almost entirely abandoned and with it much of the pointedness and poignancy of his artful, painstakingly polished prose. Let me try to show how this distinctively Hebrew rhetorical strategy works by offering an extended passage together with some detailed comment on its allusive play of language. I shall quote the opening paragraph of Agnon's long novel, *Just Yesterday* (1945), set in Palestine around 1907, when Agnon himself first immigrated; the translation is, alas, my own because, as with most of Agnon's major work, no English version is yet available:

> Like the rest of our brothers, the men of our redemption, immigrants of the Second Wave, Yitzhak Kummer left his

* The earlier section of this essay, pp. 181–194, gives a more detailed account of the gap between literary generations.

country, his birthplace, and his city and went up to the Land
of Israel to build it from its destruction and to be rebuilt
by it. As far back as he could think, our friend Yitzhak had
not let a day pass on which he failed to meditate upon the Land.
Like a dwelling-place of blessing the whole Land seemed to him
and all its inhabitants like the blessed of the Lord. Its settlements were hidden in the shadow of vineyards and olive trees,
all the fields were decked with produce, the trees crowned with
fruit, the valleys covered with flowers, while forest trees swayed
and the sky was all pure blue and every house was filled with
song. During the days, people plowed and sowed and planted
and reaped, plucked the grapes and picked the olives, threshed
the wheat and tread the winepress. At eventide, each and every
one would sit under his vine and under his fig tree, his wife
and sons and daughters around him, all happy over their work,
rejoicing in their repose, recalling the days past in the diaspora,
as one will remember in the hour of joy the days of sorrow and
so take a double pleasure in the present bounty. An imaginative
fellow was Yitzhak—out of the place his heart desired he
would conjure up imagined things.

The placid progress here of Agnon's prose through the
luminous details of a Zionist idyll to the final modest demurral
is perhaps meant temporarily to disguise but certainly not to
dilute the acid irony that saturates the whole passage. Some
notion of the subsequent course of the novel will make the
particular bite of that irony more palpable. The protagonist's
name is Kummer—which, as the verbal noun in Yiddish for
"one who comes" and as the German word for "grief," suggests
both major aspects of his emblematic role. Kummer's first name
is Yitzhak, or Isaac, and like the biblical Isaac, he will be bound
for sacrifice on "one of the mountains"—tradition identifies the
vague phrase in Genesis with the Temple Mount and he actually dies in Jerusalem—in a twentieth-century Land of Israel
where there is no heavenly voice to cry out at the critical
moment and revoke the senseless immolation. (It is worth
noting that other Hebrew novelists have since used this same
motif of the outrageous Binding of Isaac in a way that is

precisely analogous to the mythic motif of the secular Christ, the meaningless crucifixion, which so many modern writers in other literatures have employed.) The fact that this Isaac is "one who comes" only emphasizes his permanent location as an outsider, a man who comes from the outside and remains there. Though he "goes up" to the Land, in the traditional Hebrew idiom, to redeem himself and his people, his coming is actually much like that of Kafka's K. in *The Castle*—nobody expects him, there is no clear place for him or justification for his presence. Like K., the land surveyor, Yitzhak tries to demonstrate that he has a calling which connects him with the land, but his attempt to become an agricultural worker is a pathetic failure and he ends up, ironically, as a house painter, covering natural surfaces with artificial substance, hiding realities with façades. The Land itself, far from corresponding to Yitzhak's idyllic vision, is a place of spiritual confusion, cynicism, moral cowardice, hypocrisy, fanaticism. The protagonist discovers, moreover, that there is not even one Land of Israel but two: the new city of Jaffa, with its rootless intellectuals, the old city of Jerusalem, with its religious obscurantists. Yitzhak is tossed between the two like a shuttlecock, and though he dies in one, the novel suggests that both offer but different faces of the same inevitable destruction for the man who has come.

By now, the general force of the irony in the opening passage of the novel should be clear. But almost every phrase in the paragraph is a telling one by virtue of some pointed ironic reference, and in noting the allusions, which range from Genesis to Zionist catchwords, we can see how precisely Agnon characterizes Yitzhak's mental world and the quixotic nature of his ideals. Most of the reminiscences of biblical verses in the passage should be recognizable even in the English version, and they need only be mentioned briefly. Yitzhak Kummer leaves "his country, his birthplace," like Abraham, but he will find no providential God in the promised land with Whom to seal an eternal covenant. He imagines the barren, strife-ridden Palestine in language recalling the visions of pastoral harmony in Psalms and in the Prophets—"like a dwelling-place of blessing

. . ."—and he mentally invokes the verbal formula of the Book of Kings for perfect peace and prosperity—"each man under his vine and under his fig tree." A less obvious biblical reference is in the initial phrase, which echoes, "your brothers, the men of your redemption" of Ezekiel 11:15, part of a prophecy of the return to Zion.

More of the allusions, however, are postbiblical. The pioneer families sit together "happy over their work, rejoicing . . ." a parallelism that recalls a Mishnaic phrase used in a climactic prayer for the restoration of Zion from the Passover home-service. Yitzhak Kummer comes to the Land "to build it from its destruction," a recurrent idiom of messianic aspiration in rabbinic legend. Moreover, this man who is to be utterly shattered longs "to build . . . and to be rebuilt," in the words of a popular Zionist song, once danced enthusiastically to the step-hop of the hora. Even the list of verbs specifying agricultural activities is rich with associations for Yitzhak: he would know these words from having studied the agricultural tractates of the Mishnah, which preserve a vocabulary intimately connected with farming in ancient Palestine, a vocabulary that reflects the Hebrew farmer's closeness to the soil in its specialized verbs (of course, untranslatable) for the harvesting of grapes, olives, grain.

What is most difficult to describe is the subtle kind of irony generated in the passage by what might be called the allusiveness of tone. Through the amalgam of styles in the Hebrew, one gets the sense of a pious narrator—or rather, "as-if" pious—assuming the modes of address and the idioms of a traditional tale of wonders wrought for God's glory. The terms, for example, connected with "imagination" at the end of the paragraph are taken from the vocabulary of the medieval moralists. The use at the beginning of "our brothers, the men of our redemption," though it is biblical, as we have seen, also suggests something of the assumption of devout solidarity one finds in the language of the Hasidic tales: "our brothers" is a standard usage in this folk literature, and "men of our redemption" recalls in form the common Hasidic idiom, "men of our peace," so that the whole phrase becomes a kind of "translation" into the language of piety of Zionist ideals. Since the novel will show the terrifying emptiness of the new "redemption," the awful lack of true solidarity, and much more, the ultimate effect of Agnon's assuming this mask—it is his usual one—of traditional narrator writing for a God-fearing world is not only ironic but also a little eerie. Through the ironic contrast, Agnon forces us continually to feel the full nakedness of living in an inimical world shorn of the innocence and wholeness of piety.

This consideration of the beginning of *Just Yesterday* should indicate that Agnon's central achievement is not one that lends itself to definition primarily in terms of influences from European literature. Agnon does know German literature well, he lived in Germany from 1913 to 1924, and it would be surprising if he registered no response at all in his work to the exciting developments in German fiction of the earlier twentieth century. Many critics have noted affinities between Agnon and Kafka; Agnon has even written expressionist stories that are quite close to Kafka in form as well as theme. And from the outset of his career, he has been so intrigued with the possibilities of building fiction around symbolic leitmotif that he must have at least followed with great interest the experiments in symbol and motif of Thomas Mann.

Agnon's imagination, however, is too vigorously original, and his practice as a writer is too deeply involved in the distinctive literature of Jewish tradition, to make any large aspect of his work unambiguously attributable to a European source. What one can say with certainty is that there are some significant affinities—as well as decisive differences—between Agnon and many of the European writers who in the first decades of this century created the literature we still think of as revolutionarily modern. Like Kafka, Mann, Proust, and so many writers of this period, Agnon experienced in his formative years the radical breakdown of an older social and cultural order that had seemed to him to be solid, protective, relatively harmonious. The fact that he grew up in a largely Jewish town around the turn of the century, at a period when the dissolution of the traditional values of old-world Judaism was advancing rapidly, had the effect of putting him at one of the symptomatic centers of historical change and cultural decay. Themes of tragic separation and collapse of values appear even in his earliest work, before World War I, but like so many other writers, Agnon saw in the War the great symbolic embodiment of the modern reign of moral chaos, and so the War, destroyer of houses—an archetypal event for Agnon—of men, and of ways of life, became a recurrent presence in his work. He shares with Mann, Eliot, Joyce, and others a fascination with symbol and myth because for him, too, these afford a means of holding together imaginatively the pieces of a fragmented world and because he, too, participates in what Lionel Trilling has called the "spiritual" quality of modern literature—which is to say, he is always interested in relating individual experience to some ultimate order of significance, in setting man against the backdrop of eternity, and symbols help him to do this.

But if the symbolic and mythic aspects of Agnon's writing link him with the creators of the modern movement in European literature, they are also the hallmarks of his distinctiveness. His intimate acquaintance with the rich lore of Jewish tradition means that he draws many of his motifs, images, archetypes, from a body of "mythology" that is simply unknown to Western writers. His own symbolic inventiveness, moreover, is extraordinary, as is his interest in exploring a wide range of possibilities of symbolic fiction, so that while his work sometimes parallels the symbolic modes of other writers, it more often twists off in its own strange and fascinating directions. Agnon has written simple parables of consummate artistry and folktales cunningly woven with strands of motif; nightmarish expressionist stories with recurrent symbols that break off, redouble themselves, glimmer ambiguously; haunting lyric tales centered around sets of symbolic images whose meaning seems hermetic, perhaps finally private; elaborately structured poetic novels that transform social milieu into symbolic atmosphere and develop plot through variations on themes from traditional Hebrew legend.*

* For a more elaborate account of Agnon's *oeuvre*, see the essay devoted to him above, pp. 131–150.

Over against the fiction of Agnon, with its symbolic impulse, its antirealistic experiments, its intricate stylistic implication in the Hebrew literary past, the native Israeli writers have generally committed themselves to a much more direct transcription of local reality. It is true that a few of the most interesting Israeli novels of the past half-dozen years have been parabolic or symbolic, at least two of them under the clear influence of Agnon, but, for the most part, the work of the younger writers remains artistically conservative in its realism. There are, I think, good historical reasons for this adherence to realism, even to realism in some of its less imaginative, more colorless forms.

Linguistic considerations, to begin with, have made conventional realism a more challenging mode of fiction in Israel than it is likely to be anywhere else today. The writers who began to publish shortly before or after the founding of the State in 1948 were in part reacting to the avowed bookishness of the older writers' Hebrew. As the first grown generation of native speakers of Hebrew since ancient times, many of them felt a kind of responsibility to make the slangy, slurred Hebrew of the streets, the army, and the kibbutz function as a literary language. What is second nature to novelists in other countries was and to some extent still is problematic for Israeli writers because modern colloquial Hebrew is so new and so continually changing that it lacks much of the range and flexibility, certainly much of the richness of associations, of a highly developed vernacular. Lengthy transcriptions of speech, because they were linguistically faithful to actual models, seemed to be a virtue in themselves—perhaps that is why some Israeli novels are still too talky—and descriptive prose, aspiring to a tough modernity, was often no more than a literary adaptation of Hebrew journalese. At the same time, there were attempts to build a new kind of poetic Hebrew on the structural base of the new spoken language.

The culmination of all these tendencies of linguistic realism will remain, I suppose, S. Yizhar's immense stream-of-consciousness novel on the Israeli-Arab War, *The Days of Ziklag*

(1958). Long sections of Yizhar's book are made up of dialogue, as the young Israeli soldiers who are the only characters anxiously question each other about the cause for which they are fighting, the disturbing meanings of their identity as Jews and citizens of the new state; and the stylistic dividing line between these spoken exchanges and the interior monologues is sometimes hazy. In between monologue and dialogue are exhaustively descriptive passages in which Yizhar renders the most minute movements of the battle, the smallest details of the Negev landscape with all its vegetation, even the changing constellations in the desert sky at night. Because Hebrew is structurally so different from the Western languages, there have been no significant stylistic influences from without on Israeli writers—with the partial exception of Yizhar, who in both *The Days of Ziklag* and his earlier fiction tries, by a constant kneading and reworking of the language, to make it expand to the capacity of lyric plenitude of the prose of Faulkner and Thomas Wolfe. The results of this procedure in his long novel are both dazzling and fatiguing. He makes his Hebrew embrace particulars of experience and nuances of perception which the language hitherto had been unable to reach; sometimes this descriptive activity has strict thematic appropriateness, sometimes it seems merely like an overly intent exercise in absorbing as much reality as is verbally possible. Surely one of the reasons why Yizhar has written virtually nothing since *The Days of Ziklag* is that in it he had carried the linguistic impulse of exhaustive realism as far as any writer or reader would want, so that to grow as a novelist he needed to strike out in a dramatically new direction, something which, for a variety of causes, he seems still unprepared to do.

The very conscious and immediate involvement in history that has characterized the Jewish settlement in Palestine and Israel has also encouraged native writers to feel a responsibility to "report" the world around them. Yizhar's recurrence to the War, ten years after it, in the most ambitious of Israeli novels to date, suggests the general orientation of the novelists of the fifties toward recent collective experience. Every war of course brings after it a spate of war novels, but the young Israelis who fought against the Arabs in 1948–1949 felt a special urgency to convey their experience not only because it was one that had shaken their private worlds, but also because they were, after all, participants in the first armed struggle for Jewish independence since the second century A.D. This is not to suggest that the Israeli novel has been nationalistic or chauvinistic. On the contrary, many of the writers have acted as a kind of public conscience, questioning ideologies, raising the profoundest doubts about the moral and historical implications of public events. But some kind of commitment to public events generally persists, and that is a quality which tends to distinguish the Israeli novel from characteristic developments of the novel today in America, England, and France. The Zionist leadership, with an expectation of close connection between literature and politics that ultimately derives from East-European cultural traditions, would like the writers to "do" certain aspects of Israel—the great national project of Ingathering of Exiles and their assimilation, the building of new industrial cities, the reclamation of desert land, and so forth. The fiction, however, that the younger writers actually produce is often a negative image of the glowing picture expected of them by the zealously patriotic, especially among their elders. Yet, ironically, the novelists generally have proceeded to "do" the various sectors of Israeli life: in traditional novelistic fashion, they have "brought the news," and of course it is hardly ever good news, of their own personal encounters with the realities of life in the army, the kibbutz, the youth movement, the bohemian milieu of the cities, the new immigrant towns.

If one can speak at all of a single theme in the Israeli novel over the past fifteen years, it would have to be disillusionment. In this respect, the position of the Israeli writer now is rather like that of the American writer of the twenties: after the shooting is over, he finds that a national dream has faded with the gunsmoke, and he feels cheated, disheartened, a little embarrassed ever to have been implicated in the naïveté of corporate dreams. Corruption and moral stupidity are not, one would assume, any more pervasive in Israel than elsewhere, but Zionism in its classic pioneering stage was moved by a passionate utopianism, and after such visions, the confrontation with "normalcy" (itself a Zionist ideal for Jewish regeneration) was bound to be painfully disenchanting. This general sense of the passing of a heroic ideal which one finds in Israeli writers is nicely summed up by a striking moment in *The Living on the Dead* (1965), Aharon Meged's most recent novel. The protagonist, occupying the garret of a dead sculptor who, after enjoying a period of fame in the thirties, lived out his life poor and forgotten, discovers in the laundry room a junkpile of abandoned pieces of sculpture, all tributes fashioned in the old forensic style to the generation of heroic builders of the Land: "What pioneers there were in that bathtub and in those laundry pans! Hammer-swingers, wielders of hoes and rakes, bearers of rifles, working girls in kerchiefs, pregnant women, hora dancers, busts of leaders. Ah, dust has covered them all!"

The Living on the Dead provides some insight into the problems of younger Israeli writers because that is its subject and because the artistic uncertainty of its execution is symptomatic of weaknesses found in the work of many of Meged's contemporaries. In general, one is likely to find Israeli novelists a fascinating and exasperating group to follow because, till now, they have shown so much creative and intellectual ferment and so little sustained achievement. Meged is one of five or six Israeli writers who at some point in their career have given promise of unusual talent, only to frustrate its fulfillment. His previous book, *Fortunes of a Fool* (1959), is an imaginative attempt, faltering to begin with but finally quite impressive, to get to the moral core of Israel's maddeningly bureaucratized society by adopting the narrative procedures of a Kafka novel. After the misadventures of its anonymous clerk, a well-meaning weakling in a meaningless world of blind power, it was possible to hope that Meged would make this symbolic form more fully his own and go on to create an exciting new variety of the Israeli novel. In his most recent book, however, all that is left of Kafka is an unending trial—with symbolic implications, of course—that serves as a framework within which two counter-pointed stories are told in conventional fashion, one rather schematically and the other at a pace that is at times dangerously pedestrian.

The protagonist of *The Living on the Dead* is a young writer named Jonas Rabinovitch—Jonas because, like the prophet Jonah, he flees from the responsibility of a message he had been chosen to bear. Jonas has been given a large advance by a publisher to write the biography of a certain Abraham Davidov, a recently deceased hero of the old pioneering period of the Palestinian community. The would-be biographer spends his days, more or less, interviewing people who have known Davidov and his nights at The Cellar, a hangout for artists and writers. The contrast between the two is striking, although after a great deal of reiteration it becomes a little tiring, too: Davidov, in the images Jonas culls of his life from the 1920's on, is seen galloping on horseback against Arab marauders, building roads, draining swamps, ranging the countryside restlessly, singing wildly through the nights, passionately discussing Tolstoi and Gogol till the dawn; the denizens of The Cellar, on the other hand, sit slouched in an alcoholic haze, trying to impress each other with intellectual patter, striking off hollow aphorisms about Art and Reality and capping verses from Baudelaire, Breton, Ezra Pound. Davidov, it should be said, for all his fire and energy, is seen to have his own kind of inner emptiness, but it is different from the bottomless ennui of Jonas and his friends, and Jonas finds the figure of the pioneer-leader, who is supposed to be a spiritual father of the State, so alien that he simply cannot write the book about him. The publishers bring him to court for his failure to produce the promised goods, and though his attorney tries to allay his fears by assuring him that the case may go on for years, Jonas knows he can write nothing else as long as the Davidov affair remains unsettled.

The argument of the novel is quite clear: until the Israeli writer finds ways of coming to terms spiritually and intellectually with his immediate national past, he will not be able to function creatively in the present; if his roots extend only to the bottom of a shallow pool of contemporary intellectual life, he will not be able to plumb the unsettling and confusing realities of his own society, and, whatever his subject, that remains a precondition for his art. The idea surely has some validity, and the scheme of the novel might have proved to be a suggestive one if, say, Meged had developed a nuanced psychological comparison of the young writer and the old hero, or perhaps, alternately, if he had handled his whole scheme as parable and elaborated its meaning through a boldly symbolic mode of fiction. The novel he did write, on the other hand, could serve as a paradigm for the trap into which the Israeli novelist's characteristic devotion to conventional realism can lead. One senses that Meged is terribly bent upon *reproducing* bohemian cafe-society in Tel Aviv, upon reproducing the type of Jew represented in Davidov, and so we get a welter of details about both, but neither Davidov nor the habituates of The Cellar can really develop novelistically because they are, finally, only composites of details, and rather predictable details at that. One reviewer of the novel, Ada Tzemah, has made this point trenchantly in noting how the narrator's eye stays at visual surfaces, seeing its objects cinematically, so that the language itself repeatedly falls into catalogs of typifying particulars instead of being worked into artistic patterns that can show forth the realities below the details. The serious novel elsewhere seems largely to have surrendered to the camera its function of merely reproducing milieu because film, with its rapid series of comprehensive images, can do the job far more completely and less tediously than words; but this distinction between media would appear to be one that many Hebrew novelists of the fifties and sixties have chosen to ignore.

Although I have focused on problematic aspects of the enterprise of the native Israeli writers, the general prognosis is by no means bleak. Several recent Hebrew novels have shown real artistic merit, despite flaws of various sorts, and there has been some intelligent interest in formal experiment. In this connection, the novel most worthy of mention is Yehuda Amichai's *Not of This Time, Not of This Place* (1963). Although some sections of the book bog down in symbolic con-trivances, to a large extent overly conscious imitations of Agnon, Amichai's symbolic imagination is remarkably athletic, he is alert to the expressive possibilities of wrenchng narrative form from its conventional patterns, and, in his central action, he renders erotic experience vividly with a genuine lyric freshness while firmly relating it to larger aspects of cultural conscious-ness.* *Not of This Time, Not of This Place,* like Amichai's earlier volume of short stories, could benefit from some rigorous editing, but it gives evidence of a talent that could yet enable him to become a major novelist.

In any event, the case of Amichai, who is worlds away from Agnon though strongly under his influence, suggests some-thing of the special situation of the Israeli novel in general. It has been in a continual state of transition, and that makes it unsafe to generalize about, but the transition is not, as an out-sider might suppose, from bare beginnings to a first maturity. Rather, the Hebrew novel has behind it a brief but distin-guished tradition of mature achievement, and it has had to move down from the last, greatest pinnacle of that achievement and outward toward another kind of achievement. This fresh beginning is understandable and probably even commendable, but if the new Hebrew novelists are to take full advantage of the unique resources of expression indigenous to their language and cultural past, they cannot afford to turn their backs entirely on their own literary predecessors. Hopefully, as they move closer to the as yet unperceived forms of their own artistic self-realization, at least some of them will also find ways to incor-porate in their work an imaginative responsiveness to what is extraordinary in the older tradition of Hebrew fiction.

1966

* A detailed critique of Amichai's novel is offered above in "Confronting the Holocaust, pp. 163–180.

THE DAYS OF ZIKLAG—IN SEARCH
OF A CULTURAL PAST

To hell with heroism. Who needs heroism. A come-on for suckers. All this flag-waving. Our hands have got so knotted up waving old flags that they don't have the strength left to let go, to shake themselves loose, when there's nothing glorious about the flags any more. And instead of just tossing away, really and wholeheartedly, all the flags, in order to walk light and free—you go to your death for their sake, for the sake of flags that don't say anything. The hours of what's left of your life are stooped and dreary under the proud flag.

At first glance, this is hardly a surprising statement to find in a war novel published in 1958, or, for that matter, anytime during the last forty years. But the familiar theme of embittered disenchantment with causes begins to look a little strange when we realize in what war the speaker is fighting and which proud flag it is that doesn't say anything to him. This abjuration of causes is a typical moment during a discussion among a small group of soldiers on a Negev hilltop, waiting in the blistering heat of a September afternoon in 1948 for an Egyptian attack. The young men—none is older than twenty-one—are part of the first generation of Jews in two thousand years to take up arms to defend their own land. The cause for which they are fighting is the rebirth of Jewish national existence after twenty centuries of exile. But the soldiers in this novel tend to see both the glorified state and their own glorified role in another light: as the same speaker puts it a moment later, "a weight of rhetoric like a millstone around your neck."

The appearance of S. Yizhar's *The Days of Ziklag* can be

taken as one of the significant cultural events in Israel since the founding of the state. It would be a mistake to imagine that the novel marks anything like a turning point, or the sudden beginning of a crisis in Israeli thought, but *The Days of Ziklag*—together with the furor of debate raised in the Israeli press by its publication—put into a new sharp focus the whole tangle of problems of what has been standard Zionist ideology. S. Yizhar (pen name for Yizhar Smilanski) is far from being a lone, embittered voice, or even a spokesman for simply an offbeat protest group of angry young Israelis. He has for some time been widely regarded as the major writer of fiction of the younger generation in Israel. Intellectual circles in the new state waited impatiently for the completion and publication of *The Days of Ziklag*, which, at long last, was to give them the epic novel of the Israeli-Arab War, and, hopefully, the first great novel of Israel written by an Israeli-born author. Yizhar, on his part (perhaps rather too self-consciously), was laboring at his war novel with the seriousness of a man out to make literary history. By the time he completed his account of the seven-day struggle for a hill in the Negev, his on-and-off stream-of-consciousness novel had run to two large volumes and 1,143 closely printed pages. Israel's reaction to this bulky addition to its bookshelves was, in the most intense areas of debate, little short of schizophrenic. (One paper went so far as to print two different reviews of the novel side by side, one a reserved tribute and the other a violent attack.) Admirers of the book, particularly the younger critics, acclaimed it as "the literary event of the decade," "the greatest artistic creation by an Israeli-born writer." The novel's detractors (after being sure to make clear that, despite it all, they had gotten through to the end) denounced it as both unreadable and dangerously nihilistic, perhaps even subversive.

The whole dispute came to a climax in the muddle over the awarding of the Bialik Prize for belles-lettres for 1958. The Bialik Prize, given annually by the municipality of Tel Aviv, is Israel's highest honor for a work of fiction or poetry. On purely literary grounds, there could hardly have been any question about the recipient of the award. *The Days of Ziklag* had no real competitor; whatever its faults may be, it is certainly one of the few pieces of contemporary Hebrew fiction outside the work of S. Y. Agnon which deserves to be taken seriously. The majority decision of the judges was that the Bialik Prize would not be awarded for 1958, as no book had been discovered which was worthy of the honor. Both judges who refused to select *The Days of Ziklag* began their justification by declaring the book unreadable, and concluded (and it would seem that this was the real reason) by complaining that Yizhar had distorted the image of the young generation of fighters for freedom. The degree to which some of Yizhar's critics were emotionally involved in the issues under debate is suggested by the oratorical fervor that creeps into Abraham Kariv's statement to the press explaining why he voted against the novel on the prize committee. "Thousands of boys purchased victory for us with their lives . . ." and Yizhar dared to betray their memory. "*The Days of Ziklag* . . . tears down more than it builds." This notion of a literature that ought to "build" was generally implicit in the position of older critics and educators who denounced Yizhar's novel of protest. Obviously, if pushed to its logical conclusion, such a notion reduces creative literature to propaganda. But the very existence of a concept of literature as an "ought to" among members of a society's supposed intellectual leadership is symptomatic of a certain uneasiness in that leadership, of a sensed (or feared) gap between official ideology and popular conviction. It is worth noting, in this connection, one interesting feature of the *Ziklag* debate: the zealous defenders of the generation of freedom fighters were not the young people themselves but the generation that had educated them. The feeling, in the main part, among the young intellectuals in Israel was that Yizhar had written what most of them felt. One of the younger critics frankly described Yizhar's book as the "Final Inventory" that the war generation had taken of itself and its supposed ideals.

The most intelligent—and, at the same time, the most violent—attack on the novel came from the influential literary critic Baruch Kurzweil in an article which he called "The Great Disappointment." Kurzweil touched on most of the real technical faults of *The Days of Ziklag*: its unjustified repetitiousness, its lack of character differentiation, the indigence and monotony of the inner lives that we are asked to follow through hundreds of pages of interior monologue. But the real weight of Kurzweil's criticism was brought to bear against the moral quality of the book. He accused it of cynicism, nihilism, narcissism, masochism, exhibitionism, verbal onanism, to cite some of his choicer invectives. Kurzweil may have had personal motives for objecting to Yizhar, but it is nevertheless indicative of the real danger some people in Israel sensed in this book that a major critic felt obliged to bury it in such a stream of Freudian dirty names. (Criticism of the beatniks in America was, by comparison, dispassionate, perhaps because nobody sensed in the beatniks the same kind of seriously responsible and resonant protest against society that Yizhar represented in Israel.) If we put aside Kurzweil's vocabulary of pathology, his moral claims against *The Days of Ziklag* were the same as those made by the other strenuous opponents of the book: Yizhar had given a distorted picture of his own generation because of his fundamental cynicism and nihilism. If the writer whom a good part of the young Israeli intelligentsia looks on as its spokesman is really a nihilist, the acclaimed idealistic enterprise of the Zionist state would appear to be heading toward some very painful cultural dead end. How true the claims are, or what general situation could have led to the insistence on such claims, will become clear through a consideration of the precise nature of the protest made in *The Days of Ziklag*.

The plot outline of this long novel is simple enough. A squad of Israeli soldiers seizes an Arab-occupied hill in the Negev. Twice they are driven off the hill, but with reinforcements they recapture it both times. The book ends after the Israelis have succeeded in repulsing an extended attack on the hill by Egyptian forces. Judging just by this general scheme, we might conclude that *The Days of Ziklag* was following the time-honored pattern of war novels and novels of action: failure 1, failure 2, ultimate success. The book, in fact, departs radically from the tradition of the popular war novel in refusing in any way to capitalize on the inherent reportorial dramatic appeal of the events of the war. The author has worked out a narrative technique whose very purpose is to extract all trace of dramatic excitement from the action described. He accomplishes this principally by denying the continuity of experienced time. Time is fragmented into an endless succession of autonomous moments. "The whole world is nothing but the bubble of this moment. This hot moment. This cut-off moment. . . . And you exist from one moment to the next, one moment after another. . . . This sickening time, this falling bridge." Living in a world of isolated moments is bound to produce two kinds of emotional states: a sense of being becalmed in time, helplessly adrift, and a sense of apprehension at what the next, unconnected moment will bring. And throughout the interior monologues and the long discussions in *The Days of Ziklag*, boredom and fear are the two principal themes. The human will, which must assume a temporal continuity in which to operate, is paralyzed when time is completely fragmented. Action can no longer be the subject of the novel: its place is taken by a study of the emotions of boredom and fear. Now, working within this framework, Yizhar can do a rather effective job of deflating any heroic notions of the nature of war. But his novel is something more than just another debunking of the heroic, or just another protest against the debasing, stultifying effect on the individual of modern war. Both the antiheroic theme and the peculiar metaphysic of time have special cultural significance in the context of present-day Israel. An examination of the ironies bound up with the title of the novel will lead us into the ideological implications of Yizhar's attitude toward the heroic and toward time.

Ziklag was the city David used as his center of operations after he and his band of warriors had been driven into exile by Saul. The biblical days of Ziklag, like Yizhar's, were a period before the Jewish state was fully established, when survival demanded courage and skill at arms. One of the more distinctive members of Yizhar's squad of soldiers is a Bible enthusiast named Barzilai. Barzilai is a not unlikely product of secular, nationalist education in Israel. He carries with him at all times his little pocket Bible, and whenever he has the opportunity, he pulls it out to leaf through it—looking not for "inspiration," as a devout Christian might, but for an imaginative identification with biblical personages and the places they lived in. So when the group of Israeli soldiers takes possession of the hill, Barzilai becomes very excited at the thought that this very hill might be the site of King David's Ziklag. " 'Hey, if this is really Ziklag,' Barzilai insisted, 'and we're fighting on Ziklag, then it's a different story altogether!' But Nahum remained indifferent: 'It's not a different anything.' " Barzilai soon discovers, after consulting a map, that his conjecture about the identity of the hill was probably mistaken. The hill is not Ziklag, David's Ziklag, the unique Ziklag of the Bible, but merely point of elevation 244 on the military maps, distinguished from the other hills in other places only by the bland, linear distinction that makes one number different from the next. The name, however, has already stuck. The Israelis refer to their anonymous hill in the Negev as Ziklag; they capture Ziklag, run from Ziklag, are parched and frozen, maimed and killed on Ziklag—which is, after all, only point of elevation 244. The final irony is that, even if it were the real Ziklag of biblical times, it wouldn't make the least difference to them.

The most powerful exposure of the spuriousness of neobiblicism as a way to national consciousness occurs on the evening of the first day. The Israelis, with all their ammunition gone, have been forced to run for their lives in the face of a sharp Arab counterattack. They lie sprawled out on the ground, half-naked, exhausted, hungry, caked with dust and sweat. Barzilai, out of the best of intentions, chooses this moment to read to the group something "the fellows would like" from the first chapter of Second Samuel.

"Now it came to pass after the death of Saul, when David was returning from the slaughter of the Amalekites; and

David had abode two days in Ziklag; It came even to pass on the third day, that, behold, a man came out of the camp from Saul with his clothes rent, and earth upon his head; and so it was, when he came to David, that he fell to the earth and did obeisance. And David said unto him, From whence comest thou? And he said unto him, Out of the camp of Israel am I escaped. And David said unto him, How went the matter? I pray thee, tell me. And he answered, That the people are fled from the battle, and many of the people also are fallen and dead; and Saul and Jonathan his son are dead also. And David said unto the young man that told him. How knowest thou that Saul and Jonathan his son be dead? . . . " "Why don't you just get off our backs now with all your dead?" Chivi burst out in anger. "We have enough without that."

Barzilai, in this instance, is living out the neobiblical mentality to the last letter. He is trying to give depth and significance to the experience of the present moment by identifying it with a parallel moment in the heroic past of the Jewish people. This explains the innocent enthusiasm with which he undertakes a Bible-reading to his friends at such an unpropitious moment. When he is interrupted, he is drawing close in his reading to the point when David will lift his voice in the Bible's great moving elegy over the defeat of heroes—"How are the mighty fallen . . ." But against this heroic, literary image of defeat in battle, these soldiers have before them the reality of their own defeat—with the stench of their own sweat, the ache of their own tiredness, the memory of their own cowardice. Any attempt to see their dirty, distasteful world in the light of the epic grandeur of the Bible could only strike them as an infuriating falsehood.

To realize the full importance of Yizhar's attack on the notion of Israel as the Land of the Bible, it is necessary to recall the role that the Bible has played in Zionist ideology. The popular notion, to begin with, of the Jewish people through their centuries of exile as the People of the Bible, is rather misleading. The Jews were the People of the Law, a Law whose ultimate authority derived from the Bible, but which was articulated in the Talmud. The Talmud, not the Bible, was the principal text of study. And the Bible itself was always seen by Jews through the eyes of its rabbinic commentators. Modern Zionism, from its first literary precursors over a century ago, has been a distinctly romantic movement: a return to a glorious past, a break with all that life in the diaspora implied to go back to a glowing world of the Bible. But this whole romantic return of Zionism was founded on a contradiction. In the past, the Bible—or rather, the Bible and its tradition of interpretation—had remained the living book of a people because the people accepted it as God-given. Modern Zionism relegated the Bible to the position of a great humanist doctrine, and, having thrown away the one justification for "living" the Bible, proceeded to use it as the cornerstone for a new culture. One symptom of the sort of change that has occurred is Ben-Gurion's habit of referring to the Bible as the Book of Books. The phrase, which did not exist in earlier Hebrew, sounds even worse to the discriminating listener in Hebrew than it does in English. Certainly the insistence on the Bible as the Book of Books reflects a kind of huckster approach to the Scriptures, a my-book-is-better-than-your-book pitch. This spectacle of trying to "sell" the scriptures as a national book points to the whole futility of the Zionist return to the Bible; a people in the twentieth century cannot be expected seriously to take up a piece of ancient literature as its pattern for living, even if it is demonstrated that the book in question is a very good piece of ancient literature. There is no need to conclude that the founders of the modern Jewish settlement in Palestine (essentially, Ben-Gurion's generation) were simply using the Bible as an instrument of propaganda in all their talk about the fulfillment of the prophetic vision, the rebirth of ancient Israel, and so forth. The vacuity of a belief is hardly a measure of the sincerity with which people can believe it. Zionism has succeeded in fostering a secular messianism with adherents who have believed quite literally that their actions meant the realization of prophetic promise. But as a general state of affairs in cultures it would seem to be much easier to fool yourself than it is to fool your children. Yizhar's young soldiers, as we shall see, are far from the radical cynicism of which they have been accused; they are simply being confronted with the awful disparity between the high-sounding words on which they were educated and the reality they have to live in. When Barzilai unthinkingly tries to make these tired, beaten men identify with the heroic model of David, he is committing an outrage on their sensibilities, and Chivi's angry rebuke is the natural, honest reaction.

But if such young people see the falseness of linking themselves with the ancient Jewish past, and are at the same time the children of the pioneer generation that divorced itself from the immediate Jewish past, where are they supposed to stand? This is the one haunting question that the characters of *The Days of Ziklag* find themselves asking again and again.

> My grandfather, whom I never knew, was a scholar; all he did was study his Torah and his books; his life was whole and he was firmly rooted in all his relationships. Fine. My father tore himself away and came here and planted himself again. Now I and my friends are *segatiles*. Plants sprouting by the roadside. No longer scholars of the Torah, and not yet wise with any new wisdom. . . . My grandfather's wisdom came to the end of the road. A new wisdom we haven't come up with yet. . . . Fellows without forefathers. Only fathers. And anything before your father's immigration—darkness. Back to the days of King David.

It becomes clear now why Yizhar chose to represent time in his novel as a succession of autonomous moments. The technique, of course, offers a certain fidelity to the psychological reality of mechanized warfare; it is a means of reproducing the torment of endless, helpless waiting that is the main part of the modern soldier's fighting. But, beyond this, the whole extreme situation of battle affords Yizhar the opportunity to represent concretely, by means of these autonomous moments, the moral anguish of a generation that is forced to live with no past, or only a sham past, and with no goals before it that can give any very reassuring sense of the future ("time . . . this falling bridge").

(219) The Days of Ziklag—*In Search of Cultural Past*

If all that *The Days of Ziklag* did were to exhibit its wound of cultural disinheritance, the accusations of cynicism, and perhaps even of masochism, would have some justification. The truth of the matter is that Yizhar's novel is a book whose most distinctive quality is its moral soundness. The first step that Yizhar takes is to try to face honestly the world in which he and his generation find themselves: so the first purpose of his book is to do a good deal of thorough ground-clearing. Among what he was clearing away, however, were ideals to which some people in Israel had committed their whole lives, and it was inevitable that they would be able to see in Yizhar only a profaner of the nation's altars.

The young soldiers whom we get to know during the course of the novel are, for the most part, the sons of small farmers and kibbutzniks (though Yizhar does attempt to give a wider demographic sampling). Their birth dates all fall into the period between 1928 and 1930, which makes them the children of the wave of idealist pioneer immigrants who came to Palestine during the twenties. Pioneer immigrants, both of the Second Aliyah (before World War I) and of the Third Aliyah (after the Balfour Declaration) were, as a group, moved by a feeling that they were participating in the inauguration of a great millennial enterprise. First came the conviction that the modern Jewish nation was a fulfillment of an ancient Jewish messianic ideal. Then there were more specific kinds of millennial hopes founded on specific modern ideologies: the Marxist ideal of the perfect society, which the collective settlements hoped to realize; the Tolstoian ideal, preached by A. D. Gordon, of a union of the individual and the people with the cosmos through a return to the soil. The children of the pioneer-idealists, coming to maturity as their people was fighting to ensure statehood, had been educated on a vocabulary of the millennium and found themselves in a world where the millennium had not yet arrived and didn't at all seem to be on its way. As they appear in this novel, they sympathize with, even admire, their fathers, but they are simply in a different world from them.

An amazing generation, our old men. What they managed to accomplish between their youth and old age. The pathos they had, that we've lost almost completely. It's hard for us, the clear-minded ones, to follow their path. We haven't burnt any bridges behind us. We haven't exchanged one world for another. No terrors of the pogroms and drums of revolution on one side, or abandonment in a new and alien wilderness on the other side. Work intoxicated them. Both soothed them and stirred them. And then we came along.

The resentment of these young people is not so much against the parents themselves as against the education their parents gave them. They want to face the facts of their world without a vocabulary that overvalues those facts; they want, first of all, to get rid of the millstone of rhetoric that has been hung around their neck.

> Just as long as it's without talk. . . . Don't let them come to remind me of duties. Don't let them come to explain to me the situation, the nation, our youth, the role of our youth, the hour, the hour's imperative, the task—those days are finished! I have a stock that will last me forty years. Just don't let them educate me.

The very fundamental nature of Yizhar's break with the ideals of the pioneer generation becomes evident in his treatment of the theme of the seven days. Any kind of secular messianism involves the transfer to an exclusively human plane of the Judeo-Christian conception of history, a history created and directed by God. History is supposed to have meaning for man, is going somewhere, is intended to reach a posthistorical culmination. The experience of our century would tend to place in a dubious light the attempts to cling to a millennial interpretation of history while substituting man for God. Yizhar tries to show in his novel what the world must look like, stripped of illusions, when there is no faith in a God of history. The two days of Rosh Hashanah, the Jewish New Year, occur in the middle of the seven days of his novel. Rosh Hashanah is the point in the year assigned by Jewish tradition as the "birthday of the world," the anniversary of creation. The biblical seven days of creation suggest the pattern for any messianic conception of history. On each day, new things are created, and the creation culminates in the Sabbath, just as a progressing history is to culminate in the Sabbath of history. But Yizhar, by means of constant description of the changing sky from sunrise to sunset and then through the changing stars at night, is at pains to show us the complete sameness of each of his seven days. While a group of young men struggle for a hill that may or may not be important to somebody or other, nature—and nature's time—remains absolutely impassive and indifferent. In these seven days, there is no process, only cycle, no culmination, only the untiring repetition of sunrise and sunset and sunrise again.

The other major Rosh Hashanah motif in the novel offers a further indication of the intense moral honesty that motivates Yizhar's critique of traditional ideals. The Torah-reading for the second day of Rosh Hashanah is the chapter in Genesis that describes the Binding of Isaac. At the moment of the year when Jews stand before God to be judged, they recall the devotion of their forefather Abraham, who was prepared to sacrifice to God his most precious possession. The motif of the *'aqeda*, the Binding of Isaac, is taken up by Yizhar early in the novel and developed through the seven days of fighting. Without faith in a living God who will send His angel to stay the sacrificial knife, or faith in a God who, in any case, is supremely more important than anything else, including human life, the call to an *'aqeda* becomes unbearable. And when a notion like Homeland is substituted for the God that demands the sacrifice of the sons, the reaction of embitterment is still more understandable. These are the thoughts of a young Israeli machine-gunner as he waits for an Egyptian shelling to begin:

> There's no way around the *'aqeda*. You only imagine that you can leave everything and run. You can't. You're denied the possibility of running. . . . I hate our father Abraham going to sacrifice Isaac. What right does he have over Isaac. Let him sacrifice himself. I hate the God that sent him to sacrifice and closed all other paths for him—only the way to the *'aqeda* He left open. I hate the fact that Isaac is nothing but material

for an experiment between Abraham and his God. . . . To slaughter sons as a proof of love! To use force and interfere and take lives in order to win a quarrel. And that the world remained silent and didn't get up and scream: Scoundrels, for what do the sons have to die? Hate all necessity to get something at the price of causing ruin. Or destruction. Or torture. Or compulsion.

It is a hopeful sign that one of the major literary spokesmen for Israel's younger generation turns out, in the final analysis, to have deep pacifist sensibilities. Secular Zionism's assigning of ultimate value to national existence in itself was bound to carry with it the danger of making all moral values subordinate to the highest good of the preservation of the state. Yizhar and the members of his generation found themselves faced with this problem very concretely when the Israeli-Arab War put them in the position of having to take human lives in the name of the "Homeland . . . a word . . . that says everything and says nothing." *The Days of Ziklag* is a deep-felt protest on behalf of individual conscience in the face of a historical situation that often threatens to silence it. Yizhar's pacifist tendencies, moreover, are of a responsible, realistic kind. He realizes that the fighters of Ziklag do not have the alternative of simply laying down their arms. His objection to war, like all of his criticism, is made in a context of social commitment. (It should be noted that Yizhar, the great voice of protest, is committed to social action even to the extent of being a member of Knesset, representing Mapai, the ruling party.) Here, as in other areas, Yizhar's formulations bear a distinct family resemblance to those of Jean-Paul Sartre. His pacifist machine-gunner's justification for fighting sounds very much like a variation on the title-theme of *The Red Hands*:

> Always man belongs. Always he is of. Always attached to and not disconnected, by himself. . . . And for the "of" he must die. And why should he be permitted to begin making noble decisions that he won't shoot at the looters of his home, what right does he have to stand aside, to announce that he will neither do evil nor destroy, that his hands will stay clean and

won't commit murder, when his whole generation is forced to wade in blood, bound to a necessity greater than it.

The generation cannot turn its back on the necessity; Yizhar's plea is that the mind of the individual should not become enslaved to the necessity. *The Days of Ziklag* does not pretend that anyone can wish away the horror of war, but it insists again and again that we cannot allow ourselves to come to terms with a world that accepts war. Yizhar certainly has no programmatic suggestions for a road to positive action either for the individual or for the people. He has tried to remove illusions from his world, and he finds it stonily indifferent to all human enterprise. (He emphasizes repeatedly that the soldiers don't *belong* on Ziklag or in the whole natural setting.) There is little he can suggest except that, as the Sartre school of existentialism teaches, the individual must be ready to assume the terrible burden of responsibility for making his own moral decisions in a universe with no built-in values:

> You only live one time. This time. And that puts an awful lot of responsibility on you. Because there's no other time. You can't try again, a different way, like the kid in school, who, when the drawing doesn't turn out right, runs for the eraser. There is no eraser. I'm a one-time-in-the-world-and-finished creature.

This call to moral responsibility is accompanied throughout the novel by Yizhar's other major positive theme: the thirst for belief. The young generation of Israelis he portrays has not, on the whole, responded to the disenchantment with past beliefs by becoming cynical. Many of the characters of *The Days of Ziklag* are intensely conscious of the vacuum left by the loss of the old faiths, and they are anxious to find something they can believe in which will fill the emptiness. But they are not willing to settle for anything less than the genuine article.

Yet all this moral candor and courage are hardly an answer to the question of cultural continuity that is raised by *The Days of Ziklag*. If the young generation has divested itself of all the spurious connections which Zionism tried to make with the

Jewish past, are there any grounds for thinking that the developing Israeli culture will be at all a Jewish culture? One begins to suspect that Yizhar's young soldiers, during these discussions taking place under the threat of enemy arms, are led to overstate their position. It is hard to believe that for young Israelis, certainly for young Israeli intellectuals, all of Jewish history is simply "darkness, back to the days of King David." The relationship of Israeli youth to the Jewish past may be problematic, but that past is not quite a completely closed book. A dramatic instance of continuity in historical experience is supplied by Yizhar himself, perhaps unintentionally, in a striking short story called "Hirbet Hiz'ah" (the name of an Arab village). The soldier-narrator's vague feelings of uneasiness at the banishment of the villagers from their homes suddenly crystallize in a moment of nearly traumatic shock when he realizes what it is that he is witnessing: "*Galut* [exile]. Why this is *galut*. That's the way *galut* looks." It is through the centuries of pain and fear distilled in the word *galut*—a *galut* which he never experienced personally—that the narrator suddenly understands the suffering of the Arabs trudging into exile. His sympathy for them is not just the result of a humanitarian predisposition; it is made possible, and is emotionally colored, by the collective past experience of the Jewish people.

S. Yizhar has performed the service of deflating much that called for deflating in Zionist ideology. On the positive side of the ledger, it is doubtful if he, or the whole generation of Israelis he would seem to speak for, is really as completely cut off from the Jewish past as some of the characters of *The Days of Ziklag* pretend. In any case, the manifestation of such honest self-scrutiny in a culture is certainly a healthy sign. Professor Ernst Simon of the Hebrew University, in his lucid discussion, "Are We Still Jews?" in the *Ha-Aretz Yearbook* for 1951–1952, aptly describes the importance of this kind of self-criticism in Jewish national consciousness:

> The remarkable power of survival of Judaism is rooted as well in the "no" it knew how to say to every call of re-

demption that did not fit the image of the true redemption:
to Christianity, to Islam, to Sabbatai Zevi, to communism.
And through the strength of this negation the people of Israel
remained *the* people of redemption and preserved the hope of
redemption *in the world* which remained unredeemed. The
assertion of the messianic character of the State of Israel means
the loss of the criterion for true redemption. . . . The zealous
guarding of this criterion is a prerequisite for the continual
advance of the people of Israel.

The Days of Ziklag undeniably performs this function of
zealous guardianship. The criticism of Zionist messianism that
it presents is not its own innovation, but it is significant that
Israel has reached a point when such criticism could be so
completely summed up in a single book, and when such a book
could be regarded by many of the young intelligentsia as their
Final Inventory. From this point, one may hope for a time
when prevailing thought in Israel will come to a more realistic
appraisal of the purpose and justification for the Jewish state.

1960

THE KIDNAPPING OF BIALIK AND TCHERNICHOVSKY

To anyone who has been exposed to a modern Hebrew education, whether in this country or in Israel, the names of Bialik
and Tchernichovsky have the same kind of inevitable—and, for
some, wearying—ring that Milton and Shakespeare have for the
student of English poetry, or Plato and Aristotle for the student
of philosophy. During the seven decades since modern Hebrew
poetry came of age in Odessa, various efforts have been made to
fix a third luminary with the Inevitable Two. Some impassioned
pleas have been voiced for Zalman Schneur, the poet of Nietzschean rebellion who began his career in Odessa at about the
same time as Bialik and Tchernichovsky. From the next literary
generation (the writers who are now in their sixties), Avraham
Schlonsky and Uri Zvi Greenberg have occasionally been advanced as candidates, for varying aesthetic or even ideological
reasons.

But all such attempts have so far proved abortive. Though
Hebrew poetry since the 1890's, and particularly since the
1920's, has given us a surprising number of interesting figures,
Bialik and Tchernichovsky are still, in an important sense, *the*
Hebrew poets—not only for the surviving latter-day exponents
of the Haskalah, not only for the students who are subjected to
a Hebrew secondary education created in large part by such
vestigial *maskilim*, but also for discriminating readers of Hebrew who care about poetry. Young Israelis of serious literary
interests may sometimes choose to regard Bialik and Tchernichovsky as the dated spokesmen of another time and place, but
ultimately most of them must attempt to come to terms with

the two Russian-born poets because modern Hebrew poetry has as yet produced no one else of such stature, no one else with whom it is so important to come to terms.

Yet the fact is that the Hebrew reading public, or those who have claimed to speak for it and aimed to form its taste, has for the most part insisted on dictating its own terms to its two greatest poets. The result is that Bialik and Tchernichovsky—at least that part of them which is fed into the educational process and turned over in critical discourse—are often seriously misrepresented, their originality blurred, and the impact of their artistic and moral vision softened.

A glance at almost any standard reference work large enough to touch on modern Hebrew literature will reveal that Bialik and Tchernichovsky have already been assigned their place in history as "the major poets of the Hebrew national renaissance." The description is fair and accurate. Both men were deeply dedicated to the Zionist idea, and particularly to its cultural implications. Both devoted much of their lives and at least some of their poetry to the programmatic realization of that idea. It is clear that the role they played in the Zionist renaissance transcends literary history, making itself felt in the sphere of national history as well. If their poetic achievements were revolutionary, their contributions to the development of a viable Hebrew national culture in the modern world are at least imposing.

Tchernichovsky's massive efforts as a translator flung open windows for the Hebrew reader and the Hebrew language on a score of Western cultures. Bialik's whirlwind of activity as editor and anthologizer of traditional Hebrew texts, as translator, publisher, all-around literary entrepreneur, helped ensure that some of the best of the Hebrew literary past would be available to the present and that some of what was valuable in the newborn Hebrew present would be nurtured and transmitted in print to the future. One can hardly object, then, to linking the names of the two poets with the national renaissance, both through their poetry and through their extrapoetic activities. But their readers for three generations have gone further in insisting on the idea—really, almost the title—of "national poets," and this has had some unfortunate results.

Anyone in this country of my generation who grew up in Hebrew-speaking circles is likely to have sung Bialik and Tchernichovsky before actually reading either of them. The idea of singing a serious modern poet—imagine Wallace Stevens or even Robert Frost with a tra-la-la-la!—may at first seem bizarre, but it does helpfully illustrate one way in which these Hebrew poets differed from their contemporaries in other literatures. At least some of the time, they consciously wrote for the folk in its own idiom. Both were interested in folk imagination and folk poetry to a degree that has been rare in Western literature since the Romantic Movement. Tchernichovsky succeeded in making the ballad a serious art-form in Hebrew poetry, while Bialik's "Sort of Folk Songs," as he called them, gave him a ventriloquistic outlet for his poetic voice after it was virtually choked off with the last, terrible, death-ridden poems of 1916.

I don't mean to suggest that there is anything inherently wrong in Bialik and Tchernichovsky's supplying lyrics for folk songs. On the contrary, if one is going to create from nothing a whole national repertoire of folk songs, it is remarkably fortunate that two men of genius should want to contribute to the enterprise. Assuming the mask of the naïve singer, Bialik was able to write not only zestfully humorous poems but also poems of exquisite beauty. His "At Twilight" (*Lo Bayom V'lo Balaylah*), for example, a song which has been sung around innumerable campfires, has a plaintive loveliness that represents the transposition into a folk key of a major theme from his serious poetry—the forlorn longing for love. A whole series of motifs and subjects that are central to Bialik's greatest poetry, from the golden garden of paradise to the beggars' apocalypse, were transmuted into the evocative simplicity of an artful folk idiom during the last twenty years of his life.

But the fact that an acquaintance with Bialik or Tchernichovsky often begins to the strumming of a guitar and the flicker of firelight, while unobjectionable in itself, is symptomatic of the kind of misuses to which the work of the two poets has been put. Clearly, their most complex and rewarding poems are not necessarily those that can be sung in three-quarter time with a rousing refrain. In this country, for instance, an introduction to Tchernichovsky's verse frequently takes place through the sentimental strains of *"I Believe"* (*Saḥaki*), a piece of dewy-eyed idealism in rhymed clichés that was written when the poet was seventeen years old: one could hardly guess from it that the wild power of his Canaanite poems or the stunning virtuosity of his two great sonnet cycles was somewhere in the offing.

No one, of course, has attempted to limit the importance of Bialik and Tchernichovsky to their ballads and anthems. (Those who sing the ballads and anthems, moreover, are often unaware that the words are Bialik's or Tchernichovsky's.) But the fact that their poems are used to serve a public purpose does reflect a general pattern, and when the poetry is presented in the classroom, it is often still expected to fulfill a public role.

Because the educators and textbook anthologizers see Bialik and Tchernichovsky as "national poets," the pieces they typically choose to present to students are generally those with obviously national content—Bialik's hymns of praise to traditional Jewish fortitude and his songs of hope for a rebuilt homeland, Tchernichovsky's treatment of Jewish martyrdom and his tributes to the heroism of the Palestinian pioneers. In Israel, the sampling is usually somewhat broader than in this country, but that does little to discourage teachers from emphasizing the looming portion of national poems, and complaints by students about the "official" appearance of the two poets are still nearly universal. As unpromising as these patriotic subjects may sound to an outsider, each of the poets did succeed on occasion in creating distinguished literature from the explicitly national material; so the process of selection does not automatically filter out poetic greatness. And particularly in the case of Bialik, personal and national experience are often so completely fused that it is impossible to make a distinction between the two. Nevertheless, this kind of selection does exclude some of the poets' greatest work, certainly many kinds of poems that young readers would find exciting and perhaps personally relevant. And it forces upon the student poems of Tchernichovsky that are mainly oratorical rhetoric, others from Bialik's early period that were poetically desiccated by the influence of Ahad Ha-am's programmatic thinking.

Bialik, for example, wrote several important poems on the traditional study-house (*beit ha-midrash*). The greatest of these and the last, "Before the Bookshelf," is also the one whose vision is starkest, almost nihilistic. But the study-house poem most frequently adopted for classroom use is the early, declamatory paean to the *beit midrash* as the storehouse of national strength, "If You Should Seek to Know."

> If you should seek to know the well-spring
> From which your downtrodden brothers drew
> Between the straits of the underworld and the narrows of the
>   pit, among scorpions—
> Divine consolation, confidence, might, long-suffering spirit
> And iron strength to bear all adversity. . . .

The language is just as worn and abstract in Hebrew as in translation, and Bialik after the 1890's permitted nothing like this in his poetry. But just this is what is often taught.

This same limiting conception of national poetry, together with the bias of taste that is its concomitant, almost invariably dictates the choice of *The Matmid* ("talmudist") as the one long narrative poem of Bialik's to be included in a limited curriculum before all others. Now, between 1897 and 1905, Bialik completed five ambitious narrative poems, four of which are among the most extraordinary poetic creations of the Hebrew language. The remaining one is *The Matmid*. Not that it is a poem to be condescended to. It presents its ascetic talmudist in all the ambiguous implications of his cloistered heroism; its language is far richer than that of any long modern Hebrew poem before it. But set against the originality and power of the other four narrative poems, it seems artistically immature, sometimes repetitious, and near the end flawed with sentimentality.

On the other hand, *The Matmid* is the most clearly "national" of Bialik's five long poems. For *The Pond,* a myth of spiritual autobiography, concerns itself with the cycle of nature. *The Scroll of Fire* and *Dead of the Desert* touch on national material only in the most oblique, disturbingly ambiguous ways. *In the City of Slaughter* is filled with such raw anger, such horrendous images of blood-spattered corpses and cringing survivors, that it is rarely chosen as a text for young people. *The Matmid,* then, becomes for classroom purposes Bialik's monumental achievement in narrative verse—the weakest poem of the five and the one that can be misconstrued by an earnest enough teacher as a simple hymn of praise to Jewish spiritual perseverance.

I suspect that some readers never fully recover from being introduced to Bialik and Tchernichovsky in this questionably selective fashion. A few years ago, I had the opportunity to teach an informal course in Bialik at a summer camp to a group of college freshmen who had received what might be considered, by American standards, a thorough secondary-level Hebrew education. When at the first meeting I announced that we would be reading Bialik, there was a general groan, reinforced by protesting cries of "Again?" I hastened to explain that our discussions would be devoted to Bialik's love poetry, where I hoped the group would discover a different Bialik from the one with whom they were familiar. It is easy to get the impression—as these young people clearly had—that the greatest modern Hebrew poet wrote only about pogroms, hollow-eyed *yeshiva* students, old men in prayer shawls, and sweet, symbolic Birds of Zion. In point of fact, a surprising proportion of his poetry is concerned with love; passion or erotic encounter is the subject of some of his most brilliant short lyric pieces and occupies a central place in two major poems, *The Pond* and *The Scroll of Fire.* I had grand intentions of showing to the group that summer things in Bialik undreamed of in their curricula—his haunting mythic images of passional experience, the frantic oscillation between glimpses of woman as paradisiac fulfillment and nightmares of woman as demonic threat. But with more than half the group, my case was irretrievably lost from the moment of the initial announcement. Only a resolute few were willing to remain to see whether their prejudices could be shaken.

It may be objected that the presentation of poetry in secondary schools is never a fair measure of informed attitudes toward the body of poetry studied. After all, there are still many American high schools which inculcate the idea that "The Deserted Village" is the crowning achievement of eighteenth-century English poetry or that Edna St. Vincent Millay is a modern poet of towering stature. But in the case of the Hebrew poets, the treatment of their work in the classroom is curiously supported and extended through the way they have generally been handled by the critics.

A prevalent weakness in Hebrew criticism is that it so often neglects the literary text itself in a search for something behind or beyond the text. To begin with, this means that there has been very little aesthetic criticism of Hebrew literature, painfully little written on the major Hebrew poets to show precisely how they created beautiful forms through the medium of words. This lack in itself is regrettable, for good aesthetic criticism can perform a useful service in teaching us to read more attentively and heightening our enjoyment of what we read. But a more damaging consequence of these extraliterary interests is that Hebrew critics often fail to see what is actually said in a piece of literature because they are so anxious to make it a symbol, allegory, portent, or at least example of something else. Typical of this kind of reading are the standard critical comments on "Eagle! Eagle!", a well-known poem of Tchernichovsky's, which I offer here in more or less literal translation.

> Eagle! an eagle over your mountains, an eagle is flying over your mountains!
> Slow and easy—for a moment it seems merely to float,
> Floating-sailing in a sea of blue, alert to the song of exultation in the heart
> Of the heavens—of the sky, circling mutely in searing light.
>
> Eagle! an eagle over your mountains, an eagle is flying over your mountains!

Straight of back and heavy pinioned, black of feather and
   broad of wing;
Soaring tensely (arrow from the bow), an eagle circles above,
Tracking its prey in meadow and rock-crevice below.

Eagle! an eagle over your mountains, an eagle is flying over
   your mountains!
Soaring, gliding-gliding downward, and with wondrous touch,
   never moved a wing.
One moment—it froze; the next—the barest motion of its
   wings,
The slightest trembling suddenly—and it mounts to the sky.

Eagle! an eagle over your mountains, an eagle is flying over
   your mountains!
Slow and easy—for a moment it seems merely to float . . .
Land, an eagle over your mountains—over your face a gathering
   of shadow
From giant-wings passes, caressing the mountains of God.

Even in the clumsiness of this English version, without the
music and associative magic of the original words as part of the
experience of the poem, I think one can perceive in the four
stanzas a response of mingled fear and fascination to a thing of
terrible beauty in nature. There are, moreover, several important indications in the language of the poem that the eagle and
its wild beauty are meant to be seen against a vast mythic
background, very much like Blake's looming Tiger, who may
well have inspired Tchernichovsky's bird.

The critics, however, though apparently aware that the
poem represents a confrontation with some sort of arresting
presence, insist that the "real" meaning lies in a national allegory. Thus, for the late Joseph Klausner, first professor of
Hebrew literature at the Hebrew University, the poem is an
intuition of the Arab uprisings which took place a few months
after the lines were written in January, 1936. Simon Halkin,
successor to Klausner's chair, agrees in principle, actually describing the poem as "allegorical," though he prefers to extend
the scope of prophecy to include the destruction of European
Jewry: "The vulture [the "eagle" of my translation] . . . how-

ever literally a 'vulture'—a large bird of prey whose symmetrical floating in the air merely inspires [Tchernichovsky's] keen admiration—subtly transforms itself into an almost ghoulish portent." This is a clear instance of how allegorical reading—of which Halkin, incidentally, is far less guilty than other Hebrew critics—can simplify a complex poem. The speaker's profoundly ambivalent response to the bird is here separated out into two neat strands, one of "mere" admiration for the actual eagle, the other of horror for what it symbolizes. But the poem tightly intertwines these two attitudes, from the end of the first stanza (the first intimation of pain) to the last lines where the "ghoulish portent" is both threatening and curiously attractive, casting a great shadow that "caresses" the mountains of Judea.

Baruch Kurzweil, on the other hand, a critic who is constantly reminding his readers that he is a radical revisionist, offers a strikingly different interpretation. For him the bird and the mountains constitute a dialectic on the question of human freedom: "The eagle encounters the landscape which is saturated with historical significance. That is to say, the symbol of freedom—the eagle—and the symbol of this people's special history upon this special setting, i.e., 'the mountains of God'— are no longer opposed elements." *Kurzweil* is, I think, much closer to the actual concerns of the poem than Klausner or Halkin, but he insists on reducing it to an abstract formula. Every image must be a "symbol" of something, to be explained with a "that is to say" (*k'lomar*)—the very expression Rashi uses when translating a difficult idea in the text of the Talmud into its plain sense.

With this deep-rooted conviction that a poem can and should have a "translation," much of Bialik and Tchernichovsky which is not explicitly national is pressed into national shape by the powerful vise of allegorization. Bialik, after all, as Klausner proclaimed sixty years ago, was a modern-day prophet, and it would be clearly incongruous for a prophet to be caught writing mere personal poetry. One may speculate whether allegorizing is a particularly Jewish mode of thinking, perhaps an overdrawn legacy from the Middle Ages. In any case, as far as the interpretation of modern Hebrew literature is concerned, it

begins with the critics, filters down to the teachers, and sometimes infects the students as well. Occasionally I have to be
reminded how ingrained this habit of mind is, as two or three
years ago when I collided with a student at Brandeis who refused to accept one of Bialik's most warmly sensual love poems
for what it seemed to be. Surely, he argued, a poet like Bialik
wouldn't write about romping with a young girl in a sunlit
field—rather, the girl was the Community of Israel, her companion was the Divine Spouse, the dark woods were the Exile,
and so forth.

This recurrent conception of the poetry of Bialik and
Tchernichovsky as repositories of allegorical wisdom is reinforced by the tendency in Hebrew criticism to bestow on the
two poets titles which suggest that their poems were written,
not by individual persons, but by cultural or religious archetypes. Each of these titles has a core of truth around which is
wound a skein of misleading implications.

Thus, Bialik the "prophet" did assume a prophetic stance
and style in his Poems of Wrath, but the prophetic castigation
quickly breaks down into corrosive contempt under the maddening pressure of his awareness that his mission is futile, with
neither divine legitimation nor human acceptance. The logical
conclusion of Bialik's prophetic role is the naked terror in his
apocalypse of lust ("You Are Leaving Me") or in his anti-
apocalypse of cosmic ennui ("And It Shall Come to Pass in the
Length of Days"). Again, Bialik has been called (by Shalom
Spiegel) the "Mouthpiece of the Folk." Now it is true that
Bialik was able to fuse into the imaginative substance of his
poems more Jewish experience, both historical and literary, than
anyone else who has ever written Hebrew poetry. But what he
attempted to express was often intensely personal, and his attitude toward the folk was at least ambivalent, at many points
profoundly disaffected.

Perhaps the most recent of the labels for Bialik is one
suggested by Yeshurun Keshet in an article published in the
autumn of 1963; Keshet describes the poet as "the Judge of his
generation and the Builder for generations to come." This half-
truth, like the earlier ones, is more misleading than no truth at

all. The biblical implication of judge as charismatic leader is certainly false for Bialik, as is the more modern idea of moral-judicial authority, and his building for the future was achieved primarily through his activities as editor and literary promoter, not through his poetry, which, at its greatest, leaves little on which to build.

Such quasi-religious roles generally have not been attributed to Tchernichovsky: instead criticism has largely concentrated on identifying him as the embodiment of a National Spirit. Since Tchernichovsky wrote many poems concerned with pagan gods, both Greek and ancient Near Eastern, there has been much talk about the "Greek" or "Canaanite" Tchernichovsky, usually countered by more emphatic—and equally un-availing—talk about the "Jewish" Tchernichovsky. Evidence for the persistence of this pseudocritical discourse is offered by the November, 1963, issue of *Moznayim*, devoted to Tchernichovsky on the twentieth anniversary of his death. (*Moznayim* is the official publication of the Writers' Association in Israel, and in many respects can be considered the voice of Israel's literary establishment, especially its older members.) The editors managed to get together only three pieces, including the editorial preface, which actually discussed or evaluated Tchernichovsky's poetry. The three read like the development of a party line: first, the editor's statement that Tchernichovsky is not essentially a laughing Greek but a poet of Jewish martyrology; then, an article called "Martyrdom in Tchernichovsky's Work" which traces the poet's use of traditional Jewish sources; finally, a piece which concludes that when Tchernichovsky wrote of Apollo, he was not attracted to the Greek ideal but was merely concerned with resuscitating the primal God of the Jews.*

---

* Not long after writing this, I ran across precisely the same argument against official titles in Simon Halkin's long reflective poem, "Yakov Rabinowitz in Yarmouth." The relevant lines are worth quoting, both to substantiate my own case and to do justice to Halkin: "Any old label / That one of our critics happens to paste on / His victim, the writer bears with him / Till his dying day and after death as well. / Bialik's still a prophet, Tchernichovsky is / A Greek, of course. We're a strange people."

Perhaps the best argument against this whole procedure of nationalizing a poet, however serious his commitment to the national enterprise, is Bialik's own vehement objection to the procedure, both in his poetry and in his statements and actions. When the Hebrew public in 1923 attempted to celebrate the poet's fiftieth birthday with a formal jubilee ceremony, Bialik refused to participate. In response to the proffered adulation, he wrote a short poem, his first in seven years. It begins: "My soul stoops to the dust / Under the burden of your love; / Alas! I have become / A clinking penny in your empty barrel." The four remaining stanzas include a disavowal of the role of poet or prophet and a bleak view of the people's future in which, instead of rallying to causes, each man must struggle with "the burdens of his own heart."

Also in connection with the abortive jubilee, Bialik prepared a statement—published for the first time in 1963—which he apparently had intended to deliver to a small group of friends. In the formal statement, he deletes the angry impatience of the poem, even turns his refusal into a compliment to the powers of national revival. But the disclaimer of the role of national poet is just as clear: "All this stir is proof of the need that has been born for us to pinch ourselves, so that we can feel living flesh between our fingers while we say 'Me'. . . . As it happened, this time the fingers caught me. The people . . . isn't particular whether it touches the heart or some other place."

Even more instructive is Bialik's vigorous insistence that the people who adopted him as "official" national poet had stubbornly and thoroughly misunderstood his poetry. A poem he wrote in 1931, three years before his death, ought to be inserted as an epigraph to most of the criticism of Bialik that has been written:

> Even when he strips himself before your eyes, to his very
>   depths—
> Do not neigh in triumph like stallions.
> He was merely mocking you, ruthlessly,
> And reduced you all to a scornful shake of the head.

You are too worthless to bare one part of a thousand
Of his heart's meditation upon you.
Thus does he reveal himself, in order to hide the more from
    your eyes
And in order to lead you astray.
In vain will you seek him in the hiding-places of his verses—
    these too
Are but a cover for his secrets,
From among their columns, as from within the bars of a cage,
A fiery malevolent lion looks out. . . .

The remainder of the poem sustains this biblical style of de-
nunciation—the poet speaking as prophet for himself—and
expands the lion-image to a dream of freedom, with the lion,
burst from the cage, roaring scorn to his former captors from a
mountaintop. Thirty years after the death of the poet, some of
his interpreters have still not heard that scornful roar.

What has happened to Bialik and Tchernichovsky suggests
the genuine usefulness for any literature of a wide range of alert
critical activity. In America, for example, where so many reams
of criticism are produced daily, it is hardly a secret that much
bad sense, or plain nonsense, is continually written, from
pedestrian dullness in the learned journals to supercilious dog-
matism in the intellectual reviews. But at the same time, there
is also some perceptive, really helpful discussion of literature
carried on by critics and scholars. The enterprising reader at
least can find knowledgeable guides into the complexities and
obscurities of the major English and American poets of the first
half of our century. A great poet like Yeats, say, may always be
subject to tendentious, overly ingenious, or simply wrongheaded
reading, but there is enough responsible criticism of the Irish
poet to make it unlikely that prevailing opinion will substitute
an obviously peripheral Yeats for the central one.

The situation is quite different in Hebrew literature. Here
scholarship and criticism alike have been remiss. All sorts of
documents have been published, from Bialik's correspondence
and *obiter dicta* to Tchernichovsky's doodling, but there has

not yet been a minimally adequate biography of either poet. Both Klausner's book on Tchernichovsky and Lachover's biography of Bialik consist mainly of summaries of the poems (sometimes with dubious interpretations), the gaps between the summaries being filled in with biographical information, selected arbitrarily or simply at random. One can find far more reminiscences and anecdotes on the two poets, by various of their contemporaries, than responsible and consecutive biography.

As far as literary analysis is concerned, the critics of the older generation, when they are not merely explaining the poets in terms of Jewish Destiny and Jewish History, are likely to bury them under garlands of lyrical effusions—a kind of excess which would be obvious and embarrassing in English as it is now generally written, but which, unfortunately, is still easy to slip into in Hebrew. The occasional psychoanalytic reading of the poems one encounters is scarcely a relief—e.g., Bialik uses recurring images of maternal shelter because his own widowed mother sent him to live with a stern grandfather, and so forth.

There are, on the other hand, some hopefully glimmering lights within the general critical murk. Baruch Kurzweil's recent *Studies in the Poetry of Bialik and Tchernichovsky* has its illuminating moments, and it breaks vigorously from the naïvely nationalist school of interpretation. But, as in his earlier books, Kurzweil often seems to be using Hebrew literature mainly to discuss the loss of religious faith in the modern world, and his favorite procedure of interpretation—like that of his comment on "Eagle! Eagle!"—is to substitute a broad abstraction for the living poetry.

Elsewhere, Dov Sadan, professor or Hebrew and Yiddish at the Hebrew University, has written three brief but immensely suggestive essays on Bialik in which he describes the simultaneous recapitulation in Bialik's poetry of personal, historical, and mythic experience. One can only wish that the essays, the last two of which were published in 1949, had become the introduction to a detailed study of the poems. Or again, the late Ludwig Strauss did some finely perceptive structural analysis of

Bialik's verse, but his work, too, is limited to the scope of an essay.

In any case, the prospects for more frequent confrontations with the real richness of the two poets' work are probably brighter than this account would indicate. Certainly in conversation one comes across intelligent readers of Bialik and Tchernichovsky, people capable of employing critical methods of literary analysis—a few young teachers of Hebrew literature in this country, some writers, critics, and teachers in Israel, particularly of the younger generation. And in recent years, an increasing number of serious young Israeli critics have been devoting careful attention to the two poets. Useful, if not always illuminating, work has been done by Eli Schweid (who in effect tries to synthesize Sadan and Kurzweil), Reuben Tzur (who offers a New Critical reading of Bialik), Dan Miron, Tuvya Rübner, and others. Much more, however, remains to be done, not only because there is still much in the poets that calls for investigation and analysis, but especially because the inertia of prevailing opinion remains so powerful, the "official" image of the poets so entrenched in public consciousness and in the educational process.

Clearly, the critics have an indispensable service to perform in setting the Hebrew reader squarely in front of a body of poetry which he has long been led to approach obliquely. It is natural enough sometimes to lose patience with criticism in general, to suspect that the whole noisy realm of critical discourse merely intervenes between the reader and the written work. But the plight of Bialik and Tchernichovsky dramatically illustrates the need for enlightened, disciplined critics: only they can rescue the two great modern Hebrew poets from the hands of their abductors.

1964.

POETRY IN ISRAEL

Israel is probably one of the few remaining countries where verse, far from being a dying technique, has managed to stay at the vital center of literary culture. To an American, who is accustomed to having his poetry in coffeehouses, summer workshops, graduate seminars, and other suitable places of solitary confinement, it is pleasant if puzzling to discover abundant signs in Israel of the presence of a body of contemporary verse that is read as well as written. Israel may conceivably have the highest per capita production of poetry in the world—especially if you count (slim) volumes of verse and not total number of lines—and it is an even safer bet that it has the highest rate anywhere of poetry consumption. A popular book of poetry sells out a first printing of 3,000 copies within a few months. This figure in itself may not seem particularly impressive, and it scarcely suggests that sonnet cycles are hawked in the streets of Tel Aviv like hot *felaffel*. But if one considers that the Jewish population of Israel is about two million, and that, of those, considerably less than half know Hebrew well enough to read it for enjoyment, a printing of 3,000 in Israel looms as large as perhaps half a million copies of a book published in America. Compared to the success of Hebrew poets like Avraham Shlonsky and Natan Alterman, even Robert Frost looks like a mere coterie figure.

A typical Israeli bookstore window is likely to have three or four new volumes of verse in its most prominent display, along with a book or two on biblical archeology, a biography of some public figure, perhaps a popular American novel in translation. It is hard for the visiting American to get used to the idea that there actually exists something very much like a best seller in poetry. In 1965, for example, Natan Alterman published *Summer Festival*, his first book of verse in seven years. Like his previous volume, it was a sharp disappointment to most of the critics. But Alterman, who wrote some remarkable poetry back in the forties, has managed to attract a large and loyal following, and the appearance of *Summer Festival*, whatever the intrinsic merits of the book, was a real cultural event. Israel's leading intellectual monthly, *Molad*, devoted a long article to the book and its role in the poet's development, giving it the kind of attention that an American monthly would allow only to a widely discussed novelist—say, Bellow or Mailer—upon a long-awaited reappearance in print. When I was in Israel in the summer of 1965, I saw the Alterman book in almost every bookstore window, including even the little neighborhood shops whose main stock was school supplies and textbooks.

This last detail suggests one important aspect of the relative popularity enjoyed by poetry in Israel: a substantial number of Israeli poetry readers are quite young. We should not, however, jump to the conclusion that the audience for Hebrew poetry is therefore constantly growing. I suspect that many of those who become devoted to it in their high-school and university years abandon it with other sins of their youth as their lives get caught up in the more prosaic concerns of career and marriage. But even if the interest of this group in poetry is in many cases temporary, it constitutes a kind of cultural phenomenon not easy to imagine in our own country.

The distance between cultures is vividly illustrated by a story I heard from Lea Goldberg, the distinguished Hebrew poet. On a visit to Beersheba, she went into a bookstore to look for children's books. The storekeeper, as soon as he realized who she was, gave her the most cordial reception he could (something a customer can by no means take for granted in an Israeli store). In the course of their conversation, the shop owner asked Miss Goldberg if she could guess what kind of book was his biggest seller; the answer, of course, was poetry. This would not be surprising in Jerusalem or Tel Aviv, but

Beersheba is a kind of frontier city in the northern Negev, largely populated by recent immigrants. The storekeeper had to explain that most of his customers were soldiers stationed at the large army camps in the area. (In Israel, it must be remembered, this group includes women as well as men, and it would be somewhat younger than an American counterpart since the compulsory period of military service usually occurs immediately after high school.) Now, there may be some truth in the complaint often voiced in Israel that young people have abandoned the intellectual idealism of the pioneering Zionists for a narrow, self-serving pragmatism; one is in fact likely to discover considerable evidence in support of this accusation among the young Israelis with whom one talks. But the anomaly of ballads in the barracks and distichs in the duffel bags should cast some doubt upon the adequacy of such facile, moralizing judgments.

I don't mean to suggest that where hostile critics have seen young Israelis as insensitive and unreflective careerists, we should now imagine a generation of soulful seekers after truth and beauty. To begin with, this group of poetry readers, however large relatively, remains a distinct minority of all Israeli youth. The reasons, moreover, why poetry should be important to a considerable number of Israel's young intellectuals, and why it should play such a major role in Hebrew literature, are multiple, and their interrelation is neither simple nor clear. Perhaps the worst place to begin to look for an explanation is in that dubiously charted region of national character. The relative importance of poetry in Israel may be in some degree the result of cultural traditions; it surely has something to do also with the problematic role of Hebrew in the life of an educated Israeli; but the whole phenomenon must be understood ultimately in terms of the distinctive nature of Hebrew poetry.

Despite the juggernaut progress of Americanization through Israel in everything from IBM cards to supermarkets, there are important areas of cultural life still rooted in Central-European and East-European traditions. The three most significant antecedent cultures for Israel, at least as far as literature is concerned, are Russian, German, and the world of traditional Judaism. In each of these cultural milieux, poetry has been accorded a far more important place than it ever has been given in America, or, for that matter, than it has enjoyed in England since the time of Byron and Scott.

The poetry with which Jewish tradition filled the inner life of its adherents was, of course, the poetry learned from sacred texts, rabbinic as well as biblical, the liturgical verse adorning the various services, and the Sabbath and festival table-hymns. There is a real, if sometimes devious, connection between this traditional use of poetry as an expression of religious experience and the kinds of inner needs which Hebrew poetry serves today. Much Hebrew verse since Bialik has been religious in its ultimate concerns, though perhaps most often in the manner of the great Hebrew poetry of Job, quarreling with God rather than praising Him. It is a revealing fact that the two major figures in the oldest generation of Israeli poets, Avraham Shlonsky and Uri Zvi Greenberg, have produced a considerable body of deeply religious work, Shlonsky in an intensely personal mode far to the Left of institutional Judaism, Greenberg to the messianic Right of it in the language of prophetic vision and the public symbols of national destiny. Religious concerns are often at the root of poems by younger poets as well, though the expression may be more oblique, less likely to couch itself in traditional terms.

The persisting influences of German and Russian traditions are more straightforward if less substantive. There was a time, one recalls, when a furor for verse-making was expected to seize virtually every good introspective German during his student years, and a continuing acquaintance with serious poetry was something generally assumed of cultivated persons in a nation of Goethe quoters. Jerusalem is not Heidelberg, but one may see, for example, in the Israeli student abroad who makes room in his forty-four pounds of air luggage for a cherished volume of Alterman or Amichai, a shadow cast by the pale, vatic youth of a vanished Germany. Similarly, Russian cultural influences, though generally on the wane, are probably the background for the kind of public importance poetry has in

Israel. While Israel has nothing to match the passionate in-volvement of Russia's outdoor poetry readings, the public read-ing and discussion of poetry have not been entirely relegated to the esoteric audiences of poetry "centers" or to the self-con-sciously educational environment of the university. A response to poetry like the standing-room enthusiasm evoked by Yevtu-shenko's public readings in Russia a few years ago is at least still a possibility in Israel. The topical interest, moreover, of Yev-tushenko's verse suggests a further connection with Israel's cultural situation as opposed to our own. In America, serious writers have tried to come to terms with recent events of na-tional relevance chiefly through fiction and—perhaps more suc-cessfully—through reflective essays or reportage. In Israel, as in Russia, the idea persists at least in some circles that poetry can, and perhaps ought to, grapple with contemporary history. Some Hebrew poetry, to be sure, has emerged from the encounter with history very much the worse for wear artistically, but it is significant that poetry as a mode of response to life can still be ambitious, has not retreated wholly to the involutions of private experience and the nuances of aesthetic discriminations.

But what seems to me more important than any cultural tradition in explaining the vitality of poetry in Israel is the very distinctive kind of life Hebrew words assume when they are put together imaginatively in a poem. Hebrew, precisely because its resuscitation as a language for modern daily use has been so successful, is in one sense now fighting for survival. That is, the Hebrew everyone reads, writes, and speaks is to a great extent a translated language (from Yiddish, German, Russian, Arabic, English, French) in which the modes of semantic subtlety and suggestiveness indigenous to it are drastically weakened. The newspapers and popular magazines, for example, are written in a sort of international journalese that wrenches Hebrew from its native patterns of idiom and syntax and that, at its worst, makes the tongue of the prophets sound like an Esperanto imitation of the style of *The New York Times*.

On a higher level, the educated Israeli finds that his native tongue is constantly put into competition with the very differently developed Western languages in areas where it must seem less than adequate. It is easier to write a good philosophical essay, a sociological study, a piece of literary criticism, in English or German than in Hebrew, because Hebrew is deficient in certain types of specialized vocabulary and particularly in the means to discriminate subtly different levels and categories of abstraction: it lacks, in short, some of the very linguistic tools that make precise analytic thinking possible. (A very intelligent Israeli who grew up in Czechoslovakia actually told me that when he returned to Prague for an extended visit, his Czech university friends congratulated him on having established himself in Israel, but, after some conversation, regretted the fact that thinking in Hebrew had "made him stupid.") The advanced student in almost every discipline except Judaica ends up doing the bulk of his required reading in English, and this is likely to be the case with his professional reading later on. That Hebrew should be a second fiddle in such circumstances is inevitable, simply because it doesn't have all the right linguistic strings to play on. More regrettable are the many instances in which Israelis adopt or imitate a foreign cultural product mainly for its appeal as attractive, imported goods. It seems a little pathetic, for example, that to a startling number of educated Israelis, *Time* is the indispensable weekly news magazine. No conceivable form of Hebrew could compete with Timese, but it is unfortunate that the two should have to compete in anyone's mind, that an Israeli should have to follow the events of the great world in a foreign cultural idiom whose meretricious cleverness is essentially unassimilable to his own language.

The educated Israeli, in sum, finds himself maneuvering intellectually in a broad Western culture to which his own language, both structurally and lexically, is not entirely suited. He frequently has to use a de-Hebraized Hebrew that misses the best of both worlds, and for many of the needs of his intellectual life he ends up depending upon a foreign language. Now, against this general background of linguistic uneasiness, poetry offers the native speaker of Hebrew, to paraphrase Coleridge, the best Hebrew words in the best Hebrew order. In a country where so much culture is translated, both in fact and in effect, the truism about the untranslatability of poetry looms with a larger than ordinary significance. Israeli fiction in this respect is a borderline phenomenon—all the younger writers have their peculiar problems about being distinctively Hebrew stylists. But it is poetry that clearly liberates the potential expressiveness of Hebrew words, so choosing and placing them as to utilize their finest nuances of meaning, striking the rich plangencies of allusion inherent in the literary history of the words, even drawing on a large vocabulary never used in speech because it does not correspond to the practical needs of the translatable everyday world.

An Israeli with serious literary interests could conceivably find Camus (in translation) or Faulkner (in English) more deeply relevant than all the Hebrew novels on the failure of the old Zionist ideals, but there are areas of his most intimate experience which only Hebrew poetry can reach because it alone speaks to him with the subtle intimacy of his first language. It is sometimes suggested that young Israelis read poetry because they are searching for "identity." What this vague explanation actually means, I think, is that poetry gives a mouth to their muteness; feelings and thoughts partly muffled by the predicament of their language are released, crystallized into the precious clarity of artfully ordered words.

There are, moreover, some remarkable possibilities for artful ordering inherent in Hebrew words. I suppose it is absurd to claim that one language is intrinsically more poetic than another, but one can say of Hebrew that its unique history makes it a supple instrument for certain species of poetic expression that have never been, or no longer are, available to poets in the major Western languages. This of course does not mean that the use of Hebrew can in any way guarantee a poet's artistic success: even some of the most gifted Hebrew poets have been known to clutter their books with more than a fair share of metric trash. But the body of really good poetry that has been written in Israel is quite impressive, and the high quality of much Hebrew verse can be attributed at least partly to the poets' success in tapping the distinctive resources of the Hebrew language.

More than anything else, what makes Hebrew poetry different is the vital presence of the Bible—through remembered words, phrases, verses, whole passages, themes, and symbols—in the mind of every genuinely literate user of Hebrew. Though much of the biblical vocabulary, idiom, and grammar has disappeared from modern speech, the language of the Bible remains perfectly familiar in a way not easily imaginable for the average speaker of English, to whom the much more recent past of his own literature—Chaucer, say, or even Spenser—is barely intelligible. With the Bible always in the background, a skillful Hebrew poet can shift perspective or tone, introduce irony, focus two or three meanings on a single point, with a carefully weighted allusion to a biblical text, perhaps simply by means of a borrowed phrase or word. Lines of Hebrew verse which may sound flat or tritely rhetorical in translation often are charged with imaginative power through allusion. When Natan Alterman, for example, writes that "Woman's love is treacherous," a single word makes the line transcend the banality of its English equivalent. His term for "treacherous" ('aquba) never occurs in ordinary modern Hebrew; it appears adjectivally in the Bible only three memorable times, and only once, as here, in the feminine form, in Hosea—"The city of evil-doers is smeared [or "crooked," 'aquba] with blood." For the literate reader, then, Alterman's 'aquba trails after it a wake of blood (specifically, the recalled biblical word midam), and so the woman's treacherous love assumes overtones of violence and, if the whole verse is remembered, moral perversion. This apprehension of the word's darker implications is strengthened by the recollection of another biblical verse, Jeremiah's "The heart is most treacherous ['aqob] of all."

The elaborateness of my explanation for this simple turn of allusion may make it seem a difficult virtuoso trick, like writing sestinas. In point of fact, however, such coalescing of associations in a word or phrase is so natural and easy in Hebrew that poets sometimes have to struggle to keep out allusion where they don't mean to have it. Hebrew love-poetry illustrates this point with particular clarity. The power of the Song of Songs has so captured the Hebrew poetic imagination that a poet virtually has to make a conscious effort in order *not* to allude to the splendid biblical model when he writes a love lyric in Hebrew. Even a poetic expression of revulsion from a demonically carnal woman (Bialik's "The Hungry Eyes") naturally works itself out as an anti-Song of Songs, following the Canticles' convention of vertical description of the beloved's body, downward from her hungry eyes and fierce lips to the insatiable sexual darkness below. The imaginative availability of the Bible, which can make such artful parallels and inversions possible, may tempt the Hebrew poet to slide from poetry to pastiche. This was the besetting ill of the earliest generations of modern Hebrew poets, and it remains an occupational hazard of Hebrew verse, cropping up frequently, for example, in the contemporary biblicizing poet Yonatan Ratosh, the central figure of the so-alled Canaanite group that was much discussed a decade ago.

What is especially relevant, however, to our concern is that Hebrew can sustain a very viable poetic mode which looks quite like pastiche, though it differs radically from pastiche in the creative energy with which it selects, fuses, and transforms different source materials. This stanza from a poem by Lea Goldberg illustrates a kind of poetic strategy typical of Hebrew but unfeasible, I think, in most other languages:

> I life up my eyes to the mountains
> And the mountains are desolate.
> How you flowered in them, my soul,
> My wildflower in the clefts of the rock!

The section of the poem from which the stanza is taken describes a moment of existential terror, and the sudden plunge of consciousness from daylight into what the poem calls "blood-darkness" is beautifully caught by the second line here, which amputates the verse from Psalms—"I lift up my eyes to the mountains / From whence cometh my help"—and substitutes mere desolation. This kind of studied reversal of a well-known text could be done in another language, but the continuing modulation of compressed allusions in the two subsequent lines is uniquely Hebrew. The word for "how" in the third line is not the standard *eikh* but *eikha*, the variant regularly used in the Bible when the word occurs at the beginning of a formal elegy. The allusion here, through a single syllable, is subgrammatical, yet it carries with it echoes of fallen cities, scattered splendor, and Lamentations, which in turn play against both the wondering excitement of the exclamation and the gentle affection in the remembrance of Song of Songs—"My dove in the clefts of the rock . . . / Let me see thy countenance . . . / For thy countenance is comely."

It is worth noting that this mosaic of allusions occurs in the work of a poet whose prevailing tone is personal, quietly melodic or conversational, and who has rarely been concerned in her verse with tradition, history, or ideology. The traditional idiom, however, of classic Hebrew literature—not only the Bible, but to a large extent the prayer book and rabbinic legend as well—is so much the common possession of the Hebrew literary imagination, even in a post-traditional era, that it lends itself quite naturally to the most private uses of expression. In this connection, the case of Yehuda Amichai, the most popular new poet of the fifties, is especially instructive. Amichai is the most influential of the younger poets who, partly in emulation of modern British and American models, have attempted to introduce the rhythms of ordinary speech and the flatness or harshness of everyday language into their verse. Such a program was clearly necessary for the younger generation in order to close the gap they felt between poetic convention and lived experience, though the success of the program has been at best a mixed one—Hebrew Audenized can produce disastrously unrelieved poetic bleaknesses. What is interesting about Amichai is that this avowed poet of fragmented, tarnished realities—"Cripples and the unemployed / Are the songbirds in the poets' trees / And not the cuckoo and the nightingale"—should stud the jagged textures of his poems with shining bits from classical Hebrew texts.

One of the important expressive effects of Amichai's verse derives from the pointed contrast between traditional idioms and the colloquial poetic environment in which they occur. One poem, in which a soldier with orders for the front takes leave of his girl, begins, "The smell of gasoline ascended in my nostrils." After yoking ancient sacrifice and modern technology in this bizarre fashion, the speaker goes on to identify his tenderness for his beloved with that of his pious father for a ritual object: "Your soul, my girl, I'll put in my palm / Like a festival citron in soft wool—/ So, too, my dead father did." In the next three stanzas the soldier expresses his feeling for the weeping girl through disarming colloquial understatement ("Wipe your face and stand by me / And smile like in a family photo"); then he concludes by telescoping another traditional phrase into the grim menace of his own world: "The jet plane makes peace in its heights / Over us and over all those who love in the fall." The echo, of course, is from the final words of the *kaddish*— "May He who makes peace in his heights establish peace over us and over all Israel." The finely adjusted tension here between the poet's statement and the recalled text is typical of Amichai. He is neither quarreling with his source nor merely playing with it, though he occasionally does both in his use of allusion elsewhere. Rather, the fractured piece of liturgy expresses a kind of wistful regret for that world of faith in which God made peace on high—in the poet's world, lovers between battles must depend instead upon circling jets for their fleeting moments of precarious happiness together.

Yet poetry, though it may consist partly in allusions, must exist entirely in words, and the nature of Hebrew words themselves makes them uniquely suitable for the poetic rendering of certain aspects of experience. Many Hebrew words carry a distinctive force that is related to their allusiveness, but not identical with it, as can be seen in this brief piece by the gifted young poet, Dan Pagis:

Primal chaos still is twisted in the
Power-frozen rock. The rock hasn't split.
Silence, petrified, rules it.
The darkness expects.
              Imprisoned is the tremor.
And already the veins of red are running in the rock
Pounding like mute lightnings.

Some of the inadequacy of my translation is merely a result
of the rigidity of English syntax. (The quaintly poetic inversion,
for example, in the fifth line is natural and eloquent in the
original because Hebrew, even in prose, allows more freedom in
subject-predicate order.) But where the English version fails
crucially is in the first two words of the poem. They constitute a
nearly exact translation of the original *tohu reshit* (very literally,
"chaos of beginning"), with only the background of the words
—Greek cosmogony instead of Hebrew—changed. It might be
argued that the verbal connection with Genesis in the original
makes the Hebrew poem conceptually tighter: the same darkness that hovers over the chaos in the first chapter of Genesis
"expects" portentously in the fourth line here. The essential
difficulty of the translation, however, is in the taint of pretense
that clings to "primal chaos"—or any English phrase like it—
and of which the Hebrew equivalent is entirely free. Perhaps in
the seventeenth century it was still possible to use a formula
like "primal chaos" with genuine poetic resonance. But after
the Miltonizing poets of the eighteenth century, after reams of
bad Romantic and Victorian poems, after science fiction, cheap
rhetorical novels, perhaps even advertising, the words have become almost pure fake-poetic. In Hebrew, on the other hand,
the continuity between the Bible and the modern spoken language acts as a brake against this kind of progressive deterioration of words. *Reshit,* for example, is a perfectly normal conversational word, as in the common phrase, *reshit kol* ("first of
all"), and yet its appearance as the initial word of the Bible,
b'reshit, can scarcely be forgotten. *Tohu reshit,* therefore, manages to be a natural usage, with no trace of the false sublime in

it, while referring directly and precisely to a level of reality that is cosmic and mythic.

Because the whole body of ancient and medieval Hebrew literature continually sets man over against God, the created world over against the void, and time over against eternity, the language is rich in words that express ultimate things. It is worth noting, moreover, that despite the flood of Greek and Latin words absorbed by Hebrew in the Hellenistic period, most of this vocabulary of the ultimate grows from indigenous roots. The Hebrew terms for genesis, apocalypse, infinity, eternity, are all made up of simple lexical components still very commonly used in everyday speech: and in respect to their form and sound—none is more than two syllables—as well as to their history, these words are scarcely obtrusive even in a modern colloquial context. Such a vocabulary is so native to Hebrew language and literature that even the inflated pseudobiblical rhetoric of the Hebrew Enlightenment could not vitiate it as, by contrast, the English stock of terms for ultimates has been progressively cheapened since the latter part of the seventeenth century by writers following what Swift mockingly called "the high celestial road." When a contemporary English poet trots out a world-embracing word, he generally has to do it with an embarrassed grin or a defensively intellectual glare. A Hebrew poet can still use such terms with a straight face and even with unaffected, colloquial directness.

Thus Amichai, in another of his early war poems, describes his girl against a background of practice gunshots, "walking through the streets / Wearing the jewels of apocalypse." The English version of the last phrase may have its own kind of effectiveness, but the final word jolts the reader in a way not quite in keeping with the original *takhshitei ha-ketz*. The term translated as "apocalypse"—*ketz*—is one of the two simple Hebrew words for "end." Tradition has firmly linked it with eschatology—the End of Days, or *ketz ha-yamim*—but it has none of the polysyllabic pomp of the English equivalent, nor, of course, the mystifying ring of Greek strangeness and the dark aura of New Testament vision inseparable from the English word. *Ketz* is associated with the end of history and the "end of all flesh" (*ketz kol basar* is the phrase used in the Noah story), yet it has a denotative immediacy that also can suggest the end of more particular things than the whole world—the end of the poet, say, or of his beloved, the end of the brief period when the two were one flesh.

This leapfrogging between personal experience and cosmic expectations is a frequent movement in Hebrew poetry, but by no means an inevitable one. The verbal accessibility of ultimates is part of a larger pattern of distinctiveness in Hebrew vocabulary: both abstractions and traditionally "poetic" words —that is, words which characterize unusually intense inner states or highly impressive sensory data—remain quite usable poetically.

Hebrew abstractions, at least those that are not awkward neologisms, lend themselves to verse metrically, because most of them are simple iambs or anapests, and connotatively, because they generally remain much closer in form and implication to their concrete origins than is the case with the heavily latinate abstractions of English. A poem by Lea Goldberg, for example, closes with this summary of being surprised by joy: "Since then I am a pool in the night's heart—/ In their arbitrariness generous heavens / Have sunk into it all the stars." "Arbitrariness," though an exact equivalent for the Hebrew, is barbaric not only because it shatters any possible meter, but because it is associated in English with a kind of analytic discourse quite incongruous with the sensuous immediacy of the poem. The Hebrew *shrirut* does not have the same long history of use as a precise, purely conceptual term; modern Hebrew actually borrows it from a favorite idiom of Jeremiah, *shrirut-lev*, which is traditionally rendered as "hardheartedness" or "stubbornness."

Perhaps the best example of the continuing viability of "poetic" language in Hebrew is the work of Uri Zvi Greenberg. Despite his frequent diffuseness, he manages to make one repeatedly aware of the intrinsic magic of words. One central

instance is his love for brilliant and violent colors and the words
that refer to them. He calls upon half a dozen synonyms for
"effulgence," fills his pages with gold (for which there are at
least three synonyms in Hebrew), sky-blue, crimson (the biblical *argaman*, or royal purple), "shining-red" (*ḥakhlili*, an enigmatic color-word that occurs in the Bible only once, in Genesis
49:12). It is not easy to explain why, in contrast to what has
happened in other languages, such vocabulary in Hebrew
should manage to retain a high degree of imaginative life, but
surely one important reason is that the words are so ensconced
in their traditional contexts, from Genesis to the Zohar, that the
luster of their classic associations has not been dulled by
usage—the words themselves seem able to survive even the
rhetorical cheapening to which they have been subjected by
second-rate Hebrew writers from the Enlightenment onward.
In a modern Hebrew-speaking culture, then, where the language in its everyday use is flattened into gray regularity, poets
can still use descriptive and emotive words that tower splen-
didly, inviting the ascent of the imagination.

The business of poetry, it has often been observed, is to
relate the unrelated, to pull disparate fragments into significant
wholes. To the Israeli, in his peculiar predicament of apparent
but not absolute cultural uprootedness, this act of relating is
especially vital, and the language of Hebrew poetry, as I have
tried to show, renders it especially fit as an instrument for
making meaningful connections. It is not only that the Israeli
must repeatedly test out the problematic relevance of past
Jewish experience to his own emotional and intellectual life.
Like all Jews, he must also find some way to respond to the
terrible central fact of Jewish history in our time, which remains
outrageous, unthinkable, unassimilable. Some of the finest Hebrew poems of the last twenty-five years are expressions of
highly personal experiences, not directly "about" the Holocaust,
and yet finally unintelligible without reference to it. What happens in these poems is indicative of the larger uses that Hebrew
poetry serves. The past is imaginatively linked with the present;
the reverberations of historical catastrophe are caught in the

exploration of private crisis; the unassimilable elements of both individual and collective experience are thus for a moment controlled, ordered, related. Ultimately, then, what makes poetry important in Israel is that the sensitive Hebrew reader can find in it a way of responding humanly to his world—to its beauty as well as to its terror—which is simply not available to him in any other medium. At a time when genuinely human responses are not easy to come by anywhere, this function is more than a cultural luxury: the purposes served by the best modern Hebrew poetry may not fall so far, after all, from the high purposes of the great Hebrew poetry of the past.

1965

Date

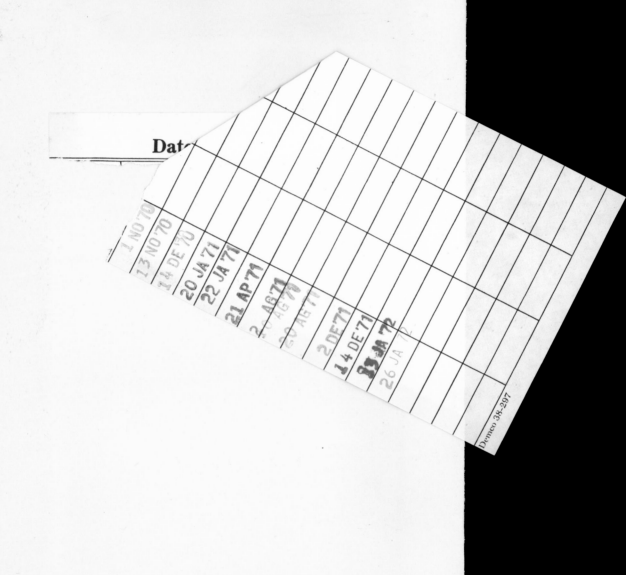

1 NO '70
13 NO '70
14 DE '70
20 JA '71
22 JA '71
21 AP '71
2 AG '71
20 AG '71
2 DE '71
14 DE '71
13 JA '72
26 JA '72